eBay®
BUSINESS
AT YOUR FINGERTIPS

Kevin W. Boyd

ALPHA

A member of Penguin Group (USA) Inc.

ALPHA BOOKS

Published by the Penguin Group

Penguin Group (USA) Inc., 375 Hudson Street, New York, New York 10014, USA

Penguin Group (Canada), 90 Eglinton Avenue East, Suite 700, Toronto, Ontario M4P 2Y3, Canada (a division of Pearson Penguin Canada Inc.)

Penguin Books Ltd., 80 Strand, London WC2R 0RL, England

Penguin Ireland, 25 St. Stephen's Green, Dublin 2, Ireland (a division of Penguin Books Ltd.)

Penguin Group (Australia), 250 Camberwell Road, Camberwell, Victoria 3124, Australia (a division of Pearson Australia Group Pty. Ltd.)

Penguin Books India Pvt. Ltd., 11 Community Centre, Panchsheel Park, New Delhi—110 017, India

Penguin Group (NZ), 67 Apollo Drive, Rosedale, North Shore, Auckland 1311, New Zealand (a division of Pearson New Zealand Ltd.)

Penguin Books (South Africa) (Pty.) Ltd., 24 Sturdee Avenue, Rosebank, Johannesburg 2196, South Africa

Penguin Books Ltd., Registered Offices: 80 Strand, London WC2R 0RL, England

International Standard Book Number: 978-1-59257-794-1
Library of Congress Catalog Card Number: 2008901390

10 09 08   8 7 6 5 4 3 2 1

Interpretation of the printing code: The rightmost number of the first series of numbers is the year of the book's printing; the rightmost number of the second series of numbers is the number of the book's printing. For example, a printing code of 08-1 shows that the first printing occurred in 2008.

Printed in the United States of America

Note: This publication contains the opinions and ideas of its author. It is intended to provide helpful and informative material on the subject matter covered. It is sold with the understanding that the author and publisher are not engaged in rendering professional services in the book. If the reader requires personal assistance or advice, a competent professional should be consulted.

The author and publisher specifically disclaim any responsibility for any liability, loss, or risk, personal or otherwise, which is incurred as a consequence, directly or indirectly, of the use and application of any of the contents of this book.

Most Alpha books are available at special quantity discounts for bulk purchases for sales promotions, premiums, fund-raising, or educational use. Special books, or book excerpts, can also be created to fit specific needs.

For details, write: Special Markets, Alpha Books, 375 Hudson Street, New York, NY 10014.

Publisher: **Marie Butler-Knight**

Editorial Director: **Mike Sanders**

Senior Managing Editor: **Billy Fields**

Acquisitions Editor: **Tom Stevens**

Senior Development Editor: **Phil Kitchel**

Senior Production Editor: **Janette Lynn**

Copy Editor: **Michael Dietsch**

Cover/Book Designer: **Kurt Owens**

Indexer: **Brad Herriman**

Layout: **Brian Massey**

Proofreader: **John Etchison**

This book is dedicated to my parents, who have always supported and encouraged my dreams.

CONTENTS

INTRODUCTION

eBay is fun. It provides a unique experience that enhances hobbies, promotes friendship, adds to or pares down living space, and fills bank accounts.

Writing this book was a distinct privilege and it gave me an opportunity to expand on themes, ideas, and strategies I teach in my eBay classes. As eBay sellers progress beyond the beginning phase, they often struggle with certain areas of their business. I have seen the enthusiasm, hesitation, and frustration on the faces of my students and clients.

This book addresses some of the most confusing and often complex components of eBay selling. It is an essential tool for all eBay sellers, whether they simply want to improve their eBay sales or launch and grow an eBay business.

You no longer have to spend time and effort researching multiple books or surfing numerous websites to find condensed, organized, and understandable eBay information. Use this book as your primary reference as you progress through your selling experiences. You now have *eBay Business at Your Fingertips*.

How This Book Is Organized

▶ Each chapter provides a table of contents so you can quickly see the areas that are covered. You can choose to read the entire chapter or flip to the particular subject of interest.

▶ This book was written with the assumption that the reader would already be familiar with the basic concepts and terminologies used in eBay selling.

◀ *SEE ALSO references are used to quickly find other sections of the book that pertain to the same subject and may further explain the topic.* ▶

WORDS TO GO . . .WORDS TO GO . . .WORDS TO GO

Words to Go are short, sidebar definitions of eBay- or business-related terms presented in each chapter. They are provided to further clarify the material covered.

All websites and resources in this book are listed in Appendix B, "Resources." They are grouped by major categories for easy reference.

Acknowledgments

A sincere thank you to Tom Stevens of Alpha Books/Penguin Group and Marilyn Allen of Allen O'Shea Literary Agency for the opportunity to write and have this book published. Genuine appreciation to editors Phil Kitchel, Janette Lynn, Michael Dietsch, and everyone else who contributed to the development of this book.

Special Thanks to the Technical Editor

eBay Business at Your Fingertips was reviewed by an expert who double-checked the accuracy of what you'll learn here, to help us ensure that this book gives you everything you need to know about running an eBay business. Special thanks are extended to Lissa McGrath.

Trademarks

1

EBAY REGISTRATION

1.1 The eBay Business Marketplace

1.2 Preregistration Preparation

1.3 Register as a Seller

1.1 THE EBAY BUSINESS MARKETPLACE

eBay offers an easy entry to online selling for individuals as well as businesses. Most eBay sellers begin as hobbyists or simply want to have a "nationwide garage sale." Others desire extra income. For many, selling on eBay is the start of an unexpected entrepreneurial venture.

Sales on eBay are not limited to individuals, hobbyists, or collectors anymore. Small businesses that have been dependent on walk-in or local customers can now reach nationwide and global buyers instantly with the access provided by eBay's worldwide marketplace.

The Business and Industrial category alone generates **B2B** sales totaling $2.2 billion annually. Many businesses use eBay as their strategic online sales channel. eBay also provides a fast way for businesses to liquidate inventory or test the sales potential for new products. Individuals and businesses often use an eBay Store as their first website.

◀ *SEE ALSO 11.1, "Advantages of an eBay Store"* ▶

There are now over 83 million active eBay members worldwide that produce sales of over $110,000 every minute, 24/7. Additionally, 1.3 million sellers around the world use eBay as either their primary or secondary source of income.

WORDS TO GO . . .WORDS TO GO . . .WORDS TO GO . . .

B2B refers to business-to-business sales versus business-to-consumer.

1.2 PREREGISTRATION PREPARATION

User ID

eBay Password and Secret Question

E-mail Addresses

Bank Account and Credit Card

ID Verify

Before registering on eBay as a seller, you have some careful considerations and decisions to make. What do you want to be called on eBay? What bank account and credit card will you use to pay eBay fees? What will be your e-mail address where eBay and potential customers can contact you? The answer to these questions should be determined before you begin the eBay registration process.

User ID

Your User ID (sometimes called your username) is the unique name that you create in order to identify yourself on eBay. Give thoughtful consideration to this decision. Keep in mind that the name you use will reflect your image as a seller. Avoid cute, silly, or weird names. Instead, create one that denotes professionalism.

If you do not own a business or have a specific product to sell, it is usually a good decision not to choose a User ID that ties you to a specific product or category. You will most likely change your products over time, and a name such as babybibs4u is too specific. After a few months of selling baby bibs, you may find that spark plugs are a better item to sell on eBay—and men may hesitate to order their spark plugs from a seller named babybibs4u.

Sellers can certainly change their names later. In fact, members are allowed to change their User IDs every 30 days. The point is to give your name careful consideration right from the beginning. Generic names are better than specific names. The name bestdiscounts4u is better than babybibs4u. A seller could sell any product under bestdiscounts4u without confusing the customer.

Sometimes, the name you have carefully chosen is already in use by another eBay member, so have three or four names ready before you begin the registration process. If your first choice is taken, you won't have to scramble to create a User ID on the spot.

There are some User ID limitations. They cannot be, or contain, an e-mail or web address. Additionally, a username must not contain spaces, symbols such as @ or &, or the name eBay.

eBay Password and Secret Question

For security purposes, you will be asked to provide a password and secret question. Good passwords must never be an actual word but rather should use a mixed combination of at least six or more letters and numbers. Make the password easy for you to remember but difficult for anyone else to ever guess. For example, say you were 11 years old when you received your first puppy, named Chippy. No one would ever guess your password of chip11pea.

It is important never to use the same password twice. For example, don't use the same password for eBay that you use for your e-mail or bank account. Never even use the same password on eBay as the one you use for PayPal. Criminals know that many people lazily use the same password for several online sites. If a login and password list is ever compromised on another site, criminals quickly try the logins and passwords on all major banking websites as well as trading sites such as eBay and PayPal. Every site you use should have a different login and password.

You will also be asked to supply a secret question that you can answer in case you forget your password. Choose a secret question that is easy for you to remember but not easy for someone else to guess.

E-mail Addresses

eBay requires an e-mail address for your eBay account. This address is how eBay and your customers will communicate with you. It would be best to have a new, separate e-mail address that is dedicated only to eBay and PayPal correspondence rather than mixing them with personal e-mails.

Think carefully before dismissing this advice. Do you really want to have important eBay and PayPal correspondence flow directly into your personal e-mail account? Your personal e-mail account is probably already flooded with joke e-mails from friends or unsolicited junk and spam e-mails. You may even be running a spam filter to weed out and discard the spam. If you run a spam filter, the one thing guaranteed is that the filter is throwing away business from potential new customers or distributors who have never contacted you before. The filter doesn't recognize the address and so doesn't allow you to see the message. That business is lost.

Open a new e-mail account and dedicate it solely to your eBay business correspondence. Allow all e-mails to flow into that account without using a spam filter. Very little spam will come to an account used strictly for business. Certainly continue to run antivirus e-mail and Internet software to protect your computer, but do not run a spam filter on this new business e-mail account. If you still aren't a believer, try it on your new e-mail account. You can always add a spam filter later, but be aware that it will most likely discard new business along with the spam.

Bank Account and Credit Card

There are fees associated with listing an item on eBay, and the seller pays the fees. During seller registration, eBay allows you to determine how you will pay for these fees. You can pay for your eBay fees with a credit card, debit card, PayPal account using a PayPal debit card, or checking account. You should carefully consider these options before you make your choice.

For the same reason you shouldn't mix personal e-mails with business e-mails, it is best not to mix any personal money with your eBay selling money. It will be less complicated for you, especially at tax time, if these payment accounts are dedicated solely to eBay sales. Seriously consider getting a separate credit card or opening a new checking account to use only for your eBay sales.

◀ *SEE ALSO 1.3, "Seller Fee Payment Setup"* ▶

◀ *SEE ALSO 3.4, "eBay Fees"* ▶

ID Verify

During registration, you can also choose ID Verify instead of (or in addition to) the credit card and bank account information. ID Verify means that eBay uses a third-party credit bureau to verify your identity. eBay accomplishes this by crosschecking the name, address, and contact information you registered on eBay with the information in a credit bureau's database. In addition, more personal information that only you would know such as your mortgage payment amount, car loan lender, and the address of your last residence is crosschecked and verified. There is a $5 application fee for this service.

The advantage of ID Verify is that your new account has instant credibility even with a **Feedback** score of zero. Sellers with ID Verify can also immediately bid on items above $15,000 and sell multiple quantities of **Fixed Price** items if they have at least 15 feedbacks and use PayPal as a payment option.

Feedback is the "self-policing" method eBay uses whereby both trading partners in a transaction can post a comment about the transaction for other members to view. New members start with a score of zero. A positive feedback comment is scored as +1 for a single transaction, a negative score is –1.

Fixed Price is a type of eBay listing where no bidding is necessary. The item is not offered at auction but for a particular stated price. When a buyer views a Fixed Price listing, they will not see a Place Bid button but a Buy It Now button.

◀ SEE ALSO 3.3, *"Listing Formats and Bidding"* ▶

1.3   REGISTER AS A SELLER

eBay User Agreement and Privacy Policy

Seller Fee Payment Setup

Multiple Accounts

Confirm Registration

You can begin eBay registration simply by clicking on the Register Now button on eBay's homepage. You will be provided with a registration page where you will enter your demographic information. Continue through this process until you have completed registration as a buyer. Next you will need to create and set up your preferences for a seller's account.

Registered buyers that want to upgrade to a seller's account should log in to their eBay account, click the Sell link on the main navigation bar, and follow the instructions to Create a Seller's Account.

During the registration process, you will be asked to provide the information covered in Chapter 1.2. Additionally, you will need to agree to eBay's User Agreement and set up your eBay Seller Fee Payment schedule.

eBay User Agreement and Privacy Policy

Before you can become a member of the eBay community, you will be asked to read and accept the terms of eBay's User Agreement and Privacy Policy. The User Agreement covers many aspects of eBay buying and selling including legalities, age restrictions, prohibited and restricted items, payment for and delivery of items, taxes, eBay fees, and unscrupulous activities.

The Privacy Policy describes how eBay collects personal, demographic, and financial information about you and your activities on eBay. It was developed for the protection of a member's private information.

Seller Fee Payment Setup

Once a month, eBay sends an invoice for the fees associated with that month's sales activity. These are the monthly totals for all insertion fees, final value fees, and any listing upgrade fees. A seller can choose four payment options:

> ▶ **PayPal:** With this option, the amount of your monthly bill will be automatically deducted from your PayPal account.

▶ **Direct Pay:** The invoice amount will be automatically subtracted from your checking account and posted to eBay within two business days.

▶ **Credit Card:** The amount owed will be charged automatically to your credit card. It usually posts five to seven days after you receive the invoice.

▶ **Check (Business Checks Only):** You must mail a check after receiving the invoice. It may take seven to ten business days to be deducted from your checking account.

If you prefer not to set up monthly automatic payments, you can make a one-time payment at any time during the month. One-time payments can be made with PayPal, credit or debit cards, or Direct Pay.

◀ *SEE ALSO 3.4, "eBay Fees"* ▶

Multiple Accounts

A member can have multiple eBay accounts. Each account must have a separate User ID, password, and e-mail address.

Some eBay members prefer one account for selling and a separate account for buying. Additionally, sellers often have multiple accounts in order to separate niche item selling from their general item sales.

This can be a good strategy in order to avoid buyer confusion. For example, a buyer who is browsing a seller's niche store that specializes in lavender beauty products would be confused to also see a set of spark plugs listed in the same store. A seller with two or more accounts would instead list the spark plugs in the store where they sell general merchandise. If later on you decide to have only one niche, you can merge the accounts so the feedback from the account you close will merge with the account you keep.

Confirm Registration

You will receive a confirmation e-mail after you finish the Registration process. Do not ignore this step. You need to click the link and follow all instructions in the e-mail or your account will not be activated.

2

PAYPAL ACCOUNT MANAGEMENT

2.1 WHAT IS PAYPAL?

Benefits

Secure Transactions

FDIC Pass-Through Protection

Buyer Protection

Seller Protection

PayPal is an online payment service provider that over 90 percent of all eBay buyers use to pay for the items they have won. PayPal was purchased by eBay in 2002 to provide an integrated payment service for its members. Other services provided by PayPal include automated e-mail notification and invoicing.

Benefits

With PayPal, eBay buyers can easily and immediately pay for the items they win with a few clicks of the mouse. This eliminates the need for sellers to physically deposit checks or money orders. Plus, sellers no longer have to wait for a check to clear before shipping the item. Payments made with PayPal are instant.

For Premier and Business account members, PayPal will also accept credit-card payments. This means that even if buyers don't have a PayPal account, they can still pay for their items using a major credit card. This feature is a key benefit to buyers and sellers.

◀ SEE ALSO 2.3, *"Registration"* ▶

Secure Transactions

Transactions on PayPal are as secure as online banking because PayPal uses the most robust encryption service available. Encryption scrambles the data between your computer and PayPal so it is understandable only by you and PayPal.

PayPal also guarantees its secure process. All transactions are 100 percent guaranteed against any unauthorized payments taken from your account.

FDIC Pass-Through Protection

All funds in U.S. dollars held in your PayPal account are placed in an FDIC-insured bank or savings institution. If that bank were to fail, your funds would be guaranteed up to $100,000. However, no interest is paid on these funds if you choose this option.

You can choose to place your balance in an interest-earning money market fund. This fund is very competitive, usually paying a comparable rate to a bank CD. Money-market funds can provide much higher returns than a typical savings account, but placing your money in a money market fund removes the protection provided by FDIC. Remember that money market funds are financial invest-ments that can increase or decrease over time.

◄ *SEE ALSO 2.5, "Using Paypal Outside of eBay"* ►

2.1

Buyer Protection

PayPal offers a Buyer Protection Policy to help eBay buyers recover payments from sellers for non-delivery or description fraud. Payments for items that **qualify** are protected under the PayPal Buyer Protection Policy up to $2,000 depending on each individual situation.

Offer Buyer Protection to Your Buyers

As a seller, you will automatically qualify to offer PayPal Buyer Protection to your buyers when you meet the eligibility requirements. There is no charge for this service and no action on your part is needed. The Buyer Protection indication will automatically appear on your listings if you have the following:

- ▶ A **Verified** PayPal Premier or Business account
- ▶ A 98 percent positive or better feedback rating
- ▶ At least 50 unique eBay feedbacks (either as a buyer or seller)
- ▶ PayPal as an indicated payment method on your listings
- ▶ The item is listed on an official eBay site

Seller Protection

The Seller Protection Policy applies only to Verified Business and Premier accounts. If a problem occurs with a phony chargeback, payment reversal, or false claim of non-delivery, sellers can file a claim. If the transaction meets the qualification requirements, PayPal will reimburse sellers for the amount of the chargeback or reversal up to $5,000.

PayPal's Seller Protection Policy qualifications are …

- ▶ At the time of the transaction, you must have a Verified Business or Veri-fied Premier account.
- ▶ The transaction must be between a United States, United Kingdom, or Canadian buyer and seller.

▶ The payment must have "Seller Protection Policy Eligible" on PayPal's "Transaction Details" page for that transaction.

▶ You must accept a single payment from one PayPal account for the purchase.

▶ You must not charge a surcharge for accepting PayPal.

▶ You must ship to the address listed on the "Transaction Details" page, and that address must be identified as a **Confirmed Address.**

▶ You must ship the item to the buyer within seven days of receiving payment.

▶ You must have trackable online proof of delivery from an approved major carrier (FedEx, DHL, UPS, USPS). For transactions of $250 U.S. or more, you must provide proof of receipt that was signed by the buyer and can be viewed online. This is known by the shipping carriers as Signature Confirmation.

▶ You must respond to PayPal's requests for information within the time period PayPal specifies.

PowerSellers in the United States, United Kingdom, Australia, Canada, Hong Kong, and France can also enroll in PayPal's Expanded Seller Protection program. Under this program, PowerSellers can ship to unconfirmed addresses to buyers in 190 countries and still be protected from false claims of items not received, or chargebacks and reversals for unauthorized payments.

WORDS TO GO . . . WORDS TO GO . . . WORDS TO GO

Items that **qualify** for PayPal's Buyer Protection program will be indicated as such in the Buy Safely section of the eBay listing.

A **Verified** account means you have confirmed your bank account (confirmed the test transactions from PayPal to your bank) during the registration process, or you were approved for a PayPal Plus Credit Card or PayPal Buyer Credit.

A **Confirmed Address** is one that has been reviewed and deemed safe by PayPal during the registration process, when it compares the account holder's shipping address to his or her credit card billing address. PayPal's Transaction Detail page will indicate to a seller whether the buyer's address is confirmed or unconfirmed.

2.2 HOW BUYERS PAY YOU

Accept Credit Card Payments

eChecks

Once your item sells on eBay, an invoice is automatically e-mailed to the winning bidder. The invoice includes transaction details including the winning bid price, shipping cost, any applicable taxes, and the total payment required.

If you chose PayPal as one of your accepted methods of payment during listing creation, a Pay Now button will also appear in the invoice during checkout. The buyer needs only to select PayPal as their payment method, log in to his or her PayPal account, and review and then approve the payment transaction with a few mouse clicks. The money for the total payment is then transferred from the buyer's PayPal account to yours.

Accept Credit Card Payments

If the buyer does not have a PayPal account but you have either a Premier or Business account, the invoice will state that your buyer can pay for the item with a major credit card. If the buyer chooses that option, a payment form appears with fields for credit card and shipping information.

Once the user completes that form, PayPal will approve or deny the transaction with the credit card company. If approved, the money will be deposited in your account and an e-mail notification sent to you. PayPal, in effect, treats you the same as a merchant by handling credit card payments from your buyers. This is a significant reason why all eBay sellers should at least have a Premier account.

eChecks

PayPal can also complete eCheck transactions. This is similar to writing a check, except it is completed electronically. Since an eCheck is a bank-to-bank transaction, it usually takes three to four business days to clear. Once it does, you will receive an e-mail from PayPal stating that the transaction has cleared.

Note that many buyers do not even realize that they have sent you an eCheck. Unless they have a Verified PayPal account, they are not eligible for instant transfers from their bank account. Therefore, if they do not have enough funds in their PayPal account to cover the purchase, the money is taken from their bank account and sent to your PayPal account in the form of an eCheck. Most buyers are also not aware that an eCheck takes several days to clear. It is good customer service to respond to any buyers who have paid by eCheck and let them know about the associated banking delay and that their item will ship only after the transaction clears.

If a buyer has a verified PayPal account but not enough funds to cover the purchase, they are eligible for instant transfers from their bank account. The funds would not only transfer immediately, but clear immediately. If there are not enough funds in the buyer's bank account, the money is charged against the buyer's credit card on file with PayPal.

2.3 REGISTRATION

Account Types

Account Confirmation

Updating Your Account

Getting Help

Opening a PayPal account is as simple as going to www.paypal.com, clicking the Sign Up link at the top of the homepage, and following the online instructions. You can select a Personal, Premier, or Business account. You may also have more than one account, but each must have a different e-mail address and separate financial information. This can be as simple as using your checking account on one and your savings account on another if you don't have two separate checking accounts.

Most eBay sellers have just one PayPal account that they use for both buying and selling. Once an account is activated, you can then add additional e-mail addresses, bank accounts, and credit or debit cards.

Account Types

The three types of PayPal accounts most common to eBay buyers and sellers are Personal, Premier, and Business. Each has a unique appeal, and you should examine them to determine which one best meets your needs.

The Personal account is most commonly used by eBay buyers. It is simple to set up and provides easy payment methods. However, it will accept only five credit card payments per year and charges a much higher percentage rate (4.9 percent) for these transactions than does Premier or Business (varies from 1.9 to 2.9 percent based on your sales volume). The Personal account, then, is best left for buyers and isn't a good choice for eBay sellers.

The Premier account is the best choice for most eBay sellers. There is no additional fee to open, or upgrade to, a Premier account, and it accepts an unlimited number of all types of payment transactions including member-to-member, credit/debit cards, and eChecks. In addition, it offers premium services such as access to PayPal's customer call center, a high-yield money market fund, an optional debit card, auction tools, and website payment products.

A Business account offers the same benefits as Premier, and you should consider it if you require two or more unique logins and security levels. For example, if you own a business and have employees who need access to the shipping information from your account, yet you do not want them to have access to the money.

Account Confirmation

Once you complete the online registration process, you will receive an e-mail from PayPal asking you to confirm your account. You must complete this process or the account will not be activated.

In addition, you should confirm any bank accounts associated with your PayPal account. You can accomplish this by using either the Instant Bank (if your bank is part of this program) or Random Deposit process offered during account confirmation. You will receive a confirmation e-mail explaining this process. Once your bank account is confirmed, you will receive a Verified status.

◀ SEE ALSO 2.1, *"What Is PayPal?"* ▶

Updating Your Account

As you progress through your eBay selling, you may need to update or upgrade your PayPal account. Using the Profile tab, you can easily upgrade your account, and update personal and financial information or your selling preferences.

Getting Help

PayPal is a financial institution and has excellent customer service. If you are unable to find the answer to your question using the Help link at the top of the homepage and you are a Premier or Business member, you can talk to a live PayPal customer call center representative at 1-888-221-1161.

2.4 PAYPAL FEES

There is no fee to open a Personal, Premier, or Business PayPal account for U.S. members, nor is there a fee to add funds to or withdraw funds from an account. Fees are charged, however, to the recipient of the payment. This includes eBay sellers who accept PayPal payments from their buyers. This is similar to the way a retail business with a merchant account is charged a fee for accepting credit card payments.

When a seller receives payment for an item from a buyer, the PayPal fee for that transaction appears in the fee column of the seller's history page.

For Premier and Business accounts, the fee is the same whatever payment method the buyer uses (credit/debit card, eCheck, balance transfer, or buyer credit). The rates for these payments to U.S. PayPal members range from 1.9 percent to 2.9 percent plus 30 cents, based on the seller's monthly sales activity. Transactions that require international currency conversions range from 2.9 percent to 3.9 percent plus 30 cents U.S.

PayPal will occasionally adjust its fees. To find the current fees, click on the Help link at the top of the PayPal homepage and type "fees" in the search field.

2.5 USING PAYPAL OUTSIDE OF EBAY

Sending and Requesting Money or Payments
Earn Interest in Your Account
View/Download Your Transaction History Log

PayPal is not limited to making payments for eBay sales, but can be used for any financial transaction among businesses or individuals. Many websites now use PayPal for their preferred checkout payment method.

Sending and Requesting Money or Payments

Individuals can pay for non-eBay-related goods and services or exchange money with family and friends by using the Send Money or Request Money tabs. All that is required to either send or request money is the PayPal e-mail address of the other party.

To send money, the member logs in to her PayPal account and clicks on the Send Money tab. A simple form appears where she then enters the e-mail address of the other member and the dollar amount to send. The money is then transferred to the recipient's account and the recipient is charged the standard PayPal transaction fee.

To request money, the member clicks on the Request Money tab and completes the form by entering the dollar amount requested. PayPal then sends an invoice by e-mail to the second member. Once that member approves payment using the invoice, the money is then transferred from his account to the requestor's account. The payment requestor is then charged the standard PayPal transaction fee.

Even if payers do not have a PayPal account, the invoice will allow them to pay using a major credit card as long as the recipient has a Premier or Business account (Personal accounts can also accept up to five credit card payments per year). PayPal then completes the transaction with the credit card company and deposits the money in the payment requestor's account. The requestor is then charged the standard PayPal transaction fee.

You can transfer funds from your confirmed bank account to your PayPal account by using the Add Funds tab. There is no charge for this service.

Funds are withdrawn from your PayPal account in four different ways: ATM draw, online transfer to your bank, online transfer to a credit card, and a check request. The ATM option requires that you have a PayPal debit card associated with your account. Clicking on the Withdraw tab can complete the other transaction options.

2.5

Earn Interest in Your Account

You can earn competitive money market interest on the funds in your Premier or Business PayPal account. Note that U.S. members will need to provide date of birth and a Social Security number (EIN tax number for Business accounts) for IRS purposes. To earn interest on your account, go to the My Account then Overview tabs. Under your Balance tab will be a link called "Earn a return on your balance".

◄ *SEE ALSO 2.1, "What Is Paypal?"* ▷

View/Download Your Transaction History Log

You can view every transaction made within the last 30 days, interest earned, and PayPal fee charged by clicking the My Account and Overview tabs. You can access historical data (for the last 12 months), sometimes used for accounting purposes by eBay sellers, and download it to a **comma-delimited** file (such as Excel) from the History tab.

WORDS TO GO . . .WORDS TO GO . . .WORDS TO GO

Comma-delimited is a type of data file that uses commas to separate the data fields from each other. This format is used to transfer data files from one application or system to another.

3

EBAY SELLING FUNDAMENTALS

3.1 SITE NAVIGATION

Primary Navigation Bar

Item Search Bar

Categories

eBay is a comprehensive, multipage, multilevel website. Its technical engine is seamlessly integrated with PayPal and must perform millions of complex financial transactions, listing creations, photo uploads, and many other disparate processes, every day.

While the engineering complexities of the eBay system are remarkable, what is most impressive is its user-friendliness. The look, feel, layout, processes, and navigation of eBay have all been carefully designed for simplicity and ease of use. This makes eBay navigation practical, functional, and understandable, regardless of a user's computer knowledge.

Primary Navigation Bar

eBay's primary navigation bar is located at the top of each page. At the very bottom of each eBay page are additional help links that are usually relevant to the current page you are viewing.

| Buy | Sell | My eBay | Community | Help |

Primary navigation bar.

The primary navigation bar includes the following links:

▶ **Buy:** Use this link to perform a keyword or category search for items on eBay.

▶ **Sell:** The process for listing an item on eBay begins here.

▶ **My eBay:** Everything that is happening between you and eBay (buying, selling, and account information) is tracked and easily available for your review.

▶ **Community:** Catch up on the latest eBay news, announcements, blogs, and discussion forums.

▶ **Help:** With this link, you can quickly search for help topics, visit eBay's Learning Center, learn about eBay University, find local eBay classes in your vicinity, link to the Security Center, or contact eBay.

Item Search Bar

At the top of the homepage is eBay's quick search bar. Using relevant keywords, members can quickly search for an item under all categories or narrow the search to particular categories.

Item search bar.

◀ *SEE ALSO 3.2, "How eBay Searches Work"* ▶

Immediately under the search field are quick links to eBay Motors, eBay Express, eBay Stores, and a drop-down menu for all of the major categories.

Categories

eBay has over 50,000 categories and subcategories of products. While most (about 80 percent) eBay buyers use keywords to search for their items, many (the remaining 20 percent) prefer to click on a particular category link and browse for products listed under that category.

The major eBay categories are found by scrolling down the left column on eBay's homepage (or using the quick link tab). Clicking on a major category will open a list of additional clickable subcategories. Buyers continue clicking to narrow their search to the particular subcategory of interest.

3.2 HOW EBAY SEARCHES WORK

Best Match and Category Expansion

One of the best ways sellers can learn how to write a good title is to study how eBay keyword searches work. A common mistake is to assume that keyword searches on eBay work the same as Internet search engines.

Unless a keyword is one of the more popular searches, eBay does not correct spelling or suggest alternative choices for a misspelled keyword. For certain categories, however, eBay may expand a search to include items that it thinks you intended rather than what you actually typed. See "Keyword Search Category Expansion," later in this section.

A few things to keep in mind about eBay keyword searches are …

▶ It does not matter what order the keywords are in unless they are within quotes.

▶ There is no need to repeat words.

▶ Searches are not case-sensitive (an uppercase, lowercase, or mixed-case search produces the same result).

Fender guitar item search results.

The following table summarizes how eBay search results can be altered based on keyword formatting.

3.2

EBAY KEYWORD SEARCH RULES

Desired Search Result	Example	Will Return
Listings that contain a particular word	guitar	Listings that contain the word *guitar*.
Listings that contain two words	guitar bass	Listings that contain both words *guitar* and *bass*. Order of the words is not relevant.
Listings that contain words in a particular order	"bass guitar"	Listings that contain *bass guitar*, in that order.
Listings that do not contain certain words	bass guitar –acoustic	Listings that contain the words *bass guitar*, except those containing the word *acoustic*.
Listings that don't contain several words	bass guitar –acoustic –amplifier –amp	Listings that include bass guitar but none that slso include *acoustic*, *amplifier*, or *amp*.
Either a Fender or Gibson bass guitar	bass guitar (fender, gibson)	Listings that contain either the words *Fender* or *Gibson* and *bass guitar*.
Listings that contain at least a portion of a word (known as a wildcard)	guitar amp*	Using the asterisk * will display listings that contain the words *guitar, amp, amps, amplifier, amplifiers*, etc.
Listings that contain a specific spelling	"gipson" guitar	Shows all listings with the misspelled *gipson guitar*. Buyers sometimes use this method looking for items with little competition because the seller misspelled *Gibson*. Without the quotes, eBay would assume you meant *Gibson* and would return *Gibson guitars* as well as *Gipson* (see Keyword Search Category Expansion below).

Best Match and Category Expansion

For certain items and categories, eBay will automatically expand a search and include items that it believes you intended rather than what you actually typed, based on relevance. If you search for a keyword that is also associated with a specific subcategory or relevant popular search items, the results from that subcategory will display even if the keyword is not in the title. So a search for *bass guitar* will bring up all of the items listed in *Musical Instruments—Guitar—Bass*, whether or not they have the words *bass guitar* in the title.

This can be either beneficial or annoying when you are purposely searching for listings that have a misspelled keyword. Placing the keyword within quotation marks ensures that eBay will not assume your intention and will only display exactly what you have typed.

eBay's Search Category Expansion list is quite comprehensive, covering many keywords and categories. You can view the list by clicking on the Help link and typing Keyword Search Category Expansion in the search box.

eBay also combines Item Specifics with keywords to provide more robust search results for many items and categories. For example, if you used the keywords "white sandals 8" in the Women's Shoes category, it would also bring up any items in that category that matched using a combination of keywords in the title and item specifics. So if an auction had "sandals 8" in the title and had "white" as the main color specified using item specifics, the item would show up in the search results even though all three words were not actually in the title.

3.3 LISTING FORMATS AND BIDDING

Auction-Style (Online Auction)

Fixed Price

Multiple Item (Dutch) Auction

Best Offer

Store Item

Proxy Bidding on eBay

Bid Increments

3.3

Even though many people think of eBay strictly as an auction site, in fact there are many different types of listing formats available. The most commonly used format remains Auction-Style (also referred to as Online Auction), which is used mostly by the casual seller. Business sellers are currently trending toward Fixed Price listings because they guarantee required profit margins and can help move product quickly. Fixed Price listings now account for 41 percent of all sales.

Auction-Style (Online Auction)

This is the most popular listing format on eBay. Buyers discover the item through keyword or category searches, place bids throughout the listing's duration, and the highest bidder at the end of the auction becomes the winner.

Auction-Style with Reserve

Sellers may choose to add a reserve price to their Auction-Style listings. A reserve is the minimum price that the seller is willing to accept for the item. If the auction ends and the highest bid was under the reserve price, the listing is considered a "No Sale" and the seller is not obligated to part with the item.

When a seller includes a reserve price, the words "Reserve Not Met" will appear under the Place Bid button in the listing. This message will remain until a bid meets or exceeds the reserve price. After the reserve is met, this line disappears and future bidders will not know that it ever had a reserve price.

Reserve prices are not revealed in the listing and are confidential between eBay and the seller. Sometimes a buyer will ask a seller to reveal the reserve price, and it's up to the seller's sole discretion whether to share the reserve price information with a buyer.

Auction-Style with Buy It Now

You may choose to add a Buy It Now button to your Auction-Style listing. Buyers then have the option to either place a bid or purchase your item immediately.

If they click on the Buy It Now button, the listing ends immediately and the buyer wins the item. If instead they place a bid, with most items, the listing converts to Auction-Style and the Buy It Now button is no longer available. Currently, in the categories of tickets, clothing, shoes, cell phones, and PDAs, the Buy It Now button remains until bidding reaches 50 percent of the Buy It Now price. More categories are being reviewed and will be added in the future. Each may have a different threshold for when the button disappears.

Auction-Style with Reserve and Buy It Now

This format allows buyers to either place bids or use the Buy It Now button. The Buy It Now button remains active until the reserve price is met, at which point the button disappears.

Private Auction

A Private Auction is one where the User IDs of each bidder are hidden from view within the listing's bid history link. A seller may choose a Private Auction when listing expensive items where the bidders may want to be more discrete or anonymous to everyone but the seller.

Fixed Price

A Fixed Price listing is one where no bidding occurs. There is one price only and the item is available for immediate sale by clicking on the Buy It Now button. Fixed Price items are displayed along with Auction-Style listings in the standard keyword or category search view.

The advantage to buyers is that they can purchase items immediately using the Buy It Now button rather than having to wait until the listing time ends to see whether they have won. The advantage for sellers is the ability to either move their items quickly or to list multiple quantities of the same item at a Fixed Price.

In order to list an item at Fixed Price, you must have a Feedback rating of 10 or more (or be **ID Verified**). It does not matter whether your feedback was obtained through buying or selling. If you accept PayPal as a payment method, you only need a feedback rating of 5 or more.

A multiple quantity (two or more) Fixed Price listing requires the seller to have been a registered user for at least 14 days (or be ID Verified) and have a minimum feedback rating of 30. If the seller accepts PayPal as a payment method, he or she only needs a feedback rating of 15 or more to sell multiple quantities at Fixed Price.

◧ *SEE ALSO 10.3, "Feedback"* ▶

◧ *SEE ALSO 1.2, "Preregistration Preparation"* ▷

Multiple Item (Dutch) Auction

A Multiple Item Auction (also called a Dutch Auction), is one where a seller lists a quantity of two or more of the same item using an "Auction-Style" format. These are auctions used by more experienced sellers who have a quantity of the same item and want to move all or most with just one auction.

The purpose of bidding on the auction is to determine how the quantity of the items will be allocated between the winning bidders, and what price they will all pay. The highest bidders have their quantities filled first. The remaining quantity goes to the next highest bidder and his quantity is filled, then on to the next highest bidder, and so on until the entire quantity demand is exhausted.

Buyers place their bids during the auction in order to ensure that they will receive their desired quantity. However, after the auction ends, all winners pay the same price as the *lowest* winning bidder's final bid. Many times, this is the starting bid price. As a seller, then, you should not create a multiple item "auction" listing unless you are willing to let everything go for the starting bid price.

Best Offer

Best Offer is an option that is added to a Fixed Price listing. It allows buyers to make an offer on the item much like an "or best offer (OBO)" listing in a newspaper. Sellers can choose to accept or decline the offer, or make a counteroffer.

Other sellers may sometimes use Best Offer to simply get rid of their items. It is not usually a good strategy to use Best Offer for **commodity items** (a seller's major product line) unless you set it to auto-reject offers below a certain amount, because it is time-consuming to respond to multiple "low-ball" offers.

Store Item

Sellers use eBay stores to list accessories, add-ons, different sizes, and different colors of their items. Store listings do not appear in a standard keyword search unless the search produces fewer than 30 findings.

Listings created exclusively for your eBay store are always Fixed Price listings. Each store listing can have quantities of up to 10,000 for one small listing fee that can be renewed every 30 days using the **Good 'Til Canceled (GTC)** option.

◀ SEE ALSO 3.5, *"Listing Upgrades and Fees"* ▶

◀ SEE ALSO 11.2, *"When to Open an eBay Store"* ▶

Proxy Bidding on eBay

When buyers place a bid on eBay, they are actually using a proxy bidding method, meaning eBay places bids on their behalf. There is no option to this. All bids placed on eBay are by proxy.

With this method, eBay favors the buyer over the seller by only bidding the minimum amount required to be either the high bidder or to reach the reserve price. If you are a buyer, eBay will place the bid on your behalf, yet will only enter the minimum amount required for you to be the high bidder—up to the maximum amount you bid.

For example, if an item has no bids and the starting bid is $1, you can enter the highest bid you are willing to pay (say, $20) and eBay will place your bid for only $1. The reason is that $1 is the starting bid and, therefore, the minimum amount required at this time for you to be the high bidder. Only you and eBay know about the remaining $19.

If no one else bids on the item, you will win it for $1 even though you entered $20. If someone else bids later, eBay will automatically place another bid for you that will again be the minimum amount required at that time. This bidding method will continue until eBay reaches $20—your highest bid. With proxy bidding, you may never even come close to the $20 you were willing to pay as long as no one else "bids you up."

The best strategy using eBay's proxy bidding is to place, just once, the highest bid you are willing to pay and then let eBay bid on your behalf throughout the auction. You win it or you lose it. Since eBay will always bid the minimum amount required, you may even end up paying much less than your maximum bid.

Bid Increments

A bid increment is the required amount that a new bid needs to be raised over the Current bid. For example, using the following bid increment table, if the current price is $2.00, the next minimum bid would need to be $2.25. The bid increments on eBay are as follows:

EBAY BID INCREMENTS

Current Price	Required Bid Increment
$0.01–$0.99	$0.05
$1.00–$4.99	$0.25
$5.00–$24.99	$0.50
$25.00–$99.99	$1.00
$100.00–$249.99	$2.50
$250.00–$499.99	$5.00
$500.00–$999.99	$10.00
$1,000.00–$2,499.99	$25.00
$2,500.00–$4,999.99	$50.00
$5,000.00 and up	$100.00

3.3

WORDS TO GO . . .WORDS TO GO . . .WORDS TO GO

ID Verified means that a third-party credit bureau has verified your identity during eBay registration.

Commodity items are products that a seller has multiple quantities of in his or her inventory stock.

Good 'Til Canceled (GTC) is the amount of time an item can be listed in an eBay store. Under this option, the item will remain in the store until sold or cancelled by the seller.

3.4 EBAY FEES

Insertion Fee

Final Value Fee

If you placed an item for sale in your local newspaper, you would be charged an advertising fee. Likewise, sellers pay the fees associated with listing their items on eBay.

There are no fees for registering as a seller and there are no recurring fees for being a seller. Fees are only applied when items are listed.

Each month eBay will e-mail an invoice to the seller for all accumulated fees for that month. The seller can automatically pay her fees by one of the methods chosen during eBay registration—usually a checking account withdrawal or a credit or debit card charge—or she can make a one-time payment using any of the payment method options.

◀ SEE ALSO 1.3, *"Seller Fee Payment Setup"* ▶

You can see the amount you owe for the current month plus invoices of the last four months. Click the View Invoices link on the Account Status link within My eBay.

There are three types of fees on eBay: Insertion Fee, Final Value Fee, and the optional Listing Upgrade Fees.

Insertion Fee

An Insertion Fee is the first fee associated with an eBay listing and is directly related to the starting price. The following table shows why so many listings on eBay begin under a dollar. The sellers are choosing the lowest Insertion Fee possible. This may not be a good decision if the item sells for the starting bid.

INSERTION FEES

Starting or Reserve Price	Insertion Fee	Insertion Fee for Books, Music, Video Games, DVDs, and Movies
$0.01–$0.99	$0.15	$0.10
$1.00–$9.99	$0.35	$0.25
$10.00–$24.99	$0.55	$0.35
$25.00–$49.99	$1.00	$1.00

Starting or Reserve Price	Insertion Fee	Insertion Fee for Books, Music, Video Games, DVDs, and Movies
$50.00–$199.99	$2.00	$2.00
$200.00–$499.99	$3.00	$3.00
$500.00 or more	$4.00	$4.00

Fixed Price listings must have a starting price of $1.00 or higher. So the minimum Insertion Fee for Fixed Price listings is $0.25 for books, music, DVDs, movies, or video games and $0.35 for all other items.

If your item does not sell, eBay gives you a second chance by allowing you to receive a credit on your Insertion Fee if you relist the item within 90 days and it sells the second time. Listing Upgrade Fees would still apply to the relisted item even if it sells the second time.

◀ *SEE ALSO 10.2, "My eBay Special Features"* ▶

Final Value Fee

This additional fee is charged only if your item sells. The fee is only applied to the item's final bid value. There is no eBay fee charged against the seller's shipping rate.

FINAL VALUE FEES

Closing Price	Final Value Fee
Item not sold	No fee
$0.01–$25.00	8.75 percent of the final value
$25.01–$1,000.00	8.75 percent of the initial $25.00 ($2.19), plus 3.50 percent of remaining balance
Equal to or over $1,000.01	8.75 percent of the initial $25.00 over $1,000.01 ($2.19), plus 3.50 percent of the initial $25.01–$1,000.00 ($34.12), plus 1.50 percent of the remaining balance

3.5 LISTING UPGRADES AND FEES

Optional Format Feature Fees

eBay Store Inventory Fees

Listing Upgrade Fees

eBay charges sellers Listing Upgrade Fees for non-standard, optional formats or enhancements to their listings. PowerSellers use these enhancements as advanced strategies to increase the item's visibility and hopefully result in more hits, bids, and ultimately a higher final price for the item.

Optional Format Feature Fees

Sellers may choose to sell with an optional format. These formats come with additional insertion fees over standard Auction-Style listings.

Sometimes sellers desire a reserve price for their listing to protect against the item selling for too low a price. The reserve price is the minimum amount the seller will accept for the item.

eBay will provide this protection and charge a fee accordingly as shown in the table below.

OPTIONAL RESERVE FEES

Reserve Price	Fee
$0.01–$199.99	$2.00
$200.00 and up	1 percent of Reserve Price (up to $50)

Buy It Now

The cost to add a Buy It Now (BIN) button to an Auction-Style listing is provided in the table below.

BIN Price	Fee
$0.01–$9.99	$0.05
$10.00–$24.99	$0.10
$25.00–$49.99	$0.20
$50.00 or more	$0.25

The Insertion Fee for a Multiple Item (Dutch) Auction or a Multiple Item Fixed Price listing is based on the fee for the starting price of your listing multiplied by the quantity of items for sale. The maximum fee is $4.00.

eBay Store Inventory Fees

There are three eBay Store subscription levels, each with a separate monthly price: Basic Store, $15.95; Premium Store, $49.95; and Anchor Store, $299.95. Additionally, the cost to list and sell an item from your store is shown below.

3.5

STORE ITEM INSERTION FEES

Starting or Reserve Price	30 days	Good 'Til Cancelled
$1.00–$24.99	$0.03	$0.03 / 30 days
$25.00–$199.99	$0.05	$0.05 / 30 days
$200.00 and above	$0.10	$0.10 / 30 days

Items in your eBay store are listed as Fixed Price items. They will expire after 30 days unless you choose Good 'Til Cancelled (GTC), where the listings and insertion fees renew every 30 days. When store items sell, a Final Value Fee is applied according to the table below.

STORE FINAL VALUE FEES

Closing Price	Final Value Fee
Item not sold	No fee
$0.01–$25	12 percent of the closing price
$25.01–$100	12 percent of the initial $25.00 ($3.00), plus 8 percent of the remaining balance
$100.01–$1,000	12 percent of the initial $25.00 ($3.00), plus 8 percent of the initial $25.01–$100 ($6.00), plus 4 percent of the remaining balance $100.01–$1,000
Over $1,000.01	12 percent of the initial $25.00 ($3.00), plus 8 percent of the initial $25.01–$100 ($6.00), plus 4 percent of the initial $100.01–$1,000 ($36.00), plus 2 percent of the remaining balance ($1,000.01—final value)

You can save up to 75 percent on your store item Final Value Fees when you drive traffic to your store from a website. For more information use eBay's Help link and type **Store Referral Credit** in the search field.

Note also that the Listing Upgrade Fees shown in the next section also apply to Store items and are charged every 30 days for Good 'Til Cancelled (GTC) listings. The only exception is Subtitle, which is $0.02 per 30-day listing for eBay Store items.

Listing Upgrade Fees

Each Listing Upgrade is described below along with the current price at the time of this writing. eBay adjusts fees periodically which is usually at the end of January each year. You can find the current fees by clicking on the Help link at the top of the homepage, typing "upgrade fees" in the search box, selecting "ebay. com fees," and then scrolling down to "show" Listing Upgrade fees.

The fees below apply to standard Auction-Style and Fixed Price auctions as well as Store items. The fees are applied once, for the duration of the listing.

Gallery—Free: Gallery displays a thumbnail picture of your item next to your title in the search results. As of February 2008, this option is now free and eBay will automatically put your uploaded photograph into the Gallery.

Gallery Plus—$0.35: Gallery Plus displays a larger, pop-up picture of your item in the search results when eBay buyers **mouse over** your Gallery photograph.

Gallery Featured—$19.95: This option will place your listing in the Featured Gallery section that is presented first, above the more commonly used Picture Gallery when viewing search results.

Listing Designer—$0.10: You can upgrade the design and layout of your listings with a variety of dazzling colors, patterns, and themes.

Subtitle—$0.50: You can place a subtitle immediately below the title in the search results to explain additional item features that are not appropriate for the title. Note that the subtitle is not searchable unless the buyer checks the box to "Search title and description."

Bold—$1.00: When viewing search results, this option bolds the title to make a listing stand out from the competition.

Border—$3.00: The Border option encases a colored border around the listing when viewing search results.

Highlight—$5.00: This enhancement places a colored background behind the listing title when viewing search results. It grabs attention much like a highlight marker does in a textbook.

Scheduled Listings—$0.10: Scheduled Listings provide sellers the opportunity to start their listings on certain days and times, up to three weeks in advance. This is a popular enhancement because it allows sellers to create their listings whenever it is convenient, yet have them start later at a better date and time.

10-Day Durations—$0.40: Listing durations of 1, 3, 5, or 7 days are considered standard. The 10-day duration is the longest option available, extends the listing for three additional days, and can cover two weekends.

Gift Services—$0.25: Sellers may want to use this enhancement if they are willing to gift wrap the item, offer next-day shipping, or ship to the address of the recipient of the gift rather than the buyer. When this enhancement is chosen, a gift-wrapped package icon appears next to the item when viewing search results. This option is more popular during the Christmas holiday season and for other popular gift-giving days such as Valentine's Day or Father's and Mother's Day.

Featured Plus!—$9.95–$24.95: A Featured Plus! listing will appear above the general listings when viewing the search results for that item's category. This option provides more visibility to buyers, since the item will always be seen first on the page before the general listings.

FEATURED PLUS! FEES

Starting/Reserve Price	Featured Plus! Fee
$0.01–$24.99	$9.95
$25.00–$199.99	$14.95
$200.00–$499.99	$19.95
$500.00 or more	$24.95

For Multiple Quantity Auctions and Multiple Quantity Fixed Price listings, the starting price used to determine the Featured Plus! fee is calculated by multiplying the starting price/reserve by the quantity available. The maximum Featured Plus! fee for any type of listing is $24.95.

Value Pack—$0.65: This selection offers a packaged discount price for the Listing Designer, Gallery Plus, and Subtitle enhancements. If selected separately, these enhancements would total $0.95.

Pro Pack—$19.95–$34.95: This selection offers a packaged discount for the listing enhancements specifically designed to attract the most attention to your listing. The package includes Bold, Border, Highlight, Gallery Featured, and Featured Plus! This option is a good value for more expensive items that can justify the cost.

PRO PACK FEES

Starting/Reserve Price	Pro Pack Fee
$0.01–$24.99	$19.95
$25.00–$199.99	$24.95
$200.00–$499.99	$29.95
$500.00 or more	$34.95

Home Page Featured—$39.95: This option will alternate your item along with other sellers' items on eBay's homepage, giving you maximum visibility to a variety of buyers. However, the length of time for your item's exposure, time of day, and day of the week varies and cannot be guaranteed. eBay will not even guarantee that your item will in fact make it to the homepage during the listing duration. For this reason, most people who use this option run a 10-day listing so they have the greatest chance of it rotating to the homepage at least once.

Quantity of Two or More—$79.95: This is the price for a Home Page Featured option if you have an item quantity of two or more.

List in Two Categories—Fees Vary: Your item can appear in two separate categories of your choice. Sellers sometimes choose this upgrade when their item is equally popular in two categories. For example, a Boat Model Lamp may be popular in both the Maritime Lamp/Lighting category as well as the Model Ship category. This option doubles the Insertion Fee as well as any Listing Upgrade fees (except Scheduled Listing and Home Page Featured).

WORDS TO GO . . .WORDS TO GO . . .WORDS TO GO

Store Referral Credit refers to a 75 percent credit on an item's Final Value Fee when sellers send buyers to eBay from their own website using a special tracking code on the link. eBay tracks this activity and provides the credit to the seller's Final Value Fee if the buyer purchases their items.

Mouse over refers to a computer user placing their cursor over an item icon or picture. With eBay's Gallery Plus, this results in automatic picture enlargement.

4

CREATING LISTINGS

4.1 Listing Preparation

4.2 Listing Creation

4.3 Top Tips for Listing Creation

4.1 LISTING PREPARATION

Conduct eBay Research

Take the Pictures

Determine the Shipping Charge

The most successful PowerSellers do some prep work to determine how best to sell their items. Before listing your item on eBay, then, some preparation is required.

Conduct eBay Research

Experienced sellers conduct research on eBay to find, study, and mimic the top sellers who are selling the same item that they are about to list. This step alone is often the key to a successful listing.

Study the keywords, categories, starting price, listing format, and other significant information used by the top sellers of a particular item. Analyze listings to determine the best choice for each component of the listing. This way, when it is time to list an item, your research will give you the details you need.

◀ *SEE ALSO 12.2, "Competitive Analysis"* ▶

Take the Pictures

Take a digital picture of your item, download it to your computer, make any necessary edits, and save it using a file name that will be easy to find when you create your listing. eBay photography is presented in Chapter 5; putting photos in a listing is discussed later in this chapter.

◀ *SEE ALSO Chapter 5, "Photography"* ▶

◀ *SEE ALSO 4.2, "Listing Creation"* ▶

Determine the Shipping Charge

Part of the listing process requires the seller to determine the shipping rate. You'll need a postal scale to weigh the item in the actual shipping box, along with all necessary packing material. Use the total weight of the packed box to determine the shipping rate from the shipping carrier's website, or use eBay's **Shipping Calculator.** Shipping is extensively detailed in Chapter 6.

◁ *SEE ALSO 6.8, "Determine the Shipping Rate"* ▷

◁ *SEE ALSO 6.9, "Postal Scales"* ▷

Once you've conducted research, taken pictures of the item, and determined the shipping rate, you're ready to create your listing on eBay using either the **Sell Your Item Form (SYIF)** or **Turbo Lister.**

WORDS TO GO . . .WORDS TO GO . . .WORDS TO GO

Shipping Calculator is a pop-up software tool eBay has developed to help sellers determine the shipping rate for their item. When the seller chooses "Calculated" rate for their listing, buyers can click the shipping Calculate link, enter their zip code, and see their shipping cost.

Sell Your Item Form (SYIF) is the step-by-step web-based template sellers use to create an eBay listing.

Turbo Lister is an eBay-developed database tool to help eBay sellers easily and efficiently create listings. Turbo Lister resides on the seller's computer hard drive and replaces the need for the Sell Your Item Form (SYIF).

4.1

4.2 LISTING CREATION

Listing Format Selection
Keywords and Title
eBay Categories
Item Description
Inserting Photos
Starting Price
Duration
Scheduled Listing
Payment Terms
Quantities
Ship-to Location, Rates, and Terms
Sales Tax
Return Policies
Listing Upgrades
Preview and Listing Revision

Begin creating a listing by clicking the Sell link on the primary navigation bar at the top of any page and completing the Sell Your Item Form (SYIF). This template-style form walks you through the required steps to construct a listing. Once you complete and submit the form to eBay, all information is then reformatted by eBay to produce an attractive listing.

This chapter is not a "How To" for listing an item, but rather a reference guide to define and clarify the steps and terms used during listing creation. If you are new to eBay, a beginners eBay selling book would be most helpful.

Listing Format Selection

You can choose from 10 combinations of listing formats for your item. Each is explained in detail in Chapter 3, but they are briefly described again here. The standard formats for eBay listings are ...

> ▶ **Auction-Style:** This is the most common format. Buyers place bids on an item and the highest bid wins.

▶ **Private Listing:** A buyer's User ID is not shown in the History page or as the High Bidder on the Auction page. It is used mostly in higher-priced auctions.

▶ **Fixed Price:** This listing format is not an auction and there are no bids. The item is for sale at one stated price.

▶ **Store Inventory:** This lists your item in your eBay Store at a Fixed Price.

You can choose to add other features during listing creation to create six additional listing formats:

▶ **Auction-Style with Reserve:** You add a minimum Reserve price, which must at least be met during the bidding, or the item does not have to be sold.

▶ **Auction-Style with Buy It Now:** Allows buyers to either bid on an item or purchase the item at the stated price.

▶ **Auction-Style with Reserve and Buy It Now:** Same as above but also adds a minimum Reserve price that must be met.

▶ **Fixed Price with Best Offer:** Buyers are allowed to make an offer for the item rather than pay the Buy It Now price.

▶ **Multiple Item (Dutch) Auction:** Used to move several quantities of the same item, to one or more bidders, using the auction format.

▶ **Multiple Item Fixed Price Listing:** Used to sell multiple quantities of the same item to multiple buyers at a fixed price.

◀ *SEE ALSO 3.3, "Listing Formats and Bidding"* ▶

Keywords and Title

The single most important component for a successful listing on eBay is the string of keywords you use to form your **Title.** It is estimated that 80 percent of buyers use keywords to search for items. Stated another way, 80 percent of your customers will find you with keywords, so your title needs to be outstanding.

You might have the best item, description, price, and pictures and offer free shipping, but if you use inadequate or poorly chosen keywords, few buyers will find your item and the results will be disappointing. Therefore, when conducting research and studying the top sellers' techniques, the vast majority of your time should be used to determine and refine the best keywords.

Title

The title consists of the listing's keywords and has a limit of 55 characters. All characters count, including spaces and punctuation, so be sure to use all 55; don't waste valuable character space by using commas, periods, and exclamation marks!

Your title should incorporate the most likely keywords that buyers will use to search for your item. The keywords are not case sensitive, and it doesn't matter what order the keywords are in or whether they are grammatically correct. However, it will be easier for your buyer to quickly understand your title if the keywords are arranged in a manner that makes sense. Additionally, your title will be easier to read if you DO NOT TYPE IN ALL CAPS, but rather use Mixed Case.

Another common mistake new sellers make is to treat the title as if were advertising space. Do not use words such as "L@@K" or "WOW" or write advertising copy such as "We offer the best deals!"

Think like a buyer searching for your item. The title is not an ad. It should be made up of good, descriptive keywords that will turn up in the most searches. In order to create powerful titles that produce the best results, it is important to understand how eBay searches work.

◀ SEE ALSO 3.2, "How eBay Searches Work" ▶

Subtitle

You can place a subtitle immediately below the title so that it will be viewed in the search results. The Subtitle feature is considered a listing upgrade and costs 50 cents. Sellers usually use subtitles to …

1. Differentiate their product from the competition. ("Auction includes camera bag.")

2. Make a great eye-catching offer, such as "Free shipping!"

3. Provide additional information that is essential but could not fit or was not appropriate for the title field.

Although it will be seen in search results, note that the subtitle is *not searchable*, unless the buyer chooses to "Search titles and descriptions."

Keyword Abbreviations

Because of the 55-character title space limitation, many sellers use abbreviations to save valuable space. For example, a seller listing clothing who wants to use "New With Tags" in her title, would use the abbreviation NWT. Abbreviations unique to eBay have become commonly known as "eBay Speak" among buyers and sellers but are formally called eBay Acronyms. A complete list of these abbreviations can be found in Chapter 9.

◀ *SEE ALSO 9.5, "eBay Speak, Acronyms"* ▶

Keyword Spamming

All keywords used in the title must be relevant to the item being sold. If you're listing a coffee mug, you can't use keywords such as iPod, cell phone, and LCD TV just to get more buyer search hits. This is known as **keyword spamming**, and the item will be found and cancelled by eBay's automated antispamming software.

You also must not use deceptive keyword titles. For example, if you're listing a Motorola cell phone, you cannot use the keywords "not iPhone." Deceitful sellers sometimes do this in order to get hits from iPhone buyers. These listings will also eventually be found by eBay and cancelled, and if the seller continues this deceptive selling method, his eBay account may be suspended.

eBay Categories

An important listing strategy is to choose the best eBay category for your item. The reason is that 15 to 20 percent of eBay buyers search for an item by browsing categories instead of using keyword searches. They may not know exactly what they are looking for, but they enjoy scrolling page by page through their favorite eBay categories.

Category Selection

eBay will help you find the proper category and subcategory for your item when you enter the item's keywords in the "List your item for sale" search box. eBay will then return the percentages of all categories that contain listings with these keywords. eBay is suggesting that you use this information to choose the category/ subcategory where most sellers list these particular items.

It is important to note that while many sellers blindly use eBay's suggested categories and subcategories, more experienced sellers will use the category they found when conducting their research. The reason is competition. The most money for an item is sometimes obtained from the category that has the least competition rather than the one that is most popular.

You can also choose to have your item appear in two separate categories or subcategories. Both category choices must still pertain to the item. Sellers sometimes choose this upgrade when their item is equally popular in more than one category.

This option will double the insertion fee and double any Listing Upgrade enhancements except Scheduled Listing and Home Page Featured.

Item Specifics

Certain eBay categories offer Item Specific searches. As a seller, you will know whether this feature is available when you choose your item's category. If item specifics are available, additional fields or drop-down menus will appear with selections such as condition, size, color, make, model, or technical specifications.

Buyers make their item-specific selections while performing a category search. For example, a buyer may not know what brand or model camera they want, only that they need a new digital camera with eight megapixels of resolution. The buyer clicks on eBay's Cameras & Photo category, and then, using the **Product Finder** search box, selects additional specifics such as resolution, condition, and optical zoom to narrow her search. eBay then displays all cameras that meet the buyer's specifications.

If you don't include item specifics in your listings, your item will not show up in the buyer's Product Finder search. Therefore, even though this feature is optional, if the item specific fields or menus appear when you're creating your listing, it is very important that you complete these fields.

Item Description

Once a buyer lands on a seller's listing, his "bid or pass" decision is based by and large on the item description. Poor descriptions are those that are too short or too long, or do not address the questions that buyers have about the item.

Descriptions are written using the Standard Tab of eBay's text editor. In the past, the text editor used to only work with Windows Internet Explorer, but it's now compatible with Firefox and Mac users.

Text Editor

Included in the text editor's toolbar are standard editing features such as the ability to choose different text fonts, types, and sizes. Additional formatting possibilities include bold, italic, highlighting, color, paragraph justification, automatic bulleting and numbering, and the all-important spell checker.

Text editor toolbar.

Next to the Standard tab is the **HTML** tab for more technical users. Sellers use this tab to insert HTML code for special desired results that the standard editor does not provide, such as inserting a table.

Pre-filled Item Information

Sellers can save considerable listing time using eBay's Pre-filled Item Information for popular books, CDs, DVDs, video games, some digital cameras, PDAs, and cell phones.

Simply enter the unique identifier appropriate for the item such as the ISBN, author, title, artist, manufacturer, and so on, and eBay automatically fills in the description and inserts a stock photo of the item into your listing. There is no charge for this feature.

When listing in these categories, sellers can use the Find Your Product link located beneath the Pre-filled Item Information section. It is also available in **Turbo Lister, Selling Manager,** and **Selling Manager Pro.**

Be careful when using Pre-filled Item Information that you also include a description that is unique to your particular item. Add the condition of the item and any accessories that might be included. Also be sure that all information is complete and correct for your particular item.

Additionally, sellers should keep in mind that, when selling in a crowded market (popular books, CDs, and so on), if most sellers are using pre-filled information, all the listings will look the same in a buyer's search view. To avoid this, consider using a different photo, or incorporate titles and subtitles that grab a buyer's attention and stand out in a crowded category.

Inserting Photos

As a seller, you should always take your own photos unless you're using eBay's Pre-filled Information feature described earlier. Upload the pictures to your computer, make any required edits, then save them in a folder and file name that will be easy to find later when you create the listing.

There are three tabs for photo insertion: Basic, Enhanced Picture Services, and Self-hosting. The Basic page offers a no-frills, quick photo insertion with a browse button. The Self-hosting tab is used to import pictures from a picture hosting website other than eBay.

The most common method sellers use to insert photos in their listing is with the Enhanced Picture Services tab. You can easily insert item photos into the listing by clicking on the Add Picture button. A browse window will appear and you select the proper folder and file name.

The first photo in an eBay listing is free. Each additional photo is 15 cents, so the fees for multiple photos in multiple listings can quickly accumulate. Carefully consider whether you really need additional photos. Most ordinary items, even expensive items, probably need only one or two photos while collectibles may need several.

For example, a $2,000 notebook computer probably only needs two photos: one with the notebook shown open, and one closed. A collectible doll, however, may need several pictures showing the full body front and back, the bottom if it is a numbered edition, and several **Macro photos** of the doll's face, clothing, or other distinguishing marks or features. Sellers should also include a photo of any flaws and mention the photo of the flaw in the description.

Never copy and paste a photo from another seller's listing. This could lead to possible account suspension. Always take your own photos. Also, never copy a photo from a manufacturer's website unless you are an authorized dealer and have received permission to use their photos. eBay's **Verified Rights Owner (VeRO) Program** has very strict rules about violating intellectual property rights.

◄ SEE ALSO 5.1, *"Photography Essentials"* ►

Gallery Picture

Gallery Picture displays a thumbnail picture of your item next to your title in the search results. This free and automatic service is the best way to gain visibility for your item and beat your competition when you insert a professional-looking photo.

Gallery Pictures.

Gallery Plus

Gallery Plus displays a larger, pop-up picture of your item next to your title when eBay buyers mouse over your listing. The charge for this feature is 35 cents.

Picture Pack

If more than six pictures are desired, a seller should choose the "Picture Pack" feature available when creating the listing. Picture Pack offers a quantity savings of six pictures, and Supersize for only $0.75 (or from 7 to 12 pictures for $1.00).

Supersize Pictures

Sellers who sell small, collectible, or valuable items such as jewelry may want to make their pictures larger than eBay's standard size (400×400 pixels). Sellers can submit pictures up to 800×800 pixels. When viewing the listing, buyers can then choose to "Supersize" the picture, which enlarges the selected photo in your listing. Note that this feature is included in the Picture Pack option price above.

Picture Manager

eBay's Picture Manager provides a subscription picture-hosting service where sellers can upload and maintain a large library of pictures. Instead of uploading and paying for pictures one at a time, you can add multiple pictures to a listing at no additional fee. Subscribers will have the ability to view all of their pictures in order to make their selection during listing creation.

The monthly subscription fee for Picture Manager storage space begins at $9.99 for 50MB, $14.99 for 250MB, and $24.99 for 1GB. Sellers who own Premium and Anchor **eBay Stores** receive discounts for this service.

Picture Show

Picture Show allows buyers to view the listing pictures in a moving slide show at the top of the auction page. This feature can be combined with Supersize to provide a large slide show.

Starting Price

The starting price for an Auction-Style listing can be as low as one cent or as high as the seller determines. The **Insertion Fee** is determined by the starting price.

One of the more subjective decisions for new sellers when creating a listing is where to set the starting price. Starting the price too low, coupled with few bids during the auction, may result in the item selling for a disappointing price.

But many new sellers make the opposite mistake by starting the auction too high. Buyers seek the more competitive listings and many times will remain there for the length of the auction. The bidding on a competitive item (where the starting price was low) will often surpass a listing that had a starting price that was set too high.

The experienced seller does not guess what their starting price should be. They determine it from their eBay marketplace research during their preparation phase.

Buy It Now Price

You can add a Buy It Now button to your Auction-Style listing. Buyers then have the option to either place a bid or purchase your item immediately.

A quantity of only one is allowed under this format. If you do not want to include a Buy It Now price, simply leave that entry box blank. There is a minimal fee for adding a Buy It Now price, which ranges from 5 cents to 25 cents.

Reserve Price

A Reserve is an optional price and should be considered the minimum price that the seller is willing to accept for the item. If the auction ends at a price that is under the reserve price, the listing ends in a "no sale."

The Reserve price is not displayed in the listing, and it's up to you whether to share the Reserve price with a buyer. If you don't want to use a Reserve, simply leave the Reserve box blank. The fee for a Reserve price is $2 if the Reserve is under $200, or one percent of the Reserve price (maximum $50) if the amount is higher than $200.

Duration

Sellers can choose a listing duration of 1, 3, 5, 7, or 10 days. One to seven days are considered standard and there is no additional charge. Ten days is considered a Listing Upgrade, and a 40-cent charge is applied.

Most sellers choose a seven-day listing. It provides maximum exposure without an upgrade charge. Shorter time frames are used to quickly move time-sensitive items, like event tickets. Some categories do not allow one-day listings because they are considered "high-risk." These include computer and cell phone categories.

Listings for 10 days are used for more expensive or collectible items. It not only provides three additional viewing days, but also gives the added benefit of covering two weekends.

Some categories do not allow one-day listings because they are considered "high-risk." These include computer and cell phone categories.

Scheduled Listing

Sellers can choose the day and time to start their auctions using a drop-down menu. This provides you with the ability to create your listings whenever you want and yet have them begin at a strategically better date and time. You can schedule listings up to three weeks in advance.

eBay is a San Jose–based company, so all times on eBay are Pacific Daylight Time (PDT), sometimes shown as Pacific Standard Time (PST). East Coast times are three hours ahead of PST, so 3:09 P.M. PST is 6:09 P.M. EST. A listing begins as soon as it is uploaded to eBay. Therefore, a seven-day listing that is sent to eBay this Tuesday at 5:21 P.M. will end the following Tuesday at 5:21 P.M.

4.2

Experienced sellers have learned that ending an auction at an odd time such as the middle of the night produces poor results. The reason is that most bids are placed at the end of the auction—sometimes in the last few minutes or even seconds. Successful sellers end their auctions at a day and time when the vast majority of buyers are at home, have free time, and can access their computers.

Most PowerSellers agree that, as a general rule, the best day and time is a Sunday evening between 5:00 and 7:00 P.M. PST. Remember that 7:00 P.M. PST is still only 10:00 P.M. EST, and your East Coast bidders will have time to participate in your auction before bedtime.

Additionally, eBay does not guarantee that your item will post as soon as it is uploaded. In fact, it can sometimes take several hours. Therefore, it is best to use the Scheduled feature when uploading Auction-Style listings so they will end when you want. It is not as important to schedule Fixed Price listings as they can end anytime.

Payment Terms

Sellers choose their accepted method of payment. Since 90 percent or more of all buyers will pay for their items with PayPal, most sellers choose PayPal as their primary method of payment. Other methods are cashier's checks, money orders, or personal checks. eBay requires new sellers (with under 100 Feedbacks) and sellers in certain categories to offer a "safe payment method," which is either PayPal or another eBay-approved payment processing service that enables the seller to accept major credit cards. There is enough evidence to argue both for and against accepting checks and money orders. Some fraud does occasionally occur with cashier's checks and non-sufficient funds (NSF) checks. It is up to the seller whether he or she wants to accept these methods of payment. The cost/benefit decision is based on the additional sales from buyers not wanting to use PayPal, versus possible loss from bad debt.

Quantities

Most Auction-Style items should have a quantity of "one." Auction-Style listings with Buy It Now *must* have a quantity of "one." Auction-Style listings with more than one quantity are called Multiple Item (Dutch) Auctions. Take care not to enter into a Multiple Item (Dutch) Auction by mistake (choosing a quantity of more than one for an auction) due to the unusual method of item distribution among the winners and the potential for low payout.

◀ SEE ALSO 3.3, *"Listing Formats and Bidding"* ▶

Sellers who have commodity items (multiple quantities of the same item) should usually sell these items in quantity using the Fixed Price format. When you enter a quantity of more than one in a Fixed Price listing, buyers can purchase as many as they want from the total quantity. eBay will adjust the total quantity available in your listing until it ends.

For example, you may have five coffee makers that you want to sell for $29 each. Use the Fixed Price listing format and enter $29 as the price, five as the quantity, and seven days as your duration. Two days into the listing a buyer clicks the Buy It Now button and chooses two as the quantity desired. The listing will now show a quantity of three and it will continue for the remaining five days or until the quantity is exhausted by other buyers.

One advantage of using a Fixed Price Multiple Quantity Listing over the Auction-Style (Dutch) version is that the buyer in a Fixed Price listing can pay immediately and you can ship the item even while the listing is still active. For a Dutch Auction, you must wait until the end of the auction to request payment and ship the items.

Ship-to Location, Rates, and Terms

Sellers will need to select the country or countries where they will ship the item. New sellers usually ship only to the United States. However, more seasoned sellers are encouraged to ship internationally in order to increase their sales sometimes 15 to 30 percent immediately.

Where Will You Ship?

The ship-to selections you make when creating your listing have a dramatic effect on your item's exposure. eBay maintains separate websites in 27 countries. In fact, 51 percent of all eBay sales are international. When using the Sell Your Item Form, you can choose to sell to certain countries or "worldwide." You also need to choose where you will ship. The ship-to selections you make determine the eBay websites where your listing will appear.

Choosing to ship in the United States will place your listing only on www.ebay.com. Choosing to also ship to Canada will place your item on www.ebay.com plus www.ebay.ca. Choosing to "Ship Worldwide" will place your listing on all of eBay's 27 international websites, dramatically increasing your item's exposure and final value potential. You may end up selling the item to a customer in Ohio, but bidders in the UK, Australia, Germany, and Italy helped run up the price. There is no extra fee to choose this valuable feature.

4.2

You should know, however, that when you list to an international eBay site using this method, there is no guarantee that your item will appear or even be seen in the search result. The reason is that priority is given to the country's residents. If there are several listings for the same item by sellers from that country's website, your item may not even appear. If it does appear, it will be in a separate section of the search result reserved for international sellers.

However, you can guarantee that your item will list on international eBay sites by choosing the "International site visibility" upgrade option when creating your listing. Not all eBay sites offer this option. To learn more about this upgrade, select the Help link and type "about selling internationally" then select "international site visibility." Before you choose the blanket "Ship Worldwide" option, you can take some steps to avoid receiving bids from countries known for fraud. These "Buyer Requirement" procedures are detailed in "Seller Preferences" in Chapter 10.

◀ *SEE ALSO 10.2, "My eBay Special Features"* ▶

Domestic Flat Shipping Rates

Choosing "Flat: Same cost to all buyers" from the drop-down menu on the shipping page means that the shipping rate you enter will be charged to all buyers no matter where they live within the United States. For multiple quantity listings, you need to enter the amount for each additional purchase.

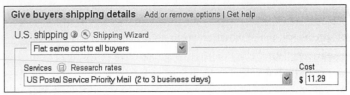

Select Flat Shipping Rate.

Note that shipping rates can be different to Alaska and Hawaii, so you should add a "Shipping Terms" section to your descriptions stating that the Flat Rate is only to the 48 states—Alaska and Hawaii buyers need to contact you for their rate. Another option is to go ahead and provide the rate to Alaska and Hawaii in this section. See the upcoming section "Shipping Terms."

To determine your flat rates you can either visit each carrier's website or use eBay's Shipping Calculator located on the Calculated Shipping page. See "Shipping Calculator," later in this section.

Domestic Calculated Shipping Rates

Choosing "Calculated: based on buyer's address" from the drop-down menu will show a different shipping rate to buyers across the United States based on their zip code. A buyer will see the Shipping Calculator (see below) in her listing and simply enter her zip code in order to see her rate. If she is logged in, it will automatically show the rates to the zip code of her registered address.

Select Calculated Shipping Rate

In order for this to occur, you need to enter the package size, weight, handling charge, method of shipment, and domestic shipping carrier (either USPS or UPS), using the drop-down menus and entry boxes you provided when creating your listing. When buyers enter a zip code, eBay uses the link to the chosen shipping carrier to determine the rate based on the seller's entries and then displays the rate for the buyer in just a fraction of time.

International Shipping Rates

Both Flat and Calculated rates for international buyers are determined the same as domestic rates except that the seller needs to choose the International shipping services option instead of Domestic. Note that international rates can be expensive and vary widely, so it is not usually a good idea to charge a flat rate to every country.

You can select a different rate for up to three different countries (or continent, such as Europe), and then use the additional Ship-to locations checkboxes to select other countries you will ship to but have not provided a specific price for. A buyer in any of these countries will be instructed to contact you directly for the shipping rate.

4.2

Shipping Insurance

Sellers can choose to include optional or mandated Shipping Insurance. For optional insurance, buyers can choose to add insurance to the item when they check out. Be careful when allowing buyers to choose not to take insurance on expensive or breakable items. Just because the buyer did not take out insurance, that will not get you off the hook if the item arrives broken. Most experienced PowerSellers choose mandatory insurance if the item is expensive or breakable.

Shipping Calculator

When you choose the Calculated tab of the shipping section during listing creation, you will see a link for eBay's **Shipping Calculator.** Simply enter the packaging type, weight, and dimensions of your package and eBay will display the estimated cost to ship your item with either USPS or UPS. You can then compare prices from the two carriers. If you choose to use a Calculated Rate, the Shipping Calculator automatically appears in your listings so buyers can determine their rates. If the buyer is logged in, eBay performs this calculation and displays the rate automatically.

Handling Cost

The ability to have eBay automatically add a Handling Cost to your shipping rate is available only when using the Calculated shipping rate option. Sellers who use Flat Rates should include any handling charges as part of their total rate. Handling rates should be kept low and reasonable, usually $2 to $3 or less per package. Be sure to cover all costs for your box and packing materials as well as any handling fee when you determine this additional charge.

Shipping Terms

It is a good idea to also include a Shipping Terms section in your description. It should include which carrier and method of shipping service you will use. If you will use a Flat Rate, describe what is included, such as "Shipping, Handling, and Insurance." The multiple possibilities and concerns of shipping are covered in detail in Chapter 6.

◀ *SEE ALSO Chapter 6, "Domestic Shipping"* ▶

Sales Tax

eBay sellers who have a business license, or even if they derive any income from their eBay sales, need to collect sales tax from in-state buyers. Simply use the drop-down menu from the Additional Information page during listing creation and choose your state and appropriate local sales tax (ask your tax advisor if unsure).

When buyers from outside your state (including international buyers) purchase items from you, no sales tax is shown during checkout. If buyers are from the same state where you reside, the tax rate and applicable tax is added to their sale during checkout. It is the seller's responsibility to report the collected taxes.

Return Policies

A reasonable return policy protects both the seller and the buyer if something goes wrong and may actually increase your sales. A 100-percent money-back guarantee can go a long way toward beating the competition. Buyers may feel more comfortable with sellers who offer return guarantees and may choose their items over competitors'.

Choose your time frame for accepting returns from the drop-down menu. Write any special conditions or policies in the space provided. However, do not use unreasonable terms or harsh, scolding language. Instead think of the Golden Rule and write reasonable terms that you would want a seller to extend if you were to purchase from them.

Listing Upgrades

During listing creation you will be asked if you want to add any Listing Upgrades. These upgrades include Listing Designer, Bold, Highlight, Border, Value Pack, and others that can help you promote your item.

However, eBay will charge a fee for each upgrade, which can impact your profitability, so think carefully before you add an upgrade. A complete review of Listing Upgrades and their associated prices are detailed in Chapter 3.5.

◀ *SEE ALSO 3.5, "Listing Upgrades and Fees"* ▶

Preview and Listing Revision

When you have completed your listing, you can click Preview to view how the item will appear on eBay. Give the entire listing a thorough review before submitting and look for formatting mistakes, description, spelling, or pricing errors. If you find an error, click Edit Listing and make the change before you submit the listing.

Listing Revision After Submission

Once your listing is posted and live on eBay, you can revise some or all of the sections to correct errors, depending on several factors. You can revise certain information depending on the selected format, whether your item has received any bids and how much time is left before the auction ends.

Sellers can revise their listings by clicking the "Revise your item" link in the top left corner of the listing. This link is viewable and clickable only to the seller. The detailed rules for auction revision are provided in Chapter 9.

◀ *SEE ALSO 9.4, "Advanced Selling Techniques"* ▶

Create Templates

When you use the Sell Your Item Form (SYIF), you can save your listing as a template to easily create a similar listing later. This will save you considerable time and effort.

For example, maybe you are selling a red KitchenAid blender but also have a blue one of the same model to sell. Create the red listing and then save it as a template. Now use the template to open the listing, change the red references to blue, delete the red picture, insert the blue picture, and save it with a new title.

To save a listing as a template, create, fully complete, and save the first listing. Next, check the "Save this listing as a template and use it to sell similar items" checkbox.

If You Get Interrupted

If you are using the Sell Your Item Form to create the listing but are unable to finish, you can save it as a draft and come back to complete it later. You can find the listing later by clicking on the Sell button at the top of each page and clicking on the title of your listing.

WORDS TO GO . . .WORDS TO GO . . .WORDS TO GO

Title includes the string of keywords sellers use in order to get the maximum number of search hits on eBay and to entice browsers to click through to their actual auction.

Keyword spamming is when the seller uses popular keywords in their title (that are not relevant to the item they are selling) in order to receive more search hits. All keywords in a title must be directly related to the item for sale.

Product Finder is an additional search tool that appears only in certain eBay categories. Buyers use this tool to further narrow their search to the particular characteristics they desire.

HTML is the abbreviation for Hypertext Markup Language, which is the code used to create web pages.

Turbo Lister is an eBay-developed database tool to help eBay sellers easily and efficiently create listings. Turbo Lister resides on the seller's computer hard drive and replaces the need for the Sell Your Item Form (SYIF).

Selling Manager and **Selling Manager Pro** are tools sellers use to easily create templates and new listings from existing listings. Selling Manager Pro has multiple features, including inventory management and communication and feedback automation.

Macro photos are extreme close-up pictures. Digital cameras have a Macro mode to ensure that the item remains in focus at such a close range.

Verified Rights Owner (VeRO) Program is eBay's policy to protect the intellectual property of copyrighted and trademarked items and materials.

eBay Stores are similar to a website in that all items shown in a seller's eBay Store are from that seller only. eBay Stores are used by sellers to sell add-on or impulse buy items such as accessories.

Insertion Fee is the first fee charged by eBay to list an item. The fee is directly related to the starting price and Reserve price (if used) of the item.

Shipping Calculator is a pop-up software tool eBay has developed to help sellers determine the shipping rate for their item. When the seller chooses "Calculated" rate for their listing, buyers can click the shipping Calculate link, enter their zip code, and see their shipping cost.

4.3 TOP TIPS FOR LISTING CREATION

General Tips

Keywords

Descriptions

This subchapter will summarize the best practices sellers should use when creating eBay listings. By following these tips, sellers will create listings that have the best chance of attracting the most bidders, thus increasing the final bid.

4.3

General Tips

Listed below are some tips to remember when creating any listing. Use these for a learning and creative process that will help you develop a pattern for successful listings.

▶ Conduct eBay research first to determine your keywords, starting price, category, and listing format.

◀ SEE ALSO 12.2, *"Competitive Analysis"* ▶

▶ Always use a professional-looking gallery picture. About 20 percent of customers browse categories instead of using keywords. When they browse, they are looking at price and the gallery pictures.

▶ Schedule your listing to end on the best day and time for your item. This is usually on weekend evenings for general items.

◀ SEE ALSO 4.2, *"Scheduled Listing"* ▶

▶ Use eBay's free Turbo Lister software to easily and efficiently create listings.

◀ SEE ALSO 13.1, *"Turbo Lister"* ▶

Keywords

Keywords are your most important component. About 80 percent of your customers will find your item based on the keywords you use. Spend considerable time researching and developing the best keywords that you think will draw the most traffic to your listing.

▶ Use all 55 characters in your keyword title. Your listing's title is the best real estate you can own on eBay. Don't waste it by leaving empty character space.

▶ Do not include punctuation in the keyword title. All characters count. Don't waste valuable character space with commas, periods, or exclamation marks. The example below shows just how limited you are with only 55 characters.

"55 total characters are in the space between the quotes"

▶ If the item is new, use "NEW" as a keyword. Many buyers eliminate listings with used items by including "new" in their keyword searches.

▶ Include the product name, model, and even the size if space allows.

▶ Do not keyword spam by using popular keywords that are not related to the item for sale. This will result in your item being cancelled by eBay.

▶ Include alternative spellings of product names if applicable for your item.

▶ Check your keywords for misspellings.

▶ Possibly include intentionally misspelled keywords if buyers routinely misspell the item or brand name. Include the brand name keywords spelled correctly and how they are commonly misspelled. For example, use "Cuisinart" and "Cusinart."

▶ To develop keywords that will appear on the most buyer searches, carefully study how eBay's keyword searches work.

◀ SEE ALSO 3.2, *"How eBay Searches Work"* ▶

Descriptions

To write a good description, sellers need to think like a buyer. If you were the buyer of your item, at a minimum you would want to know the following:

▶ Specifically, what is the item for sale?

▶ What does the listing include? Is it just the item or are accessories or giveaways included?

▶ What is the condition of the item?

▶ What is the item's color, size, weight, and dimensions?

For collectibles, you should also mention …

▶ Any distinguishing marks, numbered editions, autographs.

▶ Who made it, where, and when it was made.

▶ Any special history of the item.

For more technical equipment, you would also include ...

▶ Make, manufacturer, model number.

▶ Technical specifications. It is acceptable to use the owner's manual, product box, or manufacturer's website as the source of this information. Just don't copy it exactly as it is from the website.

▶ Warranty status.

Additionally, you would want to include ...

▶ The shipping and handling rate and shipping service you will use.

▶ The payment method options.

▶ The guarantee and return policies.

Always write your own description. Never copy and paste descriptions from websites or from other sellers' listings.

When writing descriptions ...

▶ Use the fonts, type sizes, and layout that buyers are used to seeing in books, magazines, or newspapers.

▶ Use proper grammar, punctuation, and syntax.

▶ NEVER USE ALL CAPS (all capital letters) for body text. It's too difficult to read. Use Mixed Case.

▶ Use only black and white for the description text. A colored headline may be appropriate in limited use, but not for text.

▶ Avoid using colored backgrounds, as the color many times conflicts with the text, making it hard to read.

▶ Describe the item accurately and honestly.

▶ Use the spell checker to ensure your description has no misspellings.

5

PHOTOGRAPHY

5.1 PHOTOGRAPHY ESSENTIALS

Best Camera Features for eBay

Your **gallery picture** is the single most important way to distinguish your item from the competition on eBay. Once your listing lands on a buyer's keyword search result list, it will be displayed along with all of your competition. Your listing could be nested among a few or buried in several hundred other listings.

The buyer scans the search results looking primarily at three things: price, shipping rate—and the gallery picture. If the price and shipping rate are similar to other listings, the gallery photo is the determining factor whether the buyer will click on your item title to view your listing.

Therefore, if you want to attract buyers to your listing, you need professional-looking photos. The more professional your gallery picture is, the more eyes will be attracted to your listing. Once inside your listing, the buyer will look at additional picture(s) of the item, and the better they look, the better chance you have to beat the competition. This is especially true with jewelry, clothing, and more expensive or collectible items.

This chapter presents practical advice about photography equipment, tips for taking great-looking photos, and the best practices that experienced eBay sellers use to create professional-looking photos. Keep in mind when you review the chapter that you are not trying to win a photography award, you just need to draw the most buyers to your item in order to beat your competition. Following the advice in this chapter will produce great eBay photos that attract attention to your items and help to bring the highest winning bid possible.

Best Camera Features for eBay

A multitude of digital cameras are available. Every few months new cameras appear on the market with newer, even more advanced features. Another progression has been the popularity of smaller and smaller cameras, which is great because you can slip them into your pocket. However, smaller isn't necessarily better when it comes to eBay photography. Actually, the LCD screens on some cameras have become too small to clearly see what you are photographing.

It is not necessary to cover all the available features of cameras today. The most important features are those that will be used for eBay photography and that list has been provided below. Some features and their associated benefits are explained in more detail later in this chapter.

▶ The camera must be digital. A film camera is counterproductive because all photos must be digitally rendered to eBay.

▶ The number of megapixels is not that important for eBay photography. The reason is that even three megapixels will produce a picture of excellent quality when viewed on a computer monitor. Higher resolution is important, however, when printing photos. So if you use your eBay camera for personal use, you should increase the megapixels to the quality you require that is within your budget.

▶ Adequate memory is important for higher-volume eBay sellers. Multiple pictures of several items can be taken without having to interrupt the photo session to download the pictures because the memory is full. Keep total memory in mind, then, when comparing cameras. At a minimum, a new digital camera for eBay use should have at least 512KB of memory or allow you to quickly slip additional memory cards in and out. Get as much memory as you can afford.

▶ The camera should come with an easy way to download the pictures to your computer. This is usually accomplished with smart cards, transfer stations, or **USB (universal serial bus) cables.** If you buy a camera with a USB cable and your computer is a few years old, make sure your computer has the same version as the camera's USB protocol. You can check this using the computer and camera owner's manuals or on their websites.

▶ The camera will probably come with its own editing software. Once the picture is downloaded, you will need to crop and possibly do some slight editing/adjusting before you submit the picture to eBay. You can use advanced software applications such as Adobe Photoshop, but most are not needed. Usually the standard editing software that comes with your camera or even free photo editing software available from the Internet will be sufficient.

▶ The camera should have the "white balance" feature, which allows you to adjust the camera to your specific light source. This will produce photos with colors more true to the original item, which is very important for eBay listings.

▶ A macro feature is necessary to provide the ability to take extreme close-up pictures. You will need this if selling an item that is very small, or when taking close-up pictures of collectible items.

▶ The camera must come with a zoom lens. Almost all new digital cameras now come with this feature. When comparing lenses, note that only the Optical zoom ratings are important because digital zoom will not produce a quality image for eBay photography. Optical zoom moves the actual lens forward and back. Digital zoom is just like enlarging a picture on a computer screen. The resolution will decrease the closer you zoom in.

▶ You must be able to turn off the flash. Most digital cameras today don't need a flash if there is sufficient light on the object. Flashes create "hot spots" where the bright flash is reflected off of the item and is visible in the picture.

▶ You should be able to manually focus the camera. Once you have the shot set up, you will usually produce a better picture if you manually focus the camera rather than relying on the camera's autofocus.

▶ An adequate-size LCD screen on the back of the camera will be required so you can adequately see and frame the item. Many cameras today are so small that this is difficult to accomplish. Get the largest LCD screen you can for the camera as long as it has all of your other required features. See the next bullet item.

▶ A "very nice to have" feature would be a video-output jack so you can connect your smaller camera to a 13-inch portable TV. Just place the TV next to your photography setup and you will get a much better view of your overall shot.

▶ A power source plug and adaptor for the camera is desired for extended photography sessions. Otherwise, if you are taking several pictures, you may drain your batteries. Additionally, cameras that run on batteries often automatically shut off just when you start to take the picture.

▶ Mount the camera on a sturdy tripod or camera stand. Some cameras are so small that any slight movement, such as the clicking of the shutter button, will cause the picture to blur. Be sure the camera has the screw threads on the bottom for tripod mounting.

▶ Another great feature available on some cameras is the ability to attach a remote control or thumb switch. This way, you are not touching the camera when clicking the shutter. A second choice is to use the camera's timer. A third choice is to look for a camera with stabilizer technology.

▶ A "nice to have" feature is the ability to plug in a remote flash that will bypass your own camera flash, although this is for a more professional setup.

Many digital cameras on the market will meet the requirements listed here. Moving up in price will also provide more "nice to have" features. Some manufacturers make a few models that are called "eBay Ready" but sometimes their prices are a bit high for what you really need. You should be able to find a camera with all the features noted and even more for about $150 to $300.

There is great camera comparison information at www.cnet.com. Be sure to read the Digital Camera Buying Guide. Another site loaded with information about cameras and photography equipment is Digital Photography Review at www.dpreview.com. When you are ready to buy, remember that an excellent place to shop for the camera you want is … eBay!

WORDS TO GO . . . *WORDS TO GO . . .WORDS TO GO*

Gallery picture is the thumbnail-size picture that is displayed next to the listing title from a keyword search.

A **USB (universal serial bus) cable** is the standard cable used to connect computers to peripheral equipment. The current standard interface USB protocol is 2.0. Older computers may not be compatible with this cable and may need an adaptor.

5.1

5.2 PHOTOGRAPHY EQUIPMENT

Background

Tripod

Lighting

Diffusers

Reflectors

Cubes, Tents, and Cocoons

Photo Studio in a Box

Cloud Dome

Scanners

Theoretically, the better photography equipment you have, the better photographs you will take. However, it is not practical for beginning sellers to invest large sums of money in photography equipment just to list their garden hose on eBay. It is better to have knowledge of how to get the best pictures possible with inexpensive, yet professional equipment. With a nice backdrop, proper lighting, a good camera, and computer photo editing, almost any item can display nicely on eBay.

This subchapter will examine the type of equipment needed for eBay photography at various selling levels. While more expensive equipment may be warranted for Advanced eBay Sellers (see 12.9, Phase 2, Advanced), many eBay sellers can take professional-looking photos with a minimum investment in equipment.

Background

Every eBay photography setup will require a proper background (backdrop). When browsing the listings on eBay, it becomes apparent that many sellers do not grasp this concept. They use chairs, floors, tables, towels, sofas, rags, colored bedspreads, shag carpet, and just about every other inappropriate background. These all create amateurish photos. Having a proper background is important and not difficult.

Photography can be illusion, and a nice backdrop helps to create that look. In spite of the surroundings or clutter in their studio's room, a professional photographer always has only the backdrop visible in the picture. Among many different backdrops to choose from, they select the one that will best enhance the subject. This is the same effect you want for your eBay items.

Sellers wishing to stay on the low budget side of photography can use a tri-fold poster board available from office supply stores as a table stand for the backdrop. White butcher paper or newspaper "end rolls" will perform well as white backgrounds. Use binder clips at the top of the poster board to attach the backdrop paper and let it flow down to and over the table. The paper should flow from above into a nice curve to the surface below. There should be no bends or creases, as these may show in the picture. The white background will give the illusion that the item is floating in air.

The proper background can enhance an item by giving it an appearance of greater value. More professional-looking backdrop options should include a variety of colored fabrics available from fabric stores. Be sure to purchase appropriately sized pieces of fabric for your photography setup. Photographers usually recommend these primary background colors for backdrops:

5.2

- ▶ White (matte)
- ▶ Off-white or cream
- ▶ Gray
- ▶ Black velvet (must be true velvet to photograph well)

Optional background choices include these colors:

- ▶ Royal blue
- ▶ Pale blue
- ▶ Pale yellow
- ▶ Navy or red (true) velvet

When deciding which background to use, hold the object up to each cloth. Whichever one makes the object jump out at you like 3D is your pick. You are not trying to win any photography contests, you just need the best color that will enhance the item in the photo. In most cases, the best background will be white.

For smaller items, an inexpensive yet professional background with the proper curve can be achieved with an infinity board. These boards come in different colors and can be adjusted, then locked in place with the desired curve required for the object. A perfect combination is to use an infinity board inside a photographer's cube, described later in this subchapter.

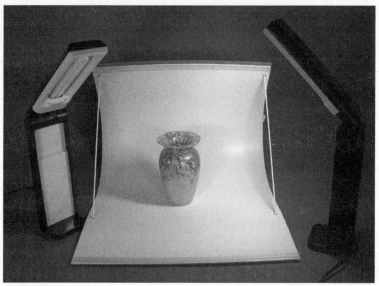

Infinity board.

Tripod

All eBay photography should require the camera to be mounted on a tripod. Tripods are affordable and come in many sizes with different features. For eBay photography, you want to be sure the tripod is sturdy and flexible so it can be adjusted to many different heights, angles, and positions.

As you progress into more expensive lighting equipment, you may also want additional tripods for mounting lights, diffusers, umbrellas, and other accessories. If the tripod is for lighting equipment, make sure you can easily attach accessories.

You will need a quick-release base that screws into the camera so you don't have to keep screwing the camera on and off the tripod. Quick-release latches for adjusting the height of the legs are usually preferred because they are more efficient than the screw-tightened legs.

Lighting

Lighting is an area of photography that has a wide range of quality and associated prices. Decide which direction to take based on the type of items you are selling. Higher-quality, more expensive items deserve better equipment.

A low-priced lighting setup can be purchased from a discount or a home-improvement store. Look for two inexpensive lamps that include reflectors (used for floodlights). These can be found with gooseneck clamps, table stands, or floor-standing designs. They should be at least a minimum of a 100-watt rating.

Bulbs for the lamps should be cool, white-balanced daylight fluorescent bulbs. These are not the strip-light fluorescent bulbs but rather energy-efficient bulbs that are shaped like corkscrews.

Fluorescent bulbs have some advantages over incandescent. Besides the problem of producing heat, incandescent bulbs can produce a yellow tint to the picture, making it more difficult to bring out the true color of the item. Fluorescent bulbs do not produce heat and can be used with a homemade diffuser without too much concern for it burning. Always use caution and do not leave any type of photo lights unattended.

The daylight rating of the fluorescent bulbs means that they will produce the light spectrum comparable to natural daylight. The additional "balanced" rating means that the light spectrum has also been adjusted to produce light comparable to the sun at noon.

Halogen lamps are very affordable and provide a lot of light. However, avoid the quartz halogen shop lamps from the local home improvement center. They are inexpensive but can get very hot. Halogens will successfully melt almost any non-professional diffusion material placed in front of them. They also present a fire hazard—not to mention an uncomfortable photo session.

Floor-standing lights.

Moving up the scale to more professional lighting equipment presents a number of options. Usually the lighting involves floor-standing or overhead floodlights with reflectors. Some will come with detachable diffusers. Professional setups include umbrellas to reflect diffused light onto the subject. This optional lighting equipment is excellent, but also more expensive, and may not be necessary for the value of the items you are selling.

If you sell expensive items, then you should explore the possibility of using professional lighting equipment. Spend some time at photography shops and browse photography magazines and popular online websites.

A popular site for equipment reviews, advice, and comparison is www.dpreview.com. Calumet Photo (www.calumetphoto.com) has a good selection of studio and lighting kits and accessories. The lighting manufacturer Photoflex (www.photoflex.com) will give you a good idea of everything that is available in photography lighting.

Diffusers

Hot spots, shadows, and inconsistent lighting challenge all photographers. Harsh or direct lighting needs to be diffused in order to remove these trouble spots. You will need to diffuse your light source to avoid the "hot spot" bulb reflections caused by direct lighting. This requires placing a diffuser between your light source and your item.

Photography stores and photography websites have professional diffusers available for purchase including a popular one called Tuff Spun. Some diffusers will even stand up to the heat of 1,000-watt bulbs. Make sure the diffuser you choose can be attached to your floodlight reflectors or lighting tripod.

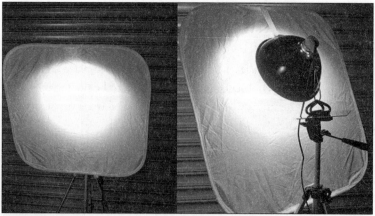

Lights with diffusers.

Simple diffusers for the fluorescent bulbs can be made with a few household items such as an opaque shower curtain or vellum (similar to crepe paper). Large fabric stores usually sell material that can be used for photography light diffusion. A good rule of thumb for any diffusion material should be that it cuts the harsh light level in half.

Reflectors

Reflectors are another way to diffuse direct lighting and eliminate bright reflections from light bulbs. A photographer's umbrella is a good example of how reflectors work. The light is not all concentrated from the bulb but spread out, eliminating the bright spots.

Reflectors don't have to be expensive either. Even white poster boards or white foam boards available from office or art supply stores can be used as inexpensive reflectors. This makes them easy to cut to the size required. The boards are then placed on the photography setup table and propped up by small but heavy items such as a soup can or a liter of pop. The reflector then is rotated to catch the light from the original light source and reflect it back onto the object or behind the object to eliminate shadows. Make sure your reflectors and props are not visible in the shot.

Cubes, Tents, and Cocoons

There are some affordable yet professional photography setups available that are popular with eBay sellers. Among them are photographer's cubes, tents, and cocoons, which work well for smaller to medium-size items.

The Cloud Cube Kit shown here utilizes a specially woven, heat-resistant, 100-percent nylon fiber mesh diffuser. This delivers uniform illumination while eliminating harsh shadows and reflective glare. The kit comes with four fabric backdrop colors—black, gray, royal blue, and white. It also includes two 5,000K flip lights.

A practical and affordable solution for eBay photography is to place an infinity board (described earlier) inside a cube or tent. The item to be photographed is then placed on top of the infinity board. Lights are located on either side shining onto and through the cube, which creates diffused light.

5.2

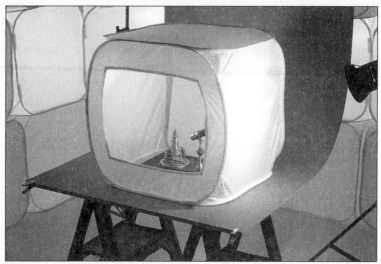

Photo cube with infinity board inside.

Photo Studio in a Box

American Recorder makes a photography cube kit complete with side lighting and camera stand called Photo Studio in a Box. For eBay sellers of small to medium-size items, this is another easy and affordable solution for taking professional-quality photos.

Photo Studio in a Box.

Photo Studio in a Box contains a soft cloth lighting diffusion cube, two professional sidelights, two colored backgrounds, and a camera stand all in one package. Being lightweight and portable makes for an easy setup on a tabletop. It folds into a box slightly bigger that a briefcase for convenient storage and travel.

The kit includes a dual-sided, blue/gray, non-reflective polyester fabric background that provides contrast with either dark or light objects. Two studio-quality, high-output 2,800K Tungsten lamps provide even color and clarity. Retractable legs allow for handheld use.

A fully adjustable, high-quality, aluminum and steel camera stand eliminates jitters and blurs commonly experienced with handheld shots. Large legs with skid-reduction pads keeps the stand firmly in place.

Note that there are imitations on the market. The most noticeable difference is that the original American Recorder product has a much sturdier camera stand while the imitations use a cheaper tripod. Photo Studio in a Box is available at multiple websites and photography stores.

5.2

Cloud Dome

The Cloud Dome is a popular choice among eBay sellers for smaller items such as jewelry and collectibles. The Cloud Dome was actually developed for use in the forensics industry and has even made an appearance in forensics lab scenes on the *CSI* TV shows.

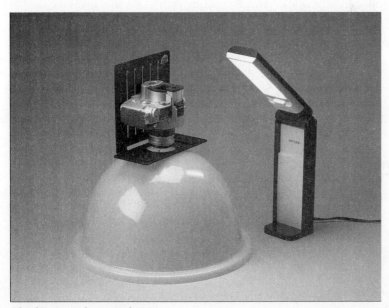

Cloud Dome with mounted camera.

Made of high-impact, non-yellowing, crack-resistant plastic, the Cloud Dome evenly diffuses natural light over the surface area of the object being photographed. You can even get high-quality digital photographs with low lighting.

Lightweight and easily portable, the Cloud Dome is outfitted with a camera mount on the top of the dome to eliminate stability problems. It is a popular tool for eBay photographers of all skill levels wanting to get high-quality digital photographs of smaller items, such as these, that lay flat:

- ▶ Sports memorabilia
- ▶ Jewelry and watches
- ▶ Stamps
- ▶ Small collectibles
- ▶ Books and magazines
- ▶ Gems and minerals

You can learn more about the Cloud Dome kits, cubes, infinity boards, and their available optional accessories from www.trainingu4auctions.com or my eBay store www.trainingu4auctions.net.

Scanners

Instead of using a camera, you can scan many flat items, save the file in a computer, and then later upload it to eBay during listing creation. Items such as books, magazines, postcards, comic books, and even some items in thin flat blister packs can all be scanned.

A scanner produces a high-resolution picture. This results in a large data file. The resolution requirement for eBay pictures is 72 dpi (dots per inch). Be sure to set the menu on the scanner to 72 dpi before scanning.

5.3 TAKING PHOTOS

5.3

eBay sellers and instructors have a popular saying: "Take the picture as if you have no description, and write the description as if you have no picture." If you achieve those two goals, you will have a solid basis for creating a great eBay listing. Chapter 4 covered how to write a great description. Now we'll provide advice for taking a great eBay photo.

Camera Settings

The new digital cameras have many automated features. Most of the manual camera adjustments such as aperture and f-stops, light meters, shutter speed, and telephoto and wide-angle lenses are now all automated. However, your digital camera still requires adjustments and procedures to create the best possible pictures.

White Balance

When you're setting up a photography session, you'll have different sources of mixed light that can interfere with each other and affect the quality of the picture. The natural light entering from the window will mix with the overhead incandescent room lighting as well as the side fluorescent floodlights. This mixture of light sources will sometimes confuse the camera and cause it to choose the wrong light as the prime light source. This causes a tint to the colors in the picture. "White balance" sets the camera to the correct "tint" setting based on the light in the room.

Make your white balance adjustment only after first setting up the entire photo shoot. Assemble the photography stand and backdrop, turn on all lighting, mount the camera on the tripod, and place it in the correct position so the camera is properly focused on the object. Now place a white sheet of paper in front of the object and use the menu button on your camera to select and set the proper white balance. Most cameras have a white balance selection of either natural, incandescent, fluorescent, or a combined source. Most of the time, you will select the combined source.

If your background is pure white, tilt the camera to focus on the background and set the white balance to the actual background you will use instead of a white sheet of paper. This adjusts the camera to view the light from all lighting sources as white. In layman's terms, you have told the camera that, based on all the light in this room at this time, this sheet of paper is white. Now that the camera understands what white is, it will take pictures with colors that are more accurate and true to the original item.

White balancing your camera is probably the single most important step you can take to achieve outstanding eBay pictures. You should set the white balance before every photography session, because the light and sources change in the room from day to day and even hour to hour. Refer to your owner's manual for the details on how to set the white balance for your camera. If you have misplaced your owner's manual, download it from the manufacturer's website.

Macro Photography

Sellers who sell small items such as coins and jewelry will need to take extreme close-up (macro) photos. Additionally, sellers of collectible items will need to take macro photos of certain sections of an item. You should probably switch from a standard camera lens setting to the macro setting when the item is about the size of a dollar bill or smaller.

Surprisingly, you do not have to physically get the camera next to the item for macro photography. In fact it is quite the opposite. Leave the camera in its normal position on the tripod, click the camera's macro mode, and use the telephoto lens to zoom in to the object. For a starting point, try using a longer lens setting by setting your camera's zoom lens from about 50 mm up to 80 mm (refer to your owner's manual).

Using the telephoto lens tends to keep the picture from distorting. This is an area for experimentation with your particular camera to determine the best distance, telephoto, and macro combinations.

Photography Setups

Your photography setup will depend on the item you are selling. If you specialize in small to medium-size items, a tabletop setup is required. Large items require more room and will most likely be photographed on the floor. Expensive items deserve better photography equipment. Most eBay sellers have several portable photography setups and use the one most appropriate for each item.

A dedicated space for your eBay photography is the best option, but many sellers use their shipping room table to set up their portable photography equipment. If you sell a lot of items each week, set aside a particular day and time for your photography. It will make your sessions less time-consuming and more streamlined.

Small Items

Photograph smaller items on a tabletop setup. Beginning or casual sellers can use the inexpensive setup mentioned in 5.2, "Background." More expensive items are worthy of better photography equipment including a photographer's cube, tent, infinity board, or cocoon.

If you sell items such as jewelry, you need the best pictures possible. Consider the Cloud Dome for jewelry or any small item of value that lays flat. Sometimes a small piece of jewelry like a ring needs to be propped up. White museum putty is perfect for this use. For other objects, use anything around the house that can be hidden behind the item. Photographers use soup cans, liter pop bottles, and Pink Pearl rubber erasers for small items.

Working with small items can be tedious. It actually can make a person tense. Get a chair and sit down when setting up the shot and taking the picture. This relieves tension and helps you to relax. You will also be at a better angle to view and adjust the camera and item.

Medium Items

Most medium-size items can also use a tabletop photography setup. The cubes and tents are good measuring sticks for medium items. If the item can fit inside the Cloud Cube (20×20×20 inches), it is medium size. If the item is too large for the cube, use the following tips for photographing large items.

For medium-size objects, use two fluorescent, balanced, daylight sidelights and possibly one diffused overhead fluorescent light on a boom stand. Use reflector boards to capture the light and reflect it back toward the object. You will need to experiment with reflector size and placement.

You will photograph most medium-size items with a standard lens setting rather than macro, but do experiment with the lens zoom setting. You want to get close but not too close. Leave a bit of background in the shot and then crop it later with the editing software. If you crop it with your camera, it may be too close and you'll have no margin left for error.

Large Items

In most cases, photograph larger items on the floor, especially if the item is heavy. You will need a large backdrop. An inexpensive source is butcher paper or one of the end rolls from your local newspaper's printing department. You can also purchase several large sizes of poster board and tape them together. You can even try using an all-white, fully ironed (with no creases) bedsheet. Once you white balance the camera, the seams will mostly disappear.

Tape a paper backdrop to the wall and let it flow out onto the floor in a nice, large curve where the wall meets the floor. Do not let the paper crease or fold. Tape the paper to the floor and place the object in the center. Note that a hard-surface floor works better than carpet. If the item is very large, consider using the garage. If that is not practical, use thin plywood over the carpet. The background paper should then cover the floor surface.

Use two side floodlights with reflectors and very high-wattage bulbs. You may even consider halogen for large items, but remember that these lights get very hot. An overhead floodlight will provide even more light if it's practical to place one.

If you are photographing in the garage, can you move the setup close to the door so natural, shaded sunlight can flood the area? You do not want direct sunlight but should take the picture in a shaded area inside the garage.

Finally, make sure your garage floor is clean before you begin the setup. You will want to be able to reuse your backdrop sheets or poster boards after this session is completed.

Clothing

Don't display clothing on hangers, floors, tables, and so on. If clothing is a part of your product line, consider purchasing a half-body mannequin (torso only). These are available and relatively inexpensive on eBay.

You can place shirts or blouses with sleeves on a white, thick poster board. It should be ironed, laid out on the board, and held in place with straight pins.

Some eBay sellers use models, but sometimes the model distracts from the item. A torso mannequin is probably the better choice—you don't have to worry if they blink or smile. But if you use a model, make sure their appearance is understated, so the clothing gets noticed. Another tip is to crop off the head during editing. When photographing skirts or pants on a model, crop the picture just above the belt. Study magazines and catalogs that sell clothing and observe how professionals photograph clothing.

Collectibles

Most items on eBay need only one picture. If the item is very common and the buyer should know what it looks like, there is probably no need for more than one or two pictures. For example, you only need one picture of an iPod unless a second picture is required to show the included accessories or excessive wear.

Collectibles, however, may need several pictures showing a full front shot, full back shot, and several close-ups of the item. Use macro photos for collectibles to show distinguishing marks, characteristics, or features such as autographs or the number if a limited edition. If there are flaws in the item, take a picture of the flaw and mention it in your description.

Artwork

It is best to prop up artwork with heavy hidden items such as liters of pop and shoot it straight on. You should not wipe artwork but a few bursts of non-residue air from compressed cans will remove dust and lint.

If the artwork is framed behind glass, reflections and glare can become a problem. Diffused lighting will remove much of the glare. Reflector boards or even black poster boards can then be adjusted to remove as much glare as possible. Some photographers use a black poster board with a hole cut in the middle just large enough for the camera lens. The black poster board is placed about 1 to 3 feet back from the artwork. Pictures are taken with the camera lens inserted in the pre-cut poster-board hole. The black poster board will now significantly reduce transient reflective light and glare from the artwork's glass.

Note that without special equipment or photo-editing software, you may not be able to entirely remove the glare in the photo. This is acceptable for eBay photography. Just be sure that the glare is more to the side or edges and does not interfere with or distract from the main subject in the artwork.

Set the Shot

One of the more confusing elements for eBay sellers with limited photography experience is how best to display the item. There is no need to agonize over this. What you need are relevant, professional photography examples to emulate.

Go to a large bookstore and browse the magazine racks. Look for several magazines that advertise items similar to the items you sell on eBay. Study the ads to learn how professionals photograph similar items. Some use props while others are quite creative in how they arrange the item(s). Study the background, camera angles, and how close they crop the item. Learn from the pros and then mimic them.

Take the Shot

You have chosen the properly sized photography setup for your item. You've set the shot by carefully arranging the item, props, camera angle, and lighting.

Before you snap the picture, go through the following mental checklist. Don't dwell on it—just give each area some careful thought and make the necessary adjustments.

- ☐ Observe how the item looks with the background.
- ☐ Look at the way the item is placed or arranged with other items or props.
- ☐ Check the sidelights to ensure they are diffused and point at about a 45-degree angle to the item.
- ☐ Check the fill lighting and camera angle.
- ☐ Sit down in a chair to remove tension.
- ☐ Examine your lighting again while looking through your camera viewer and try to remove any shadows with reflectors.
- ☐ Set your white balance.
- ☐ Manually focus your camera.
- ☐ Hold your breath to eliminate shaking, or use a timer or remote. Take 2 to 3 pictures for ordinary items. Collectibles usually need 6 to 8 different shots (close-up, full front shot, back shot, and so on) and for each shot, you should take 3 to 5 pictures.

5.4 EDITING PHOTOS

Transferring Pictures

Photo-Editing Software

eBay's Picture Manager

The photography and lighting setup is the most difficult part of eBay photography. When set up properly, by following the tips outlined in this chapter, you should have several excellent pictures to choose from. Editing and preparing them for eBay should then be a "snap."

Transferring Pictures

Transfer pictures from your digital camera to your computer by either a smart card or a USB cable. The computer USB cable is connected to the camera or its transfer base or reader.

Usually the transfer is as easy as the push of a button on the transfer base or a few simple mouse clicks from your computer. Each camera is different, so follow the instructions in your owner's manual to transfer the pictures properly.

Photo-Editing Software

After you transfer the pictures to your computer, edit them and prepare them for submission to eBay with photo-editing software. Most digital cameras today are sold with their own photo-editing software for the computer. Usually this software is sufficient for the simple edits required for eBay. Because different manufacturers use different editing software, you should refer to your owner's manual for specific editing procedures and techniques. If you are selling more expensive items, you may want to purchase more sophisticated (and more expensive) photo-enhancement software such as Adobe's Photoshop.

Crop and Rotate

Use your editing software to review all the pictures you took of the item and choose the one that looks the best. Sometimes the picture is rotated by 90 degrees and the horizontal becomes vertical. Use the rotate control to realign the picture to its proper horizon before you begin any editing.

The first step in preparing the photo for eBay is to crop the picture. Use the crop feature to eliminate most, but not all, of the background. The item should fill most of the picture, leaving only a small background to "frame" the item. This will make the viewer focus on the item and not be distracted by the background.

Brightness and Contrast

Sometimes a picture can be enhanced slightly by adjusting the brightness and contrast levels. However, before you touch those levels, make sure your computer monitor is set properly. Most digital cameras will produce very good brightness and contrast, but if you find that many of your pictures need adjusting, it may be your monitor.

Usually computer monitors' factory settings have the brightness too high and the contrast too low. The color also needs to be set properly. PC World magazine recommends the site www.epaperpress.com/monitorcal for monitor calibration. It is also a good idea to Google "Calibrate Computer Monitor" and read several opinions and procedures.

Sharpen the Photo

Many pictures could use just a touch more sharpness to really make the item "pop." Some editing software comes with a sharpen or enhancement adjustment. Check the before-and-after sample pictures your software will provide to ensure that it does indeed enhance the photo and not cause it to fuzz due to oversharpening or overenhancement.

Watermarking Photos

To keep other sellers from copying your photos, you can use a **watermark.** This is especially important if you sell artwork.

Usually the watermarked name is that of the seller's business, such as "Courtney's Art World" or your eBay User ID. The image or name is faint enough that it does not distort the picture, but visible enough that another seller could not use it.

Be sure you do not place the watermark over the main subject of the picture. This will distort the image and make it less desirable. Most professionals place the image in a corner of the picture. This will make it difficult for another seller to capture your picture and edit out just the corner, as the picture would then be "out of frame."

Some photo-editing software programs include the watermark feature. If yours does not, more advanced editing programs such as Photoshop provide this feature. If you are an artist, you already should be using Photoshop or another advanced program for your pictures.

Resizing

All photos should be properly sized for eBay. The standard size for eBay photos is usually 400×400 pixels. However, sellers can upload pictures with more pixels in order to increase the quality and detail of the photo. Likewise, it is best not to resize the picture to less than 400 pixels or the lower resolution may result in a poor-quality picture. The maximum picture quality allowed for standard-size submission is 800×800 pixels. If a picture larger than 800×800 pixels is submitted, eBay will automatically resize the picture down to a standard size.

Sellers who sell small, collectible, or valuable items such as jewelry should select the Picture Pack option when creating their listing so that they get the Supersize feature. This option will allow a buyer to click the Supersize link and enlarge the picture on their screen. Pictures submitted for Supersize using the Picture Pack feature should increase the resolution to 1000 pixels or more on the longest side. This will ensure a quality photo when Supersized.

◄ *SEE ALSO 4.2, "Listing Creations"* ►

5.4

Save the Photo

eBay's photo protocol works best with the JPEG format. Be sure to save your pictures in the .jpg (JPEG) format.

Most editing programs label pictures by number. This provides no help to you later when you have 300 pictures and you need to insert the correct one for your eBay listing.

The solution is proper picture naming and computer file management. You should start by creating a proper file folder for related pictures. Name the file folder either for the week you will be listing or for type of product. For example, if the products you are selling change every week and are a one-time sale, use a file folder named for the week you will be using them, such as 11.23.09. Then use a file name for the particular item that you can easily find later, such as "white iPod," and save that picture under the 11.23.09 file folder.

If you specialize in a particular niche and you will be selling the item repeatedly, then it is best to name the file folder after the type of product. For example, create a file folder named Stuffed Animals. Then save a picture of each particular product under file names such as beaver, otter, and chipmunk.

If this is confusing to you, then you should brush up on your computer file-management skills. A good way to accomplish this and learn more about photography at the same time is to take a class on digital photography from your local community college or Parks and Recreation department.

eBay's Picture Manager

eBay provides a subscription picture-hosting service where sellers can upload and maintain a large library of their pictures. With Picture Manager, a seller can add multiple pictures to a listing at no additional fee. For sellers who use many pictures, this service can save them considerable money over eBay's standard picture-listing insertion fee of 15 cents per picture after the initial free first one.

The monthly subscription fee for Picture Manager storage space begins at $9.99 for 50MB, $14.99 for 250MB, and $24.99 for 1GB. Sellers who own Premium and Anchor eBay Stores receive discounts for this service.

WORDS TO GO . . .WORDS TO GO . . .WORDS TO GO

A **watermark** is a faint, translucent image, name, logo, or title that is cast over the photo to make online photo theft difficult.

5.5   TOP TIPS FOR EBAY PHOTOGRAPHY

Author's note: I have a good friend, Al Tanabe, who was a professional photographer for many years. He specialized in still-life photography for magazine ads and catalogs and has won numerous awards for his work. His background is perfect for eBay photography. I asked Al if he would provide additional photography tips for eBay sellers, and he agreed. Following are Al's tips for your eBay photos:

▶ Make sure that your camera has been "white balanced" after each setup so your camera will capture the true colors of the item (refer to your owner's manual). This is one of the most important steps in digital photography. Don't ignore this step. It can be the difference between an off-color picture and a photo with true colors.

▶ There is no such thing as "too much light." Light brings out the texture, color, and character of the object. Modify the "quality" of the light with diffusers and use reflector cards.

▶ A photo of a shiny object can be a photo of the reflections. When photographing a shiny object such as silverware or jewelry, use reflector cards profusely.

▶ On an overcast day, move your photography stand out to the patio. Natural light will bring out the true colors of your item. But avoid direct sunlight.

▶ Wipe the item clean before taking the pictures to remove lint and fingerprints. Wipe the lens clean with an approved lens cloth. Cover the lens with the lens cap when not in use.

▶ To help keep items upright that would normally roll or fall over, use a small beanbag underneath the background cloth or a pink pearl eraser behind the object. You can also use Wacky Tacky or museum putty as long as it does not leave residue on the object.

▶ Check your owner's manual to see if there is a close-up or macro setting. Use it for small objects or items about the size of a remote control.

▶ Watch for stray reflections on the shiny surfaces. They can usually be removed with reflectors.

▶ For small collectibles, construct a "pedestal" by placing a box or even better, a Quaker Oats (cylinder) box, under a true velvet backdrop and placing your object on top. This creates a point of focus for smaller objects. It also gives an impression of greater value.

5.5

Keep in mind that you are not trying to win awards for your eBay photography like Al has won. So don't agonize over your photos. However, following the tips presented throughout this chapter will definitely set your photos apart from your competition and help to increase the perceived value of your items. That is *exactly* what you are trying to accomplish with eBay photography.

6

DOMESTIC SHIPPING

6.1 SHIPPING CARRIERS

Out of the three major components of an eBay business—product sourcing, selling, and shipping—the most complex, multifaceted, and often misunderstood component is shipping. Shipping rates are multidimensional and therefore vary tremendously. They also have a direct impact on a seller's bottom line, so choose your carrier carefully.

The primary carriers available to eBay sellers are UPS, USPS, FedEx, and DHL. We'll look at each carrier in this chapter, but note that the vast majority of eBay sellers use UPS, USPS, or both primarily because these two are integrated in eBay's Shipping Calculator.

If you're an advanced eBay seller, set up an account with all the carriers you will use. This will prove valuable for available discounts, notifications, and newsletters or help when resolving shipping problems or claims.

Each carrier has strengths, specialties, and weaknesses. There is usually no one-size-fits-all decision when it comes to choosing a carrier. Experienced eBay sellers use a combination of carriers and services depending on the items they ship. For example, rates for medium-size packages are competitive among all carriers within the contiguous 48 states. For small, lightweight packages or for items that can fit inside a bubble pack or padded envelope, USPS usually offers the best rates. There's a comparison table at the end of this chapter to help you decide which carrier to use depending on the size, weight, and contents of your package.

This chapter quotes several rates and services that are current at the time of this writing, but the point of this chapter is not to present current rates but to compare carriers. Rates will change, and the charge for a particular service may no longer be current. However, the comparison between different carriers and their services relevant to eBay sellers will still be valid.

6.2 FEDERAL EXPRESS (FEDEX)

FedEx Benefits and Services
FedEx Contact Information

Many people still think of FedEx as the carrier that only provides overnight deliveries. However, FedEx also offers business and home ground delivery rates that are quite competitive with UPS Ground or USPS Parcel Post.

FedEx Benefits and Services

FedEx has over 50,000 drop-off locations, including drop boxes for Express shipments. For additional convenience, FedEx has teamed with the copy center giant Kinko's (now called FedEx Kinko's Office and Print Centers), for counter and drop-off services.

6.2

FedEx is known for its excellent express delivery services. Most eBay sellers, however, use more economical FedEx ground services to businesses and residences.

Express Services

Packages can be up to 150 pounds, with a size limit of 119 inches in length or 165 inches in length plus girth (L + 2W + 2H) using the following delivery services to/from most cities:

▶ **SameDay:** Packages that make the local morning cutoff can be delivered the same day, 365 days a year.

▶ **First Overnight:** Delivered next business day from 8:00 A.M. to 10:00 A.M. depending on destination.

▶ **Priority Overnight:** Delivered next business day before 10:30 A.M.

▶ **Standard Overnight:** Delivered next business day before 3:00 P.M.

▶ **2Day:** Delivered second business day before 4:30 P.M.

▶ **Express Saver:** Delivered third business day before 4:30 P.M.

FedEx Ground

This is the service used to ship items to U.S. businesses. Packages have a weight limit of 150 pounds and size limit of 108 inches in length or 165 inches in length plus girth (L + 2W + 2H). The packages are usually delivered between one to five business days depending on the distance to the final destination.

FedEx Home Delivery

Packages up to 70 pounds can be delivered to businesses or residences within one to five business days. The box size limit is 108 inches in length or 165 inches in length plus girth (L + 2W + 2H). FedEx does not deliver to post-office boxes in the United States.

Tracking and Insurance

Tracking is automatically included on all FedEx packages at no additional charge. Items can be tracked worldwide. Proof of delivery is provided online at no additional fee.

Packages are automatically insured up to $100 for loss or damage. Additional insurance coverage can be purchased at the time of shipment and applicable fees will be applied.

Home Pickup

Pickups can be scheduled for either the same day (if made before the cutoff time in your area) or the next business day. The driver will pick up the item at the location you specify. Pickups can be scheduled up to 10 days in advance.

FedEx charges $4.00 *per package* for a courier pickup. For FedEx ground shipments, "regular pickups" can be scheduled daily or for specific days of the week. The rates for daily pickups are $8.00 per week if your weekly shipping totals $60 or more, and $12.00 if less than $60.

You can print labels for your packages using the FedEx Ship Manager software. This is especially convenient for home pickup.

Delivery Signatures

Signatures are required for FedEx deliveries unless the recipient has at some time signed a door tag authorizing delivery to their residence without a signature. You should state this in your eBay listing **shipping policy** so there is no confusion with your buyer later.

Rates

Rates vary widely and are dependent on package size, weight, shipment method, destination, and any additional services requested. Use the comparison table at the end of this chapter to determine how FedEx compares to other carriers.

Packaging Guidelines

FedEx boxes and shipping supplies are for Express shipments only. For ground shipments, you must provide your own corrugated box.

◀ *SEE ALSO 6.7, "Packing Materials and Corrugated Boxes"* ▶

If the box has been previously used to ship an item, make sure there is no damage and remove all previously used labels. Use packing material specifically made to cushion items during shipment. Multiple items in one package require that each item be wrapped in separate packing material. Use approved packing tape to seal the box.

Freight Services

eBay sellers who ship large items or pallets can choose FedEx Freight service. FedEx also offers a refrigerated service for temperature-sensitive items. Many large-volume sellers choose the Freight Service not to ship items, but to receive pallets of merchandise from distributors.

◀ *SEE ALSO 6.7, "Packing Materials and Corrugated Boxes"* ▶

6.2

Claims

Undeliverable packages that are refused by the recipient or have an incorrect address are returned at the sender's expense. Packages refused because of damage are returned to the sender at FedEx's expense. Refunds for damaged goods are handled through the customer service department.

FedEx Contact Information

Sellers wanting more information should visit www.fedex.com and download their FedEx Welcome Kit. Additional links and phone numbers follow. You may want to save these links as favorites in your web browser for quick access.

U.S. customer service	1-800-GoFedEx (1-800-463-3339)
International customer service	1-800-247-4747
Billing questions	1-800-622-1147
Packaging advice	1-800-633-7019

FEDEX QUICK LINK INFORMATION

Desired Service	Link Map (go to FedEx.com, then click)
Track a U.S. package	Track
Drop off locations	Ship, find locations
Ship a package	Ship, prepare shipment
Schedule a pickup	Ship, schedule a pickup
U.S. rates	Ship, get rates
Content restrictions	fedex.com/us/services/terms/groundtariff.html
Order supplies	Manage, order supplies
Billing	Manage, view bills online
International tools	Ship, prepare an international shipment
New U.S. customer account	New, customer center

WORDS TO GO . . .WORDS TO GO . . .WORDS TO GO

A **shipping policy** should be included in the listing description and provide a clear explanation of the seller's method of shipment.

6.3 DHL

DHL Benefits and Services
DHL Contact Information

Headquartered in Plantation, Florida, DHL was formed in 1969 and merged with Airborne Express in 2003. The DHL initials represent the last names of the founders, Dalsey, Hillblom and Lynn.

DHL Benefits and Services

DHL specializes in express and global shipments plus multiple delivery warehousing and fulfillment services that appeal mostly to high-volume businesses. The most popular DHL services for eBay sellers are ground and home deliveries. DHL rates are very competitive with other carriers for U.S. deliveries.

Express Services

DHL offers multiple express services from/to most cities that include ...

- ▶ **Same Day Service:** Any size or weight on the next flight out of town.

- ▶ **Next Day 10:30 A.M.:** Packages up to 150 pounds delivered the next business day by 10:30 A.M.

- ▶ **Next Day 12:00 P.M.:** Packages up to 150 pounds delivered the next business day by 12:00 P.M.

- ▶ **Next Day 3:00 P.M.:** Packages up to 150 pounds delivered the next business day by 3:00 P.M.

- ▶ **Ship Ready:** A flat-rate delivery, arriving the next business day by noon for envelopes, or delivered the second business day by 5:00 P.M. for packages.

Ground

Available in the 48 contiguous states, delivered within one to six business days depending on the origination and final destination. Package limitations are 150 pounds and sizes up to 108 inches in maximum length and 165 inches total length plus girth (L + 2W + 2H).

DHL@Home

This option offers business-to-residence delivery to the 48 states. Packages are picked up by DHL and delivered to the customer's home by the local post office. Packages are accepted up to 70 pounds and are delivered within two to seven business days. DHL does not deliver to post-office boxes in the United States.

Mediamail@home

This is a business-to-residence delivery service to the 48 states for media-related material such as books, CDs, and DVDs. Packages are picked up by DHL and delivered to the customer's home by the local post office. Packages are accepted up to 70 pounds and are delivered within two to seven business days.

Tracking and Insurance

DHL offers tracking at no charge through its website. Additional insurance, referred to as Shipment Value Protection, is determined at the time of payment.

Home Pickup

If scheduled online, home pickups can be scheduled for $3 per pickup no matter the amount of packages. This is an advantage over UPS and FedEx, which charge $3 to $4 per package. DHL account holders can also schedule weekly pickups for $9. You can print prepaid shipping labels at home and have the shipping cost added to your monthly bill once you have established a DHL account.

Delivery Signatures

Signature Preferred DHL deliveries will require recipient signatures unless the recipient has signed a door tag authorizing delivery without a signature.

Rates

Shipping rates depend on size, weight, shipping method, and destination. DHL usually offers the lowest rates for ground services compared with other carriers. They have also formed an alliance with Office Max to provide additional, convenient counter service. There is an extra charge for home pickup. Use the comparison table at the end of this chapter to determine how DHL compares to other carriers.

Freight Services

DHL specializes in freight storage and shipping services. Some eBay sellers use DHL to substitute for their own warehouse. They contract with DHL to warehouse their items and perform order fulfillment.

Claims

Claims with DHL for lost or damaged items are relatively simple to file by calling 1-800-CALL-DHL.

DHL Contact Information

Sellers wanting more information should visit www.dhl.com. Essential links and phone numbers are provided below.

New U.S. customer account	1-866-345-2329
Billing	1-800-CALL-DHL
Customer service	1-800-805-9306

DHL QUICK LINK INFORMATION

Desired Service	Link Map (go to dhl.com, then click)
Track a U.S. package	Track, track by number
Drop-off locations	Ship, find drop-off locations
Ship a package	Ship, prepare a shipment
Schedule a pickup	Ship, schedule a pickup
U.S. rates	Ship, get rates
Order supplies	Ship, order supplies
Freight	Ship, solutions
International shipping	Ship, ship internationally

6.3

6.4 UNITED PARCEL SERVICE (UPS)

UPS Benefits and Services

UPS Contact Information

United Parcel Service is a very popular choice among business owners and many eBay sellers. UPS Ground is the service chosen most often and competes directly with USPS Parcel Post, DHL@Home, and FedEx Ground.

UPS Benefits and Services

UPS has large customer centers in all major cities around the country for package drop-off. It also offers convenient drop-off boxes in multiple locations as well as its smaller stores, usually located in strip malls, called The UPS Store. Locations are easily found on the www.ups.com website.

The office-supply store giants Staples and Office Depot have formed an alliance with UPS so sellers can ship with UPS directly from their stores. Staples and Office Depot offer promotional discounts that are often cheaper than shipping from a UPS customer center. Ironically, sometimes the best UPS rates are not from the UPS customer centers or from the UPS stores but from Staples and Office Depot.

eBay has also formed a partnership with UPS, making it easy for sellers to print discounted shipping labels directly from their My eBay tab. You'll find more about this partnership later in this chapter.

◀ *SEE ALSO 6.11, "eBay Shipping Center"* ▶

Express Services

UPS offers multiple competitive rapid-shipping services, to/from most cities including ...

▶ **Express Critical:** Best available flight, 24/7, 365 days a year to all 50 states.

▶ **Next Day Air Early A.M.:** Next business day delivery by 8:00 A.M. to 48 contiguous states.

▶ **Next Day Air:** Next business day to all 50 states by 10:30 A.M., noon, or end of day depending on destination.

▶ **Next Day Air Saver:** To residential destinations by end of day in 48 contiguous states.

▶ **2nd Day Air A.M.:** Delivery by second business day by noon to 48 contiguous states.

▶ **2nd Day Air:** Delivery by end of day to all 50 states.

▶ **3 Day Select:** Delivery by end of third business day to 48 contiguous states.

UPS Ground

UPS Ground is their most economical service and provides domestic shipping usually within one to five business days to all 50 states. Ground deliveries to residential addresses occur anytime between 9:00 A.M. and 7:00 P.M. Monday through Friday.

Tracking and Insurance

UPS provides automatic tracking as well as insurance of $100 for every package. Additional insurance can be purchased if required.

Shipping Labels

You are able to easily print and pay for professional looking labels directly from your My eBay tab. Payment is easily made using your PayPal account.

◁ *SEE ALSO 6.11, "eBay's Shipping Center"* ▷

Home Pickup

There is a $3.00 *per package* pickup charge for ground packages scheduled for next day pickup when scheduling online. Daily pickups can be scheduled once you open an account. The rates are dependent on your weekly shipping volume as follows:

UPS WEEKLY RATE FOR DAILY PICKUP

Weekly Bill	Rate
$0–14.99	$17
$15–59.99	$12
$60+	$8

6.4

Rates

UPS rates vary widely dependent on multiple factors such as the shipping method, weight, size, and destination. You can make a quick shipping estimate by visiting www.ups.com, clicking on Shipping, and choosing "Calculate Time and Cost."

The UPS Store locations are independently owned and operated by Mail Boxes Etc. franchisees, a subsidiary of UPS. These stores provide a convenient drop-off service, but it is important to note that they also add a premium charge that is in addition to standard UPS rates. This makes them one of the more expensive shipping options for eBay sellers. Use the comparison table at the end of this chapter to determine how UPS compares to other carriers.

Packaging Guidelines

UPS provides boxes and shipping supplies for Express shipments only. For ground shipments, you must provide your own corrugated box and packing material.

SEE ALSO 6.7, *"Packing Materials and Corrugated Boxes"*

Packages have a 150-pound weight limit. Box sizes must not exceed 108 inches in length or 165 inches in length plus girth (L + 2W + 2H). Packages over 70 pounds carry an additional handling charge.

Freight Services

eBay sellers who ship large items (over 150 pounds) or pallets of product should investigate UPS Freight Service. This is a very economical alternative to the major trucking lines. A comparison of shipping quotes reveals that UPS Freight rates can sometimes be half the cost of major trucking companies. Ironically, UPS sometimes subcontracts with these same trucking companies to deliver the freight. Shippers then get the same quality service at half the price. Shippers need a UPS account in order to use UPS Freight.

SEE ALSO 6.7, *"Packing Materials and Corrugated Boxes"*

Claims

UPS is one of the easier carriers to deal with when making a claim, but easier to deal with does not mean it is more lenient in approving claims. It just means the process to file and resolve a claim tends to be smoother and faster than it is with the USPS. It also helps to have a business account with UPS, where you will have an assigned representative to deal with.

UPS Contact Information

Sellers wanting more information should visit www.ups.com. You can view or download its comprehensive Daily Rate and Service Guide by clicking on Shipping, choosing Continental U.S., and then scrolling down to the guide link.

Additional UPS links and phone numbers are provided below. You may want to visit and save these links as favorites in your web browser for quick access.

Customer service	1-800-PICK-UPS (1-800-742-5877)
Freight service	1-800-333-7400

UPS QUICK LINK INFORMATION

Desired Service	Link Map (go to UPS.com, then click)
Track a U.S. package	Tracking, track shipments
Drop-off locations	Locations
Ship a package	Shipping, create a shipment
Schedule a pickup	Shipping, schedule a pickup
U.S. rates	Shipping, calculate time and cost
Content restrictions	Support, preparing your package
Make a claim	Support, customer service claims
Order supplies	Shipping, get UPS labels, packs
Billing	Support, customer service e-mail UPS
International tools	Shipping, use international tools
New U.S. customer account	Shipping, open a UPS account

6.4

6.5 UNITED STATES POSTAL SERVICE (USPS)

USPS Benefits and Services

USPS Contact Information

The United States Postal Service (USPS) is an obvious favorite among eBay sellers. Its Priority Mail delivery options are especially expedient and Media Mail is most practical.

USPS Benefits and Services

While the other carriers specialize in shipping medium to large packages, USPS offers economical shipping of smaller items that can fit in bubble packs and padded envelopes. It also offers free home pickup, Saturday deliveries, and reasonable rates to military **APO/FPO addresses.**

Post offices and their satellite service counters are conveniently located in nearly every city in the United States. To help alleviate long lines, many larger post offices now offer Automated Postal Centers (APC) in their lobbies that are open 24 hours a day, seven days a week. Shippers can use the APC to weigh an item, print a label, and drop off a package.

Express Services

USPS offers a variety of domestic shipping services to businesses, home addresses, or post-office boxes. Its expedited services to/from most cities include …

- ▶ **Express Mail Next Day, Noon:** Delivered the next day by noon, 365 days a year, for packages or envelopes under 70 pounds. Includes $100 insurance and automatic tracking.

- ▶ **Express Mail Next Day, 3:00 P.M.:** Delivered the next day by 3:00 P.M., 365 days a year for packages or envelopes under 70 pounds. Includes $100 insurance and automatic tracking.

The USPS services more commonly used by eBay sellers are Priority Mail, Flat-rate Priority Mail, Parcel Post, and Media Mail. The USPS is not a good choice to move large items or pallets of freight.

Priority Mail

Priority Mail packages or envelopes can usually be delivered to all addresses in the United States within two to three days. Package restrictions are 70 pounds and a total length plus girth (L + 2W + 2H) of 108 inches. Free Priority Mail boxes can be ordered online.

◁ *SEE ALSO 6.7, "Free Priority Mail Boxes"* ▷

There is an interesting behind-the-scenes secret as to why most Priority Mail packages can travel coast-to-coast and be delivered in just two to three days with minimal problems: USPS *subcontracts the air transportation segment for most of its Priority Mail packages to FedEx!* The packages are then transported to the recipient's local post office for final delivery.

Flat-Rate Priority Mail

An economical option for small, but heavy items is to use the Flat-rate Priority Mail service. The flat charge is only $8.95 as long as the contents can fit within the provided boxes and do not exceed a weight of 70 pounds.

6.5

There are three different sized Flat-rate Priority Mail boxes. They measure 11" × 8½" × 5½", 13⅝" × 11⅞" × 3⅜", and 12" × 12" × 5½", and are free from your local post office or can be ordered online.

◁ *SEE ALSO 6.7, "Free Priority Mail Boxes"* ▷

Parcel Post

Parcel Post is an economical method to ship medium to large items and competes directly with FedEx Ground, DHL Ground, and UPS Ground. Package restrictions are 70 pounds and a total length plus girth (L + 2W + 2H) of 130 inches.

First-Class Mail

This service is ideal for envelopes, bubble packs, and small packages up to 13 ounces. In some cases, first-class rates are even cheaper than Parcel Post for small, lightweight packages. For items more than 13 ounces, use Priority Mail or Parcel Post.

Media Mail

Formerly known as Book Rate, Media Mail is the most economical rate for sending CDs, DVDs, videotapes, computer disks, books, manuscripts, printed educational charts, printed music, loose-leaf pages, three-ring binders of medical information, film, and sound recordings. Package restrictions are 70 pounds and a total length plus girth (L + 2W + 2H) of 108 inches.

A common mistake by eBay sellers is sending all printed material by Media Mail. The USPS does not allow any advertising material within Media Mail packages. Advertising includes paid advertising as well as advertising inserted by the shipper. This includes newspapers, magazines, comic books, and catalogs.

Additionally, never send a package Media Mail in order to save shipping costs if the package contents are not indeed media. The USPS reserves the right to open any Media Mail package to examine the contents. This could create an embarrassing predicament.

Delivery Confirmation and Insurance

Delivery Tracking and Confirmation and $100 insurance is included for all Express Mail packages at no additional charge. Delivery Confirmation (not tracking) can be purchased for other packages or is included if the shipping label was purchased online (see Shipping Labels below).

Some sellers confuse Delivery Confirmation from the USPS with Tracking from UPS, DHL, and FedEx. They are not the same. While the other carriers allow shippers to track the progress throughout the item's journey, USPS Delivery Confirmation will only report when the item has reached its destination.

Remember also that the USPS does not require a signature for smaller package deliveries unless they are sent Express Mail. Therefore, confirmation means only that the package was placed in the mailbox or on the doorstep. A recipient can easily claim non-delivery, as the package is vulnerable to walk-by theft. **Signature Confirmation,** although inconvenient, may be the best choice for higher priced items. Signature-required deliveries are not standard but are available for purchase as a shipping upgrade.

◀ *SEE ALSO 2.1, "What Is Paypal?"* ▶

Shipping Labels

You can easily print prepaid shipping labels from a home office using the USPS Click-N-Ship service. In addition, you can print USPS shipping labels from your My eBay page. This is the most efficient method since eBay fills in the shipper and recipient's addresses and payment can be made using PayPal with just a mouse click.

◀ *SEE ALSO 6.11, "eBay's Shipping Center"* ▶

Home Pickup

With USPS's Carrier Pickup service, eBay sellers can schedule a pickup from home free of charge, regardless of the number of packages. This is available for all types of packages up to 70 pounds each, as long as there is at least one Priority Mail package included. Free home pickup is a significant advantage over all other carriers and is especially helpful in avoiding long lines at the service counter during holidays and tax time.

Rates

Shipping rates vary for the services and shipping method chosen, along with the destination, package size, weight, and dimensions. Media Mail is the most economical way to ship media-related items. Flat Rate Priority Mail can be an economical way to ship small but heavy items quickly. Use the comparison table later in this chapter to determine how USPS compares to other carriers.

Claims

Insurance or damage claims can be filed no sooner than 21 days and no later than 180 days after delivery. If the package was lost or damaged, the USPS will pay for the insured item plus shipping within 30 days. While the 21-day delay appears to be a distinct disadvantage for using USPS over other carriers, remember that claims are rare and other comparison factors such as shipping rate are more important.

USPS Contact Information

The USPS provides a comprehensive website (www.usps.com) that explains all shipping services in detail. Quick links and phone numbers are provided below.

U.S. customer service	1-800-ASK-USPS (1-800-275-8777)

USPS QUICK LINK INFORMATION

Desired Service	Link Map (go to usps.com, then click)
Track a U.S. package	Track and confirm
Drop-off locations	Locate a post office
Ship a package	Shipping products and services
Schedule a pickup	Schedule a pickup
U.S. rates	Calculate postage
Content restrictions	Shipping products and services
Order supplies	Shipping tools, supplies
Click-N-Ship	Shipping products and services, click-N-ship
International shipping	Shipping products and services

APO/FPO addresses is the abbreviation for Army, Air Force, and Fleet post offices for the U.S. military overseas.

Delivery tracking and confirmation means only that the carrier has placed the item at the doorstep of the destination address.

Signature confirmation requires that a person at the destination address must sign for the package.

6.6 CARRIER COMPARISON CHART

Carrier Comparison Conclusions

This chart assumes that packages are dropped off at service counters, therefore no charge for home pickup. The shipper uses his or her own box. No extras except Delivery Confirmation for USPS. All items are shipped to residential addresses. No dimensions were used for the shipping box.

CARRIER COMPARISON CHART

Service (Purchased online)	FedEx	DHL	UPS	USPS Ground	USPS Priority Mail
Home pickup	$3 per package	$3 for a pickup	$3 per package	Free with 1 Priority Mail package	Free
Convenient drop-off locations	Usually	Depends on city & state	Usually	Yes	Yes
Free boxes	Express only	Express only	Express only	No	Express & Priority
Flat rate for heavier items, using flat-rate box	No	No	No	No	Yes ($8.95)
Free tracking	Yes	Yes	Yes	Delivery Confirm. (online)	Delivery Confirm. (online)
Free $100 insurance	Yes	Yes	Yes	No	No
Free Saturday deliveries	No	No	No	Yes	Yes
Deliveries to post-office boxes	No	No	No	Yes	Yes
Freight services	Yes	Yes	Yes	No	No
2 lb., ground, Seattle to Miami, track + $100 insur.	$8.80	$7.88 w/ DHL account	$11.11	$6.90 + $2.05 for $100 insurance	$8.15 + $2.05 for $100 insurance

6.6

continues

CARRIER COMPARISON CHART (CONTINUED)

Service (Purchased online)	FedEx	DHL	UPS	USPS Ground	USPS Priority Mail
5 lb., ground, Seattle to Miami, track + $100 insur.	$10.53	$9.30 w/ DHL account	$13.42	$11.25 + $2.05 for $100 insurance	$16.50 + $2.05 for $100 insurance
10 lb., ground, Seattle to Miami, track + $100 insur.	$13.24	$11.98 w/ DHL account	$16.93	$16.92 + $2.05 for $100 insurance	$25.70 + $2.05 for $100 insurance
35 lb., ground, Seattle to Miami, track + $100 insur.	$34.73	$28.98 w/ DHL account	$45.41	$33.17 + $2.05 for $100 insurance	$55.10 + $2.05 for $100 insurance
Days Required 5 lb., Seattle to Miami	7	8	7	7	2–3
5 lb., air, Chicago to Anchorage, track + $100 insurance	$28.63	$30.39 2nd day	$37.40	$11.25	$16.50
5 lb. air, Chicago to Honolulu, track + $100 insurance	$32.10	$33.79 2nd day	$37.40	$10.50	$15.85 (Note: $8.95 or $12.95 flat rate)
eBay/PayPal online discounts available. (See 6.11, "eBay Shipping Center")	No	No	Yes	Yes	Yes

Carrier Comparison Conclusions

No single carrier will meet every eBay seller's needs. Carriers specialize in particular services and the right choice depends on what, where, and when you are shipping. There are, however, some carrier comparison conclusions to keep in mind when making the decision.

FedEx

FedEx offers competitive rates with USPS and UPS for heavier ground shipments. Free boxes are available for express shipments only. FedEx charges for home pickup, does not deliver to post-office boxes, adds a fee for Saturday deliveries, and is not a good choice for shipments to Alaska or Hawaii. FedEx does offer competitive services for freight shipments.

DHL

DHL usually offers the lowest rates for standard ground shipments, but is not as convenient for drop-off locations when compared with all other carriers. Free boxes are available for express shipments only. DHL charges for home pickup, does not deliver to post-office boxes, adds a fee for Saturday deliveries, and is not a good choice for shipments to Alaska or Hawaii. DHL specializes in business and freight services and offers competitive rates for storing and shipping larger freight.

6.6

UPS

UPS provides multiple, convenient drop-off locations. Its rates are the least competitive for items weighing 2 to 10 pounds. Free boxes are available for Express shipments only. UPS also charges for home pickup, does not deliver to post-office boxes, and adds a fee for Saturday deliveries. UPS usually is not a good choice for Alaska or Hawaii shipments. However, UPS does offer discount shipping and home pickup rates to eBay sellers.

◄ *SEE ALSO 6.11, "eBay's Shipping Center"* ►

USPS

The USPS offers free boxes for Express and Priority Mail shipments. It offers a flat rate for small but heavy items and free flat-rate Priority Mail boxes. USPS provides free home pickup and Saturday deliveries at no extra charge. It can certainly deliver to post-office boxes. It does not charge a premium for deliveries to remote, rural destinations.

USPS rates usually beat all other carriers for small, lightweight packages (under two to three pounds) or for packages to neighboring destinations (within a state). USPS rates are also competitive with FedEx and UPS for ground deliveries and highly favorable for shipments to Alaska.

Remember also that for small packages (under 13 ounces), first class may be the best choice. USPS also offers significant discounts for Media Mail. The USPS is not a good choice for freight services.

6.7 PACKING MATERIALS AND CORRUGATED BOXES

Free Priority Mail Boxes

Corrugated Boxes

Padded Envelopes

Packing Materials

Shipping Large Items

Packing Tips

A considerable portion of the shipping cost to eBay sellers can be the cost of packing materials and corrugated boxes. This section investigates the practical options available when purchasing shipping materials and provides packing tips and guidelines to minimize shipping problems.

Free Priority Mail Boxes

USPS and eBay have formed an alliance to provide free, co-branded Priority Mail boxes. From eBay's Shipping Center, sellers can link to the USPS website to order variable-weight and flat-rate co-branded boxes. The boxes are stamped with phrases such as "Buy it on eBay. Ship it with the U.S. Postal Service."

Priority Mail Flat Rate box.

There are currently four different sizes of variable-weight boxes and two sizes of flat-rate co-branded boxes. They are ordered in quantities of 10 or 25. Sellers can order one quantity of each box size every day. The boxes are shipped flat in a corrugated shipping box and are delivered to your door, free of charge. Sellers can order the boxes from eBay's Shipping Center (see 6.11) or by using the link ebaysupplies.usps.com.

There are other sizes of Priority Mail boxes available that do not have eBay branding (nine sizes total). These can be ordered for free at shop.usps.com and click on For Mailing and Shipping. You can also order labels and forms on this site.

Corrugated Boxes

Sellers sometimes need to provide their own shipping boxes. Some sellers seek out retail or grocery stores and take their discarded boxes. Others reuse boxes in which they received shipments from their distributors or other product sources. Sometimes you can cut a larger box down to fit an item.

6.7

These "box reuse" methods are okay as long as the box is not damaged or there is no excessive printing on the box. Remember, the box is the very first impression of your service to your buyer. A box that has labels and printing blacked out with a black marker, or too much packing tape that was not fully removed gives a poor, unprofessional impression. It could be a determining factor for a meager or less-than-glowing Feedback comment.

Purchasing corrugated boxes from office-supply stores is an expensive choice. A box from these sources at retail prices is usually many times the cost from corrugated-box suppliers when purchased in bulk. This has a direct effect on a seller's bottom line. For example, a seller has a part-time eBay business selling seven items a day. The boxes required cost $6 each from an office-supply store and 80 cents from a corrugated-box supplier. That is a *savings* of $36.40 per day ($5.20 × 7) or a surprising $1,092 per month ($36.40 × 30 days)!

Check your yellow pages under Corrugated Boxes to find a local source. Compare their prices with online suppliers such as ULINE. Visit www.uline.com and request a catalog. ULINE's box selections are comprehensive and it has nearly every size you will ever need. It has six locations spread around the country to help reduce the shipping costs.

It is best to order in bulk when ordering from ULINE or any other corrugated-box supply company. Don't order one or two boxes—order 50, 100, or more and receive a bulk discount. The boxes are sent to you in flat stacks for cheaper shipping and easier storing. Even when including the price of shipping, purchasing in bulk will reduce the cost per box sometimes five- to tenfold over purchasing from an office-supply store.

Many times eBay sellers discover after an exhaustive online search that some of the best prices for their boxes, mailers, and packing materials are on eBay. In addition, shipping supplies such as tape, tape dispensers, shipping labels, scales, shipping box dividers, and rubber stamps are all found on eBay.

Padded Envelopes

Padded or bubble envelopes are best used for small items that are not vulnerable to breakage. These types of mailers can also be purchased at a discount from online suppliers such as ULINE or on eBay.

CDs, DVDs, and sometimes books are shipped with padded envelopes. This may work most of the time, but expect some occasional CD jewel box breakage or damaged book corners. Collectible, expensive, or breakable items should always be shipped in a box.

Packing Materials

Experienced sellers will often purchase their boxes in bulk from a corrugated-box supplier but use free sources of packing material. Bubble wrap and Styrofoam wedges or peanuts can sometimes be too expensive to order and have shipped.

If you don't have a local supplier of inexpensive packing materials, consider visiting local retailers. This is another way you can pass along the act of recycling. Retailers receive daily shipments in boxes that contain packing materials. For small bubble wrap, visit trinket stores such as Hallmark. For large bubble wrap, visit furniture stores. Styrofoam peanuts are used to pack trinkets, lamps, fine china, figurines, and other breakable items.

If you're not sure what packing material to use for your item, learn how online retailers pack them for shipment. The way they pack the item is how you should pack yours.

You should pack expensive or breakable items in bubble wrap and place in Styrofoam peanuts. Note that large bubble wrap should be used for breakable items as the smaller bubbles do not provide adequate protection from breakage. If you cannot find a local source for bubble wrap, try uline.com, papermart.com, fast-pack.com, or ebay.com.

You can wrap less expensive and non-breakable items in a variety of other packing materials. One of the most practical is newspaper; a few lightly crumpled sheets will fill the empty space of a box quickly. It's also very lightweight, easily available, and inexpensive. If the item you are shipping is vulnerable to the ink on the newspaper, simply place the item in a sealed plastic bag.

If you would like to use clean white paper for a more professional presentation, consider butcher paper or industrial tissue from a local source or ULINE. Moving companies also sell clean white wrapping paper. Visit your local newspaper and ask if you can either have (for free) or possibly purchase their "end rolls."

Shipping Large Items

Shipping larger items and freight can be a source of confusion and concern for the average eBay seller because of the apparent complexity. In reality, shipping freight is quite simple, manageable, and affordable with the following services.

6.7

Freightquote.com

Founded in 1998, Freightquote.com provides small businesses with free, quick comparison quotes for freight services among all carriers. This service is similar to airline comparison sites that search for the best ticket prices.

A shipper simply completes the required web-based information page and Freightquote.com returns a rate comparison of all relevant carriers. Once a shipping option is chosen, the Bill of Lading (BOL) forms are automatically printed, a pickup date is established, and the selected carrier dispatched. During transit, the shipment can also be tracked directly through your Freightquote.com account.

There is no charge to use their service. The freight company that wins your business will pay their fee.

Uship.com

Uship.com is an auction-style shipping site that provides a unique solution to shipping larger items, vehicles, animals, household items, and freight. You can list your shipment details at no charge and then receive shipping quotes from among 40,000 transportation service providers.

Many times these quotes are from mainstream carriers that have empty space in a truck passing through your area. Typical savings can be 50 percent to 60 percent off standard carrier rates. Uship.com also offers an array of tips, blogs, forums, and services to meet the shipping needs of small businesses.

DSI and U-Pic

Experienced sellers sometimes use private insurance companies such as DSI and U-Pic to insure freight shipments. Typical savings can be 50 percent off the standard carrier rates.

◀ *SEE ALSO 6.11, "eBay's Shipping Center"* ▶

Packing Tips

The following packing tips and guidelines are a summary of the best practices suggested from all carriers. Use these guidelines to minimize shipping problems or damage.

Boxes

▶ Use durable shipping boxes with no punctures, tears, or corner dents and with all flaps intact.

▶ Ensure that the box strength has not been weakened from rain, humidity, or label removal.

▶ For heavier items, use double-wall boxes.

▶ Do not exceed the gross weight limit for the box. This is usually displayed in the "box certificate" that is stamped on one of the bottom flaps.

▶ Do not wrap the box in paper.

Labels

▶ If reusing a box, carefully remove all labels.

▶ Black out all printing with a marker or place your shipping label over printing.

▶ Place only one address label on the box.

▶ Place the label on the top of the box.

▶ Do not place the label over a seam or closure.

▶ Do not place the label on top of the sealing tape.

▶ Clearly label whom the package is "from" and "to."

▶ Place a strip of clear packing tape over the shipping label to protect it from moisture.

Tape

▶ Do not use cellophane tape, masking tape, duct tape, electrical tape, or string.

▶ Use pressure-sensitive plastic or nylon-reinforced, two-inch or wider tape specifically made to seal shipping boxes.

▶ Tape the box end to end on both the top and bottom flaps.

▶ For heavy items, seal with heavy-duty or reinforced tape. Apply additional tape to the bottom of the box since it will bear the weight. Once the box is closed, seal the box by placing additional tape on the top and bottom edge seams.

▶ For water-activated paper tape, use pressure sensitive packing tape with a 60-pound grade and at least 3 inches wide or use water-activated, reinforced tape.

▶ Water-activated reinforced tape usually only needs two center-seam strips on the top and bottom.

6.7

Packing Materials

▶ Use 2 to 3 inches of cushioning packing material on the bottom, sides, and top to ensure the item does not move during transit.

▶ Close box and gently jiggle the box to ensure the item does not shift in the box.

▶ When shipping multiple items in one box, wrap each item individually and place additional packing material between the items.

▶ Use inflatable air bags only for lightweight items that do not have sharp corners or edges. Do not use air bags for expensive items, as they are not dependable and can break, shrink, or burst from extreme hot or cold temperatures.

▶ Styrofoam peanuts can settle or allow the item to settle during transit. Ensure that you provide at least 3 inches of peanuts around the item and then completely fill the box to the top.

▶ Take special care when shipping highly breakable items. Use two or three layers of different packing materials and possibly double box the item.

▶ Be aware that many of your customers may not like Styrofoam peanuts and could be annoyed if you use them. It is best to use them only for expensive or fragile items. One of the newer types of peanut is now made from biodegradable cornstarch. You can wash them down the sink when finished.

6.8 DETERMINE THE SHIPPING RATE

Flat and Calculated Rates

During listing creation a seller must determine the shipping rate. The first decision is which method to use, a flat rate or calculated rate? Each method has advantages and disadvantages.

Flat and Calculated Rates

With a **flat rate,** the same shipping charge will apply for all U.S. buyers no matter where they live. However, a flat rate to ship a mini-refrigerator from Flint, Michigan, to Detroit, Michigan (60 miles), should not be the same rate that would be charged for shipping it to San Diego, California (2,000 miles).

The shipping rate for larger-size items should be determined using the calculated rate option. Selecting the calculated rate during listing creation, the seller must enter the weight and dimensions of the box. eBay will automatically perform a calculated rate based on the buyer's zip code.

This requires the potential buyer to click on the "calculate" link in the listing and enter his or her zip code. This can be discouraging to a buyer because it requires more clicks to discover the shipping rate. If the buyer is logged in to their eBay account however, the rate will be displayed automatically. Flat rates will always display on the results page while calculated rates will only appear if the buyer is logged in to their account.

When should a seller use a flat or a calculated rate? A consensus among many eBay sellers is that the delineation weight is about 4 or 5 pounds. Items under that weight are usually charged a flat rate and for items over that weight, sellers prefer the calculated rate.

To determine the rate, the item should be placed in its shipping box along with all the required packing materials. The box is then placed on the seller's postal scale and the weight noted.

For a calculated rate, the weight and size of the package are entered into the Shipping Calculator during the listing process. eBay will then handle the calculations when a buyer clicks the Calculate link in the listing.

For a flat rate, the seller goes to the carrier's website and enters the weight and package dimensions. Sellers who will use UPS or USPS to ship the item can look up the rates directly from the Sell Your Item Form during listing creation. The seller uses his zip code and then a zip code in the United States that is farthest from where he lives (example, Chicago would use a San Diego destination zip code). He then immediately receives the quoted rate and adds any handling charge. The shipping quote and the handling charge become the flat rate. This is what the seller will enter into the proper shipping form for "Flat Rate" during the listing process.

A little-known but relevant fact is that the rates for all carriers are determined by the pound, not by pounds plus ounces. Any ounce over a particular pound will be regarded as the next pound. For example, a package weighing 2 pounds, 1 ounce will be charged a 3-pound rate.

A detailed explanation of calculated and flat shipping rates is provided in Chapter 4. For either method, the seller will need a postal scale to determine the proper weight.

◀ SEE ALSO 4.1, *"Listing Preparation"* ▶

◀ SEE ALSO 4.2, *"Listing Creation"* ▶

6.8

WORDS TO GO . . .WORDS TO GO . . .WORDS TO GO

Flat-rate is a listing option that allows you to charge the same shipping rate for all the United States or to a specific international destination.

6.9 POSTAL SCALES

Postal Scale Features

A Popular Scale for eBay Sellers

Postal Scale Scam Warning

There are two tools essential for eBay sellers, a digital camera and a digital postal scale. Before a seller can determine what shipping rate to charge, she needs to know the combined weight of the item, the shipping box, and all packing materials.

Postal Scale Features

A variety of postal scales are available on the market today. Surprisingly, a comparison reveals that many have either too low a weight limit, too few features, or too high a price for eBay sellers.

Listed below are the desired essential features to look for in a postal scale to be used by an eBay seller.

▶ It should have a weight rating that exceeds the typical items you will be selling. Suggestion: 50+ lbs.

▶ Displays a digital readout.

▶ Ability to display oz./lbs. or grams/kg. (for international sales).

▶ You should be able to "zero" the weight if you are weighing envelopes, tubes, liquids, or other items that need to be placed in a holding container. You place the container on the scale and zero the scale to remove the **tare weight** reading, and then add the material. Now you know the weight of the liquid or material.

▶ Provides a "hold" feature to save the weight for a few seconds after you remove the item when placing large items on the scale that cover the readout.

▶ It should be portable and have the ability to run on batteries. Forget the AC adaptor. As an eBay seller you will use it in your shipping room, next to your computer and throughout the house and garage. Be sure to purchase one that can run on batteries (usually C batteries for longer life).

One thing to keep in mind is that there is nothing magical about the word "postal" in "postal scale." It is a scale, not a postage meter. It simply weighs items.

It can be used around the house to weigh items in the kitchen, garage, and basement. For example, you can use a scale rated over 50 pounds to ensure your suitcase does not exceed the 50-pound airline weight limit.

A Popular Scale for eBay Sellers

While at first it may seem that there are several scales available, few scales will have the desired features listed previously. Scales available at retail office-supply stores are surprisingly short on features, low on weight limits, and high in price. Even the scales on the USPS website carry ratings of only 5 and 10 pounds. This falls far below the weight limit needs of the average eBay seller who ships even medium-size packages.

One of the more popular scales among eBay sellers is the UltraShip scale from My Weigh. They have several scales at different weight ratings. The scale that meets all the desired features listed previously is the UltraShip 55 (pound) scale.

It also has a very nice additional feature. That is the ability to physically separate the digital readout section from the scale by use of a retractable cord. This is ideal for weighing items in large boxes that cover the readout.

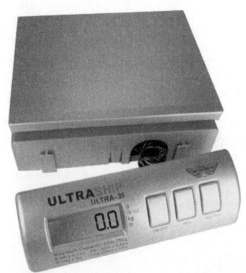

UltraShip scale.

These scales are available on eBay and online. However, be aware that because of their popularity, these particular postal scales are also a popular choice of bait for scammers. Be sure and read the next section before you purchase.

Postal Scale Scam Warning

Be aware that many Internet and eBay postal scale sellers are disreputable. In fact, the problem had become so bad at one time that My Weigh, the manufacturer of UltraShip scales, mentioned the scam on its website.

Deceitful sellers claim to be authorized dealers of My Weigh and list an Ultra-Ship scale online. The price is at a ridiculously low price (under $15) when compared with a common standard price (about $40 to $45). This seems to be a great deal for the buyer, until she receives the unit. Upon careful examination, she sees that the scale she received is not the same as advertised. In fact, sometimes it does not even have the My Weigh name. The scale is a very cheap knockoff with horrible weight readings and tolerances.

Checking the seller's feedback before you buy is not always a good indicator; many buyers leave positive feedback when they receive the scale and before they actually use it. A better clue is the price itself. Ask yourself this question: "How can a seller who claims to be an authorized dealer sell the scales below wholesale?" The answer is simple: the scales are refurbished units, liquidated older models, used models, or knockoffs (a scam).

Before you purchase online or on eBay, it is a good idea to be safe and find a reputable dealer. You can visit My Weigh's website at www.myweigh.com to find its higher-volume, authorized retailers.

Note: Disreputable postal scale sellers have been reported to eBay many times. They will "go away" for a while, but then eventually return. I had heard so many complaints from my eBay students that I was determined to help solve this problem. I contacted the distributor and discussed the dilemma. I now feel confident to supply the legitimate UltraShip scales specifically recommended for my students and readers on my website www.trainingu4auctions.com or my eBay store www.trainingu4auctions.net.

WORDS TO GO . . . *WORDS TO GO . . . WORDS TO GO*

Tare weight refers to the weight of the box and packing materials and excludes the weight of the items it will contain.

6.10 RESOLVING RETURNS AND CLAIMS

Damage

Item Doesn't Work

Buyer Doesn't Like Item

Non-Delivery Claim

A buyer might have one of several reasons to return an item. This is a good reason to provide a detailed **return policy** when creating a listing. Some of the more common return claims are examined here.

Damage

When shipping damage occurs during transit, usually the box will have holes, rips, or crushed corners that are obvious. However, even with irrefutable evidence of rough handling, the particular carrier can also claim that the item was not properly cushioned or packed. Therefore, if it is obvious that the item has been damaged, it is best to have your customer not fully unpack the package but leave the item wrapped in the packing material if at all possible or practical.

6.10

In every case, the carrier should be contacted first to determine the specific claim process for the item. Many times the carrier will return to the customer's home, pick up the item, and take it to the central office for examination and a refund decision.

Whenever possible, the seller should be the one to deal with the carrier. Take the customer out of the claims loop, and refund their money or send a replacement. Deal with the carrier separately.

The lesson here should be obvious. Pack the item carefully and professionally. This will minimize breakage and maximize the chance for refund approval from the carrier.

◀ *SEE ALSO 6.7, "Packing Materials and Corrugated Boxes, Packing Tips"* ▶

Item Doesn't Work

A mechanical or electronic item that does not function properly upon receipt is the responsibility of the seller. Provide clear instructions in your return policy whether you will refund the money or replace the item. Requiring the buyer to send the item in for repair, even under warranty, is a poor choice that can lead to negative feedback. A new item should function properly. If it doesn't, replace it or refund the money. Then you send it in for repair and resell it as a factory-refurbished unit.

Always wait, however, for the item to be returned first before refunding money or replacing the item. A buyer can always claim it doesn't work, wait for a refund, and never ship the item back, because ... it actually works and now it is free!

Buyer Doesn't Like Item

Solve this problem upfront when writing your return policies. The cost to return items because the buyer didn't like the color, it didn't match the wallpaper, or other reasons beside damage is the responsibility of the buyer. You can offer a 100-percent money-back guarantee but the buyer should pay the shipping to return the item.

Non-Delivery Claim

Packages lost during transit are very rare. They may be late but almost never are lost. Many times a claim of non-delivery is because of an undeliverable address. As soon as a customer contacts you with the dreaded "Where's my package?" you should take immediate investigative action.

FedEx, UPS, and DHL have online tracking throughout the transit process. Simply enter the tracking number and you will immediately find where the package is and if there is a delivery problem. Contact the carrier and possibly the buyer and resolve the problem. The buyer will be nervous at this point. Keep him or her in the loop as you resolve the problem. This will relieve tension, earn confidence in you, and result in great feedback even after the shipping delay problem.

Note that USPS only offers tracking for Express Mail shipments. Delivery confirmation (an option for most other USPS shipments) only confirms that it has been delivered. You cannot determine where the package is during transit, only if it has been delivered to the final destination. This is a distinct disadvantage over other carriers.

Sometimes a buyer will claim non-delivery even when the carrier has reported making the delivery. Is the buyer trying to cheat you? Not necessarily. Delivery means the carrier has placed the item on the buyer's doorstep at sometime during a particular day. A dishonest neighbor or someone walking by can be tempted to take the package. Packages are especially vulnerable when left in multifamily home complexes such as condos or apartments.

While this is a tough mystery to solve, many times it can be resolved. If the shipment contains a commodity item that is not expensive, ship a replacement—but this time require a signature confirmation delivery. It is difficult to claim a non-delivery whenever there is an actual signature on record from the person receiving the package.

Next, see whether the item qualifies for Seller Protection from PayPal. If it does, request a refund through PayPal.

◄ *SEE ALSO 2.1, "What Is Paypal?"* ▶

The lesson here is to always use tracking or delivery confirmation for packages. For one-of-a-kind or expensive items or items shipped to multifamily complexes (those with unit or apartment numbers in the address), consider requiring signature confirmation. If you choose this option for multifamily addresses, be sure to mention it in your shipping policy.

6.10

WORDS TO GO . . .WORDS TO GO . . .WORDS TO GO

A **return policy,** developed during the listing process, should provide a clear understanding about the seller's guarantees, refunds, and associated time limits.

6.11 EBAY'S SHIPPING CENTER

Print Prepaid Postage with PayPal

USPS Discounts with PayPal

UPS Special Pricing Program

Tracking Packages

Combined Shipping Discounts

Handling Charges

Excessive Shipping Charge Policy

Insuring Packages

Private Third-Party Insurers

Third-Party Printing Hardware/Software

Shipping Tips

eBay's Shipping Center provides detailed information on many essential and advanced shipping features available to eBay sellers. This includes UPS and USPS shipping discounts for sellers who pay for their shipping online with Pay-Pal. eBay's Shipping Center can be located by clicking on the Site Map link at the top of any page, then under Selling Resources.

Print Prepaid Postage with PayPal

You can print prepaid postage labels for the USPS or UPS directly from your My eBay page. The shipping charge is automatically deducted from your PayPal account.

From your My eBay page, click the Print Shipping Label link next to the customer's name. You will be taken directly to PayPal where the customer's address and the sender's return address will already be automatically filled in. Simply choose your carrier and shipping options and print the label. You can even choose to hide the shipping or postage charge and the label will print without revealing the dollar amount.

Print Shipping Label from My eBay.

The label is designed for printing on specific peel-off/stick-on labels for a few models of Pitney Bowes, Brother, Zebra, and DYMO Label Writer printers. For details, refer to Third-Party Printing Hardware/Software later in this chapter. While this can save time and effort for medium- to large-volume eBay sellers, the cost for equipment and labels is a more expensive option for lower-volume sellers.

Therefore, with no additional printer setup, the labels can also be printed directly on standard 8.5 × 11 paper using an ordinary home printer. Simply trim the label with a pair of scissors and adhere it to your package using a few strips of clear packing tape.

You should also know that when you print a shipping label through PayPal, the buyer will automatically receive an e-mail stating you have printed the label. This is done automatically to save you time and effort. However, the problem is you haven't really shipped the item, just printed the label, and the buyer will most likely assume the item was shipped. If you use this service, it is a good idea to send a follow-up e-mail and mention when the package will be shipped.

6.11

Use this label-printing service in conjunction with home pickup to save time traveling and standing in line at the post office or UPS counter. Remember that free USPS home pickup requires that at least one of the packages is Priority Mail.

USPS Discounts with PayPal

PayPal has formed an alliance with USPS for discounted domestic services and international shipping rates to eBay sellers. Free Delivery Confirmation is automatically provided for Priority Mail packages when purchasing prepaid postage online with PayPal (Express Mail always provides free tracking). USPS offers discounted rates for Delivery Confirmation for First-Class, Parcel Post, and Media Mail. Up to $500 in USPS insurance can also be purchased online with PayPal.

Sellers can also save 5 percent on USPS Priority Mail International and 8 percent on Express Mail International. Additionally, sellers can print customs forms directly from their PayPal accounts. When printing prepaid postage shipping labels, PayPal will also generate customs forms with pre-filled information with the international address of your customer.

◀ SEE ALSO 8.3, *"International USPS Shipping Rates"* ▶

UPS Special Pricing Program

UPS offers a Special Pricing Program to eBay sellers who purchase their shipping online. Discounts vary but can reach up to 31 percent for UPS ground. Slightly lower discounts are available on several other services including home pickups.

Shippers can also purchase up to $999 of additional UPS insurance with PayPal. If you have a UPS account, you have the option to bill the amount to your account rather than paying with PayPal.

To sign up for the UPS Special Pricing Program offered to eBay sellers, visit the eBay Shipping Center by clicking the link located in Seller References under the Site Map link at the top right of any page.

Tracking Packages

When purchasing shipping labels using PayPal, UPS tracking and USPS Delivery Confirmation can be viewed directly from both the buyer's and seller's My eBay page. They can also be viewed from their PayPal Account Overview page.

USPS Delivery Confirmation will designate when the package has reached its final destination. UPS and USPS Express Mail tracking will show the detailed progress throughout transit. Both of these features qualify as the online tracking requirement for PayPal's seller protection. Note, however, that for items over $250, you need signature confirmation in order to qualify for seller protection.

◄ *SEE ALSO 2.1, "What Is Paypal?"* ►

Combined Shipping Discounts

eBay's Combined Shipping Discounts service allows sellers to offer shipping discounts for buyers who purchase multiple items. This is a tremendous benefit to buyers wanting to save money on shipping as well as sellers who will profit from add-on or impulse-buy sales.

This feature can be set up for either flat-rate or calculated shipping rate using your own custom discount rules based on each item's weight and size. You can also set promotional shipping discounts for purchases that total or exceed a designated sum.

Simply select the Preferences link under My Account in your My eBay page. Click the Show link for Combined payments and shipping discounts and then click on Edit. As buyers browse your items they will now see messages automatically generated by eBay informing them of your combined shipping discounts.

Handling Charges

Experienced eBay sellers have different views about handling charges. Some think that customers should only be charged the actual cost of shipping. Others actually try to profit from shipping. The majority of experienced sellers, however, charge a reasonable fee for handling that covers the cost of packing materials, the shipping box, and the labor to pack the box, and in some cases travel to the shipper's drop-off location. The consensus on a reasonable handling charge is no more than $2 to $3 per package.

Excessive Shipping Charge Policy

Sellers are allowed to charge a reasonable fee for shipping and handling, but they are not allowed to gouge their customers or try to make their profit from the shipping rate rather than the product. Disreputable sellers sometimes list their item for a very low starting price and then make their profit from an excessive shipping rate. This is because eBay fees correlate only to the product and not the shipping.

It is clearly a disadvantage for a legitimate, policy-abiding seller to have to compete with deceitful sellers who list items at ridiculously low Starting or Buy It Now prices with an unreasonably high shipping rate. Most of these excessive charge violators are eventually discovered and reported to eBay from upset buyers or competing sellers. Sellers who are caught using this deceptive practice will have their listing cancelled. If they continue this practice, they can lose their PowerSeller status (if they are a PowerSeller) or have their account suspended.

6.11

◁ SEE ALSO 9.3, *"Account Problems or Item Delisting"* ▷

Insuring Packages

Packages are automatically insured up to $100 with UPS, DHL, and FedEx. For USPS packages, no insurance is included except for Express Mail deliveries. However, up to $500 of insurance can be purchased online.

Should sellers purchase additional insurance? This decision must be made for higher-value items. The fact that carriers end their free insurance at $100 is a big clue. That is the dollar amount when the need for insurance really begins. This is especially true with expensive, breakable items.

Some sellers let the buyers decide whether to buy insurance and make this choice an option during **eBay Checkout.** This is not a good business decision. Allowing the buyer to opt out of buying additional insurance will not let you off the hook if the item is lost or damaged during transit.

Keep in mind that it is very rare for any carrier to lose a package. Shippers are really buying insurance for damage. With this in mind, the insurance decision becomes clearer. The item either needs insurance for damage or it doesn't. If it does, add the amount to your total shipping charge and write in your shipping policy that your rate includes insurance.

Finally, do not try to profit from insurance. This tactic is usually more obvious to the potential buyer than trying to profit from shipping. Sellers who do this will be viewed as less than credible, because they're gouging their customers.

Private Third-Party Insurers

Shippers can purchase up to $500 of insurance online with USPS and $999 with UPS. Additional insurance can be purchased at their service counters. A less expensive option for additional insurance or for insuring international bound packages is to purchase from private, third-party insurers.

The two most popular private, third-party shipping insurers among eBay sellers are U-Pic and DSI. Many times their shipping insurance rates can be purchased for a substantial savings compared to standard carrier rates. This becomes a very popular insurance alternative for shippers of high-volume items, high-value items, or freight.

> ▶ **U-Pic:** Provides substantial insurance discounts for FedEx, DHL, UPS, or USPS domestic and international shipments. Typical savings are 50 percent and can be as high as 60 to 80 percent off carrier insurance rates for higher-volume shippers. eBay sellers should visit www.u-pic.com and read the FAQ document to learn how this private insurance process works and how to set up an account.

> ▶ **DSI:** Discount Shipping Insurance, found at www.dsiinsurance.com, also provides discounted insurance coverage for small to large items with all major carriers. The rates are sometimes 90 percent lower than standard carrier insurance rates and tend to be a bit less than U-Pic's rates. eBay sellers should visit the website and click on the Questions link for more information.

Third-Party Printing Hardware/Software

As their eBay sales volume increases, advanced sellers may progress to other professional shipping label printing hardware and software. Membership with some of these companies comes with additional perks from their partners such as discounts from shipping carriers.

Software

Many software companies offer prepaid shipping label services. The two that are affordable and have become most popular among eBay sellers are listed here.

> ▶ **Endicia:** Web-based software for the trouble-free purchase of shipping labels and postage for packages and letter mail. Provides discounted pricing for tracking, delivery confirmation, and shipping insurance.

It automatically generates customs forms for international shipments. Provides automatic e-mail shipping notification to shippers' customers, complete with tracking information. Different monthly rates are available depending on your shipping requirements. A free 30-day trial is available at www.endicia.com.

▶ **ShipWorks:** Provides customizable desktop software that simplifies all aspects of the shipping process. It can automatically download sales from eBay as well as other popular online sites including Amazon.com, Yahoo! Stores, and eBay's ProStores. Once downloaded, paying for and printing shipping labels are a mouse click away since it automatically connects to FedEx, USPS, and UPS.

ShipWorks also offers integrated services with Endicia, Marketworks, ChannelAdvisor, Stamps.com, and the private shipping insurer DSI. Additionally, it comes with different components that provide other services such as inventory tracking, low-supply notification and customer communication (e-mail) automation.

6.11

Monthly fees vary depending on shipping volume. Developed by Interapptive software, ShipWorks offers a free 30-day trial available at www.interapptive.com.

Hardware

Sellers who want to print directly on convenient peel-off/stick-on shipping labels should compare prices and features of the following manufacturers. Note that the models listed for each manufacturer are compatible with PayPal's prepaid shipping label service. If you use Endicia, ShipWorks, or another label-printing software, you should contact the software company to ensure compatibility with the particular label printer models.

▶ **Pitney Bowes:** Manufactures professional shipping-label printing equipment. Their model LPS-1 is designed specifically to work with PayPal's prepaid postage program. Check www.pb.com to compare features of the LPS-1 with other manufacturers and to find a dealer near you.

Join Pitney Bowes' PriorityPerks program at www.pbpriorityperks.com for savings on supplies or products and services from its program partners. Most notable is the ability to save 12 percent on FedEx Ground shipping and up to 20 percent on services from FedEx Kinko's Office and Print Centers.

▶ **Brother:** Another giant in the label printer business. Its models QL-500 and QL-550 are specifically designed to print the prepaid peel-off labels with your PayPal account. For more information or to find a dealer near you, visit www.brother.com.

▶ **Zebra:** A lesser-known brand, but offers the largest selection of competitive printer models that are compatible with PayPal's prepaid printing service. The models that qualify are Zebra LP 2844-Z, TLP 3842, HT-146, TLP 2844, and TLP 3844. For more information or to find a dealer near you, visit www.zebra.com.

▶ **DYMO:** Provides home, office, and industrial shipping label printing solutions. DYMO offers two label printers that are compatible with PayPal's prepaid label service, the Label/Writer 330 and Label/Writer 330 Turbo. Visit www.dymo.com to compare features with other manufacturers and to find a dealer near you.

Shipping Tips

By following the tips below, you will maximize your odds for successful shipments.

▶ **Shipping area:** If possible, set up a separate shipping area as well as an inventory storage area.

▶ **Supplies:** Be sure to always stock enough shipping boxes, supplies, and packing materials.

▶ **Receive payment first:** Never ship until you are paid. Checks and money orders must clear the bank first before shipment is made.

▶ **Print labels online:** Save time, trouble, and money.

▶ **Schedule home pickup:** Save more time, trouble, and money.

▶ **Pack carefully:** Follow the Packing Tips guide provided in section 6.7.

▶ **Ship quickly:** Ship packages as soon as you can within reason. Professional eBayers should try to ship every day, and part-time sellers at least two to three times a week.

▶ **Shipping rates:** Charge only the actual cost of shipping plus a reasonable $2 to $3 handling charge. Remember, shipping rates are now shown on search result views.

▶ **Insurance:** Buy shipping online to qualify for $100 insurance for UPS, DHL, and FedEx. Use private, third-party insurers to minimize insurance costs for items with a value over $100.

▶ **Invoice:** Include an invoice or a copy of the PayPal packing slip in the package placed on top of the item just before you seal the box.

▶ **Returns:** Allow for easy returns and provide quick refunds. Returns are rare, so consider them part of the business.

▶ **Refund shipping:** If you discover you have charged too much for shipping, an unsolicited refund goes a long way to winning a long-term, loyal customer.

WORDS TO GO . . .WORDS TO GO . . .WORDS TO GO

eBay Checkout is the post-auction process, when the buyer pays the seller for the item.

6.11

7

PRODUCT SOURCING

7.1 WHAT TO SELL

The eBay Selling Progression

What Not to Sell

Determine What to Sell

Most sellers begin their eBay experience because of a need to get rid of a few things around their home. In effect, they are having a nationwide garage sale. For many, this is the extent of their selling experience. For others, this is the beginning of a part-time or full-time eBay career.

Continuing sellers, at some point, want to move from their garage-sale mode to profit mode. The most common questions sellers have at that time are …

▶ What should I sell?

▶ How and where do I get my products?

▶ How can I know a product supplier is reputable?

Many eBay books recommend sourcing products from local garage and estate sales, flea markets, surplus or thrift stores, and storage unit auctions. These are legitimate sources of products for eBay sellers, but they've been covered in detail in other books and we will not repeat them. These product sources tend to appeal more to antique dealers, collectors, or the casual eBay hobbyist seller who has the time and enjoys the hunt.

This chapter is primarily for eBay sellers who have already tried those sources and now want to move beyond them. They are looking for a more formal relationship with product suppliers. This is indeed part of the natural eBay selling progression. These sellers are becoming more serious and are now sourcing product for profit, not for fun. They should no longer have their product choices and eBay sales for the next week dependent on what they found over the weekend at a garage sale.

You should make product sourcing decisions through a methodical process, to find products that are proven profitable on eBay and consistently available from a reliable and reputable product supplier. This chapter will present the procedures, tools, and resources that many professional eBay sellers use to determine their product selection and product sourcing.

The eBay Selling Progression

Many people think of eBay as selling individual items, one at a time, to a single person, for minimal profit. This is indeed how the vast majority of sales are made on eBay. It is not, however, the business plan for the serious, successful eBay entrepreneur.

As eBay sellers progress from amateur to professional, they move away from small-profit items ($5 to $20) and begin selling more expensive items, for a larger profit. The next natural selling progression phases tend to be as follows:

1. Selling higher-priced items ($50 to $200) to several customers (higher volume).

2. Selling even higher-priced items ($200 to $2,000) to businesses.

3. **Drop shipping** expensive items to save inventory costs.

4. Selling **lots** to individuals or businesses (B2B).

SEE ALSO 7.5, "Drop Shippers" ▶

SEE ALSO 12.9, "Strategies for eBay Business Phases" ▶

What Not to Sell

There are many misconceptions about eBay selling. Before discussing what to sell, you need to know what a professional eBay business owner should not be selling. Following are a few products a professional seller should avoid.

Cheap Products

Avoid products that are cheap in both quality and price. So many people think of eBay as the place for buying cheap items. However, there is not a good reason that a seller who makes even a part-time living from eBay should be selling items, one at a time, for under $10. It takes just as much time to list, pack, and ship a $100 item as it does a $10 item. Leave the cheaper items to hobbyists and amateur sellers. You are in this for the money now, not a hobby.

There is another reason to avoid selling cheap products. The troublemakers tend to shop there. Sell to a select customer base by selling better-quality, higher-priced items.

Unprofitable Products

Do not sell any product if it is not profitable. If the product does not return a profit, you are wasting your time. Not every product that is popular on store shelves is a moneymaker on eBay. Additionally, not every product you sold for a healthy profit last year (or in some cases, last month) is profitable now. eBay markets change considerably throughout the year.

Products and Categories with Tough Competition

It is very easy to sell on eBay—sometimes too easy. Some amateur sellers are very happy to make a $2 profit on a $100 sale. This is not the place for serious eBay business owners. Why list, sell, pack, and ship any product for such a small profit? Also avoid saturated marketplaces with too many competitors all listing the same items.

Mass-Market Products

New mass-market items are rarely profitable on eBay. It is very difficult to compete with giant retailers and Internet sites that sell these items.

When you study the "What's Hot on eBay" report, you will notice that items that appeal to the mass market, such as consumer electronics, are where the action is on eBay. However, a **niche market** is usually where the profits are.

◀ *SEE ALSO 15.1, "Finding What's Hot"* ▶

Many new eBay sellers want to sell either the glitz products or products that they are more familiar with because of their retail appeal and popularity. With most new mass-market items, though, your competition is so large and the margins so small that there is little profit for the average eBay seller.

Generally speaking, it is not a good business model to plan on selling new, latest-model, mass-market items such as consumer electronics on eBay. Your competition is not only the large electronic stores such as Best Buy and Circuit City, but also thousands of other online retailers who are also selling the same items below the prices of these major stores. Additionally, many wholesalers of these products require sellers to have a very high credit line and make large minimum-quantity purchases. That is too much competition and overhead to be profitable on eBay.

Products That Are Difficult to Ship

Selling refrigerators on eBay may be profitable, but you will then have to pack and ship them. Look for items that are smaller and much more manageable to ship.

Determine What to Sell

The most asked question by a new eBay seller is "What should I sell?" However, this is really the wrong question. The eBay marketplace is constantly shifting and changing, so what was selling a year ago may not be moving today. What is hot and a big money maker today may not be profitable even six months from now.

The question is not "What should I sell today?" but rather, "How can I determine what to sell?" The biggest difference between an amateur and a professional seller on eBay is the way they select their products. The amateur chooses his products based on a hunch—"I think these items will be a winner on eBay." The results are hit or miss.

The professional makes her product selection based on a product's proven profitability. This chapter will take you through the process that many eBay professionals use for product selection and sourcing.

◁ *SEE ALSO 7.2, "Niche Markets"* ▷

◁ *SEE ALSO 7.6, "Product Analysis"* ▷

WORDS TO GO . . . WORDS TO GO . . . WORDS TO GO

Drop shippers are wholesalers that will ship individual items directly to customers for online sellers. The seller doesn't stock, pack, or ship the product.

A **lot** refers to items sold by suppliers in bulk and in a certain quantity. A buyer may purchase a lot of 25, 50, or even 1,000 of a particular item. Sellers on eBay may sell a group of non-identical items to one buyer as a lot (such as 25 different articles of clothing in a particular size).

A **niche market** is a much smaller segment of a larger market category.

7.1

7.2 NICHE MARKETS

General Selling vs. Niche Selling
Finding an Ideal Niche Market

A niche market is a much smaller segment of a larger market. Most eBay sellers sell to a product category level, not a niche level. For example, selling a variety of sporting goods equipment is a category level. Selling only baseball equipment is a smaller market segment but the competition may still be too large to be considered a true niche on eBay. Specializing in selling only baseball bats is a niche.

Many eBay professionals have learned to take the niche one step deeper to considerably reduce their competition and increase their sales and profit. In the example above, specializing in devices that help Little League batters time their swings is an **ideal niche market.** That is the level where big money can be made on eBay as long as your competition stays away.

An ideal niche market is one where there is very high demand but little competition for a particular product or group of products within that niche. If the competition is nearly non-existent but there is still high demand for the product, you can corner the market. Ideal niches are more rare, but are great marketplaces for an eBay seller to begin their product selection process and build a solid business.

General Selling vs. Niche Selling

It is important to know that not everything sold on eBay needs to be in a niche market. Specifically, selling **liquidation** items that may change from week to week does not need to be niche—only profitable. So the decision must first be made which direction you want to go with your eBay business, general selling or niche selling?

If your business plan is to sell items that you have purchased from surplus, close-outs, and liquidators, you want to **general sell.** Customers will probably buy from you just once and move on. Your products will change from week to week depending on what is available from the liquidators.

If your plan is to specialize in certain items and build a business from returning, satisfied customers and referrals, you want to **niche sell.** If you want to make the top profit margin in a niche, you should sell in ideal niches.

◀ *SEE ALSO 7.4, "Wholesalers, Liquidators, Importers"* ▶

◀ *SEE ALSO 12.1, "Develop Your High-Level Business Plan"* ▶

Finding an Ideal Niche Market

You have no doubt heard the phrases "Find a need and fill it," "Find a problem and solve it," or "Find out what they want and give it to them." All of these phrases are the template you should use in product selection to find a truly profitable ideal niche on eBay.

The first step in finding an ideal niche market is the product idea. Product ideas can come from a variety of sources including an educated hunch, products found in a retail store, the Internet, magazine, newspaper, or radio advertisements. The professional eBay seller also finds a niche a bit more methodically with help from technical product analysis.

A good first step is to find what is hot and in demand on eBay in the category where you may want to sell. This can be accomplished by reviewing eBay's free "What's Hot on eBay" report from Seller Central.

◀ *SEE ALSO 15.1, "Finding What's Hot"* ▶

In order to have products fall into an ideal niche, there should be high demand and little competition. Therefore, once you have a category or product in mind, you need to conduct competitive analysis to determine the demand, competition, and profitability of the item.

7.2

This is a daunting task to accomplish manually. There would be days and weeks of research combing through the categories and products on eBay. Professional sellers use software tools to accomplish the marketing analysis quickly and efficiently. The method and tools used to find an ideal niche market and guarantee that the items they want to sell are profitable are summarized below. Note that the software tools mentioned are detailed in Subchapter 7.6.

1. Determine a product or category to investigate. Start with Seller Central's "What's Hot" list for the category you are interested in.

   Software tools: HammerTap Research, Terapeak, and eBay Marketplace Research can also provide a report for what's hot on eBay for the categories you are interested in.

2. Determine if the products or categories are a niche or ideal niche.

   Software tools: Worldwide Brands' OneSource package provides Demand, Competition, and Instant Product Analysis tools to quickly determine if you have a niche or ideal niche.

3. Determine the profitability. Just because an item is a hot seller doesn't mean it is profitable.

Software tools: HammerTap Research, Terapeak, and eBay Marketplace Research can quickly determine how the item has been selling on eBay in the last 90 days. Sellers compare the going price on eBay with the wholesale cost. If unsure, assume 45 percent off of the retail price.

◄ *SEE ALSO 7.6, "Product Analysis"* ►

◄ *SEE ALSO 12.2, "Competitive Analysis"* ►

WORDS TO GO . . . WORDS TO GO . . . WORDS TO GO

An **ideal niche market** is one in which there is very high demand but little competition for a particular product or group of products within a niche.

Liquidation items are usually older-model, surplus, or closeout items that a major wholesaler or retailer needs to clear out of a store or warehouse. Many use professional, online liquidators to offload the items.

General sell refers to selling all types of unrelated items much like a general store. The plan is to build a business not from related niche items, but from variety and value.

Niche sell is when all items sold by a particular retailer are related, complementary, and from the same niche.

AVOIDING MIDDLEMEN

Seminars, Magazine Ads, and Infomercials
Legitimate eBay Courses
Middlemen

There is no shortcut to eBay success. It takes dedication and hard work to start or grow any business. As you advance through your eBay selling phases, you will need to expand your product line with new items, categories, and niches. To accomplish this, additional product suppliers are needed. However, if you conducted a Google or Internet search for eBay product suppliers you would receive from thousands to millions of hits.

Some of these sites are legitimate and others are scams. Many, however, are middlemen who place themselves between you and the actual wholesaler and add a surcharge when you order their products. As an eBay seller, you will need to be able to identify and separate legitimate product suppliers from scammers and middlemen.

Seminars, Magazine Ads, and Infomercials

Use caution with any company claiming to be a product supplier for eBay or Internet sellers. The more a company claims to be the single source for all of your eBay or Internet products, the more suspicious you should be.

These companies are often found on the Internet, in the back of home-based business magazines, and on late-night TV infomercials. Some may have traveling road shows that come to your city. They may even take out full-page ads in your local newspaper or blitz the radio advertising a free two-hour eBay or Internet seminar.

These seminars are usually bait-and-switch. The seminar attendees arrive expecting a free seminar on eBay or Internet selling. The free seminar is actually a commercial for a paid seminar. At the paid seminar, the true pitch is revealed. The company is there to sell you an Internet website and supply all the products for you. It can "get you started today for only two to six thousand dollars!" If you don't sign up for the deal, expect high-pressure follow-up sales calls.

If a company claims to be a source for your eBay products and then tries to sell you other services besides the products, you should consider it highly suspect. Genuine **wholesalers** sell retailers (you) products at true wholesale prices.

Legitimate eBay Courses

If you are considering attending an eBay seminar, check if the company is also offering advice on Internet selling. If it mentions anything about the Internet in the ad, it is not an approved eBay course. Another clue is the length of the seminar. You cannot learn about selling from an eBay-sanctioned instructor in 1.5 hours. That time frame is just right for a sales pitch, not a class.

There are legitimate eBay seminars and courses that are held around the country. These courses use eBay-authorized presentations, books, and instructors. The instructors have the title "Education Specialist Trained by eBay." You can find eBay-approved classes and instructors in your area by visiting eBay's Education Specialist site: www.poweru.net/ebay/student/searchIndex.asp.

Middlemen

Many of the companies on the Internet that claim to be a product supplier for eBay sellers are actually **middlemen.** They buy products wholesale, mark them up, and sell them to unsuspecting eBay sellers. Products that are purchased from a legitimate wholesaler would be at actual wholesale prices.

Middlemen accomplish this by first applying as a dealer (retailer) to several legitimate wholesalers. Once accepted, they now have access to hundreds or thousands of products. Their next step is to open a website and place those products for sale, but at a marked-up price. Their website claims to be the source of all these products at special pricing available only to their members. When you see such claims, be wary. The company is probably a middleman, because legitimate wholesalers do not advertise in this way.

Middlemen companies are able to get away with this because they are not actually doing anything illegal. Their members do in fact get the products that they order, but at marked-up prices. There is nothing technically or legally wrong with this—just deceitful.

The other problem here for eBay or Internet sellers is that so many others are trying to sell the same products that, in most cases, eBay is saturated with these item listings. There is little to no demand for the product, which results in no sales or no profit.

Since most of these items go unsold, the eBay seller is stuck with the inventory. She may try several different products, but all of her eBay listings end with about the same result: no sale. When she finally realizes the full extent of what has happened, she may have spent hundreds or even thousands of dollars on products that will never sell.

Membership Fees

Since few products are actually being sold, how do these middlemen make any money? Membership fees. Most middlemen require a membership fee to have access to their "exclusive" product line. Some of these memberships are several hundred dollars annually.

Legitimate wholesalers do not require hefty upfront membership fees. They may require a small processing fee along with your dealer application, but even this practice is rare. Legitimate wholesalers usually forgo any dealer application-processing fee, but may require a set minimum amount for your first order.

Before you become overly concerned about dealing with any product supplier, be assured that many are 100 percent legitimate. Just remember that true wholesalers rarely advertise, require membership fees, or make any claims about your chance for success selling their products.

◖ *SEE ALSO 7.4, "Wholesalers, Liquidators, Importers"* ▶

Identifying Middlemen

Remember that middlemen are not doing anything illegal. But they are deceitful by charging you more for their products than you should pay and limiting you to only the products they carry. Their services are of no real benefit to any serious eBay businessperson. Here are a few clues to help you distinguish legitimate wholesalers from middlemen:

▶ How did you hear about the supplier? From a TV infomercial, magazine, or newspaper ad? Legitimate wholesalers don't advertise in this manner.

▶ If they claim to be the only source required for all of your product needs, and that they will handle everything for you, they are probably middlemen.

▶ If they make any claim about how much money you can make selling their products, or if whatever they claim sounds too good to be true, it is and they are middlemen.

▶ Companies that require an annual membership fee to have exclusive access to their products are most likely middlemen.

▶ What are the requirements to become one of their dealers? Any retailer who purchases items from a legitimate wholesaler must have a business license. The dealer application must require a copy of your business license and your tax ID. If this important step is not required, they are middlemen.

▶ Do they try to sell you anything other than their products, such as add-on services, consulting, websites, and so on? Wholesalers sell products at wholesale prices, period.

▶ Google the company's name along with the keyword "scam" or "fraud." If there are complaints, you will find them.

Beware of any site that appears from this type of search, complains about the middleman, and then tells you that it has the only true solution. While it may be legitimate, it is definitely a clever sales pitch.

Finally, the main problem with using a middleman's method is that it is completely backward from how an eBay seller should source products. Sellers should not make product decisions based on what is available from a supplier's basket of goodies. This is much too limiting. Professional eBay sellers analyze the eBay marketplace first to determine what products sell well and are profitable. Only then do they contact the wholesalers of those products and set up an account. That is the process required for true eBay profitability.

WORDS TO GO . . .WORDS TO GO . . .WORDS TO GO

Wholesalers buy products from manufacturers and sell only to retailers who have a business license. Consumers cannot buy from wholesalers.

Middlemen are deceitful product suppliers who claim to be wholesalers. In fact, they are retailers who purchase products wholesale, add a markup, and sell them as wholesale to unaware online retailers.

7.4 WHOLESALERS, LIQUIDATORS, IMPORTERS

Wholesalers

Liquidators

Finding Legitimate Wholesalers and Liquidators

Importers

Become an Importer

Fulfillment Centers

eBay sellers must first determine the category or niche where they will sell. They then conduct product analyses to determine the associated products that are profitable. Finally, they find a solid, consistent, reputable, and reliable source for those products. This process is known as **product sourcing.** For the eBay professional, the sources for their products are usually from wholesalers, liquidators, and importers.

Wholesalers

A manufacturer is set up to produce and ship substantial quantities of product. The minimum quantity of product that is required when purchasing from a manufacturer is usually too large for a single retailer to carry. So manufacturers sell to wholesalers, who are equipped to order and store large pallets of the same product and move it out quickly. Multiple retailers then order the product in smaller quantities from the wholesaler and sell to the end customer. The complete process from manufacturer to consumer is called the distribution **supply chain.**

In the distribution supply chain, the wholesaler is between the manufacturer and the retailer. A consumer cannot purchase a product directly from a manufacturer or wholesaler except in rare cases.

The wholesaler is not the dreaded middleman that people say they want to eliminate. In fact, as a retailer, *you* are. When consumers think of cutting out the middleman, they want to get their products from wholesalers. In practice, however, this rarely happens. Most large wholesalers require that their customers be a licensed business owner with a sales-tax ID number. Only very small product suppliers will consider selling directly to the public. Even then, the items are sold at full retail price.

Wholesalers require a retailer to have a business license and tax ID for two reasons. First, this shows that their customers are genuine businesses who will most likely be purchasing from them for a long time. Second, the tax ID is required so they do not charge sales tax to the retailer. Sales tax is only charged once, by the retailer, and only to the end consumer.

Wholesaler or Distributor?

The difference between a wholesaler and distributor is subtle but noteworthy. Distributors usually employ a sales staff that calls on retailers to take orders. Distributors also usually accept smaller minimum-quantity orders than wholesalers. A wholesaler is usually a larger fulfillment center that does not actively pursue retailers but waits for the retailers to contact them to place orders.

For this book, the differences are not significant. eBay sellers purchase from both wholesalers and distributors in essentially the same manner and for the same purpose. For this book, then, the term wholesaler is meant to include both a wholesaler and distributor.

Buying Lots

Many of the large wholesalers sell their products to retailers in bulk. This is known as buying a lot in certain required quantities. Retailers may be required to buy a lot of a particular item in quantities of 25, 50, 100, 500, or 1,000 items. Purchasing items in lots usually comes with a bulk order discount.

eBay sellers, however, need to be careful not to purchase too much of one particular item unless they are certain they can move that quantity in a short amount of time. Their money is best used for purchasing a variety of items to sell now, not hoarding inventory of just one type of product for sales six months in the future.

Some wholesalers will sell to retailers in smaller minimum order quantities. These are sometimes referred to as light bulk wholesalers. They appeal to small business owners such as eBay sellers because they have much smaller minimum-quantity order requirements.

◀ *SEE ALSO 7.5, "Drop Shippers"* ▶

Buying Wholesale on eBay

On eBay's homepage, scroll down the left column and select the product category you're interested in. Now select the Wholesale Lots link for that category.

Here you will find an assortment of products, many sold in lots, from a variety of sources. Some are small manufacturers or retailers who are liquidating a certain product. Maybe the product was not selling in their store or a new model has now replaced the older item. Before you purchase any products sold as a lot from this category, do your research first to be sure the items can be sold individually and for a profit on eBay.

Make sure you also look at the shipping terms and costs and factor that into your profit margin. Pallets of products can be expensive to ship across the country, so you might find it more economical to buy from a supplier in your state, or at least on the same coast or region.

eBay's Reseller Marketplace

eBay's Reseller Marketplace is a separate site from ebay.com but is owned and operated by eBay. It is open only to PowerSellers and provides a B2B exchange with a dynamic variety of inventory available in multiple categories.

◁ *SEE ALSO 9.8, "PowerSellers"* ▷

The Reseller Marketplace provides a source of new and refurbished products to **PowerSellers.** The hundreds of product suppliers are from every link in the supply chain, including manufacturers, wholesalers, liquidators, and retailers, and must first be approved by eBay.

7.4

This service is limited to PowerSellers because it is for the eBay professional. Most products are sold in lots, so the buyer would need storage space. The average wholesale lot sale is between $1,000 and $5,000.

PowerSellers are able to purchase directly from these legitimate product suppliers without the normal dealer application approval process required when dealing with wholesalers. If you are a PowerSeller, you can sign up for this service by going to www.ebay.com/reseller, and registering for a buyer's account.

Liquidators

Large manufacturers and retailers often use professional liquidators to clear out older-model surplus and closeout items. The items can be new, restocks from customer returns, or factory-refurbished products. Many of these liquidators are now online and use auction-style listings for small businesses to bid on the items. This can be a great source of products for the eBay seller who wants to general sell.

Liquidators usually sell their items in lots. The condition of the items (new, used, refurbished, restock, and so on) is stated in the available Bill of Lading (BOL). You can't return items purchased from liquidators, so be sure they are indeed sellable and profitable on eBay, and that the source you are about to purchase from is reliable.

An eBay seller can find products at significant discounts off even the wholesale price when buying from liquidators. Buying in lots provides items at pennies on the wholesale dollar when viewed on a per-item cost.

More advanced eBay sellers with available storage space order large quantities of product by purchasing in lots from a liquidator. They then break the large lots down to smaller lots and sell them in the Wholesale Lots category on eBay for a nice markup. Other eBay sellers purchase these smaller lots and then sell the individual items on eBay. Being the large-lot buyer is a good strategy when you're moving into the professional selling phases of your eBay business plan.

SEE ALSO 12.9, *"Strategies for eBay Business Phases"* ▶

Finding Legitimate Wholesalers and Liquidators

Finding legitimate, reputable wholesalers and liquidators rather than middlemen or scam artists is the most difficult task for an eBay seller. An Internet search for wholesalers or liquidators will produce tens of thousands of hits. To eliminate trial and error, or the enormous task of sifting through thousands of suppliers, eBay professionals usually subscribe to product trending and analysis service providers such as What Do I Sell and the product sourcing research provider Worldwide Brands.

SEE ALSO 7.5, *"Drop Shippers"* ▶

What Do I Sell

What Do I Sell (WDIS) was founded and is managed by Lisa Suttora, and her site is certified by eBay as a legitimate service provider. Lisa was a featured speaker at eBay Live in 2005, 2006, 2007, and 2008. She is a contributing editor to *Entrepreneur* magazine and the "Product Sourcing Radio" show, and is a published eBay author. Lisa is considered by many insiders as the guru of product sourcing and trend analysis information for eBay sellers.

WDIS is a product trending and analysis site. It provides a full range of information, educational materials, and resources about product sourcing and trending that is specifically targeted for eBay sellers. Included on the site is the following information:

▶ How to find the products buyers want.

▶ How to locate legitimate suppliers.

▶ How to sell profitably in the eBay marketplace.

The WDIS Advantage program also provides ...

▶ Updates and trends of today's consumer.

▶ Tutorials for growing an eBay business.

▶ Professional, practical retail strategies.

▶ Tips on how to gain a competitive edge.

Most valuable are the links provided to reputable, legitimate wholesalers and liquidators. Lisa locates, investigates, and interviews possible product sources for eBay sellers and records her findings and recommendations on her site. On average, for every 40 distributors or product sources investigated, only one will meet her rigid approval process.

What Do I Sell product sourcing links.

Lisa also provides predictions for the latest product trends on eBay. Armed with her information, you can stay several steps ahead of your competition and sell items that are on the rise of the demand curve rather than the fall as most eBay sellers do.

WDIS is a members-only monthly subscription service. She also offers a significant discount off her standard rate at www.whatdoisell.com/studentrate.

Importers

Advanced eBay professionals may want to expand their marketplace sales and experience **economies of scale** by purchasing items from importers or actually importing the items themselves. Importers are wholesalers who buy directly from overseas manufacturers in bulk and at significant discounts.

Finding legitimate importers can be another daunting task for an eBay seller. Many websites claim to be importers but are middlemen. Use the list in 7.3, "Identifying Middlemen," to run the same test for importers. A popular website to learn how to find and work with reputable importers is www.importexporthelp.com. A popular site that provides access to legitimate importers is again Worldwide Brands.

SEE ALSO 7.5, "Drop Shippers" ▶

Become an Importer

Some professional eBay sellers who have the financial resources actually contact international manufacturers and become importers. The advantages to being an importer are the tremendous discounts available when buying directly from a manufacturer. The disadvantages are the required bulk quantities, storage, and **lead times.**

As an importer, you must work either directly with a manufacturer or through an import agent who works on commission. You also need to work within the time constraints of production runs and international shipping—which is literally by ship. Most of these items are shipped in the large cargo storage containers you see stacked on ships and on trucks. You will need to arrange for shipping and storage once the container arrives in the United States. Importers either supply the warehousing space themselves or rent it from fulfillment centers, which we'll talk about next.

When ordering from a manufacturer, always be sure you get a few samples first before you place a large order. Until you have a sample, you can't be sure of the product's quality. Be careful also when working with any manufacturer that claims it can manufacture brand-name items for you. Many Asian manufacturers produce cheap knockoffs. These cannot be sold on eBay. You can only purchase brand-name items for resale on eBay from an authorized wholesaler.

Importing is not for the beginning eBay seller. It should be reserved for eBay sellers who have a solid business and the financial resources, with proven products that are profitable enough to warrant the trouble of importing and leasing warehouse storage.

A free website that connects eBay sellers with Asian manufacturers is www.globalsources.com. Global Sources also has several reports available for purchase that explain how to deal with Asian manufacturers. The reports are specific to the type of items you wish to import, and most are in the $300 to $600 price range.

Michigan State University offers a very helpful informational site on importing at globaledge.msu.edu. Once there, click on their Resource Desk page. Other sites that are helpful for anyone wanting to work with or become an importer are www.busytrade.com and www.rusbiz.com.

Fulfillment Centers

At some point, the inventory needs for a successful eBay business will grow beyond the boundaries of the home-based business space. The progression tends to move from a bedroom to the garage to a local storage facility. When business owners require more room than a storage facility, they usually rent space from a local business, lease a small warehouse, or use fulfillment centers.

7.4

There are several fulfillment centers around the country. It is usually best to pick one that is either near the coast if you are importing, or near the center of the United States if you are not importing but buying lots from wholesalers or liquidators in the United States. Being in the center of the United States reduces the cost of shipping individual packages elsewhere in the country.

Amazon.com now offers fulfillment services to businesses called Basic Fulfillment. eBay sellers can order bulk quantities of product from any wholesaler, have each product individually prepackaged, and then have them shipped and stored safely at one of Amazon's warehouses. After one of the items has sold on eBay, the seller places a fulfillment order to Amazon using a simple web form. Amazon's fulfillment center then ships one of the prepackaged items to the customer. Amazon can even include a customized note to the buyer on the packing slip.

The cost for Amazon's Basic Fulfillment is multifaceted. To learn more go to www.amazon.com/gp/seller/fba/fba_pricing.html.

Fulfillment services are not cheap and are only for eBay businesses that have the volume and resources to justify the cost. Remember when receiving quotes that, although the cost may seem high, you must compare this with the cost of renting warehouse space and hiring your own employees. Two popular fulfillment centers are www.moultonfulfillment.com and www.mfpsinc.com. Mentioning these sites is not an endorsement, but they are provided for you to compare their services and prices to others to find the one that best meets the needs for your items and budget.

WORDS TO GO . . .WORDS TO GO . . .WORDS TO GO

Product sourcing is the methodology sellers use to find their products and product suppliers.

The **supply chain** is the method by which products move, from manufacturer to wholesaler to retailer to consumer.

PowerSellers are eBay sellers that have attained a certain level of selling or volume status (Bronze, Silver, Gold, Platinum, Titanium) based on average sales maintained over a three-month period.

Economy of scale is a business term that refers to the per-unit cost savings of a product when introducing new manufacturing improvements or bulk procurement discounts.

Lead time is the total time required from the product order to final delivery. When ordering from overseas manufacturers, it can take weeks or even months.

7.5 DROP SHIPPERS

How Drop Shipping Works

Advantages of Drop Shipping

Disadvantages of Drop Shipping

Finding Reputable Drop Shippers

Worldwide Brands

Drop shippers are wholesalers that will ship an individual item to a single end customer for an online retailer. This provides financial leverage to the seller because he or she does not have to pay for the item until it sells. It also eliminates the need for extra storage space, since sellers do not have to physically stock the items in their own inventory.

Website owners and eBay sellers use drop shippers as their fulfillment centers for many of the products they sell. The drop shipper views the eBay seller as their salesperson.

How Drop Shipping Works

eBay sellers who use drop shippers create a listing for the product and wait for the auction to end. When it ends, the customer will pay the seller for the amount of the item plus the shipping charge as required in the listing. Most often the payment is via PayPal, in which case the seller will receive an e-mail notification of payment from PayPal. The seller then places an order with their drop-ship wholesaler to have the item sent directly to their customer. The wholesaler's fulfillment center ships the item and charges the wholesale cost of the item plus shipping and any drop-ship surcharge fee back to the seller. The eBay seller keeps the remaining profit without ever having touched the product.

Since eBay sellers purchase drop-ship products at a wholesale cost, a minimum **profit margin** must be met when selling the items. Therefore, sellers should list their products on eBay at Fixed Price or Auction-style with a Reserve to achieve the desired margin.

◀ SEE ALSO 12.6, *"Success Is Profit, Not Sales or Feedback"* ▶

◀ SEE ALSO 3.3, *"Listing Formats and Bidding"* ▶

Advantages of Drop Shipping

Because little to no inventory is actually stocked, eBay sellers who use drop shippers can definitely benefit from economy of scale. Theoretically, the savings are
sizable because there is no inventory cost until the item is sold. Even a part-time
eBay seller can list a lot of products if the inventory cost for the item is zero. If
the item does not sell, the only cost to the seller is the eBay listing fees. This is
a considerable savings advantage compared to the cost of stocking all of these
items.

Many advanced sellers use drop shipping to test a new product or marketing idea
before placing a bulk order. They try a few test listings and drop-ship those items.
Only if the new product proves successful do they purchase from the wholesaler
in bulk, and at a discount, to stock their own inventory.

Disadvantages of Drop Shipping

When drop shipping, you are placing your eBay feedback in the hands of the
wholesaler. You need a reliable drop shipper that will pack and ship the items
promptly, carefully, and dependably. You can be caught short if the drop shipper
is out of the item you just sold. If this happens to you, negative feedback is coming. Scanning the feedback on eBay reveals that this does happen. Occasionally
you may read feedback that says, "Seller is selling items they do not have!" When
you see that, the seller was probably caught selling a product that was on back-
order from their drop shipper.

While this seems like a showstopper, it is not. Most problems associated with
eBay selling have simple solutions, and this one does as well. A seller who uses
drop shipping should stock a minimum of one or two of each item they drop-ship
in their own inventory. If their wholesaler is out of stock, they ship from their
own inventory and do not list the item again until their wholesaler has a replen-
ished supply. The best way to prevent this problem is to always be aware of your
drop shipper's inventory and never list an item that is in short supply.

The biggest problem for eBay sellers wishing to drop-ship is not about becoming
a dealer, learning the drop-ship procedures, or stocking personal inventory. The
biggest problem is finding a trustworthy, recommended, and reputable drop shipper in the first place.

Finding Reputable Drop Shippers

How do you find a reputable drop shipper? If you conducted an Internet search
using the keywords drop shipper, you would receive over 3 million hits. Many
of these are the middlemen or scammers mentioned previously in this chapter.

What an eBay seller needs is a drop-ship directory that is constantly, carefully, and methodically scrubbed to include only the reputable drop shippers.

◄ *SEE ALSO 7.3, "Avoiding Middlemen"* ►

At the time of this writing, the only published drop-ship directory that is certified by eBay is provided by Worldwide Brands. This is a members-only site with the charter to find legitimate drop shippers, wholesalers, importers, and other reputable product suppliers for their members.

To be clear, Worldwide Brands does not sell you any products. You become a member of the site to find the legitimate, reputable wholesalers or drop shippers and then purchase your products directly from those suppliers. This is a big difference compared to middlemen who require that you can only purchase items from suppliers through them.

Worldwide Brands

Worldwide Brands (WWB) is a product sourcing research website. It actually started its business appealing to website owners who needed a way to find reputable wholesalers, liquidators, and drop shippers. A few years ago, eBay sellers discovered WWB; drop shipping began to catch on among several advanced eBay sellers, and Worldwide Brands began marketing to eBay sellers as well as website owners. It is also the creator and host of Product Sourcing Radio and eBay Radio's official product sourcing editor.

Worldwide Brands is known mainly for the valuable information it offers about wholesalers in several databases that it maintains. Each wholesaler in any of the WWB databases must first pass a very stringent proprietary analysis in order to be deemed "reputable." WWB's full-time research staff is dedicated exclusively to keeping these databases updated with all wholesalers willing to work with online business owners, including eBay sellers.

WWB's databases are invaluable to online sellers looking for reputable product sources. For example, as a member of the site, when you need a drop shipper you simply enter the drop-shipping database and type the brand or product name you are looking for into the keyword search box. The search tool will then scour the databases to locate a reputable drop shipper for the item. Note that not every item has a WWB-approved drop shipper, but most common and popular items do.

Worldwide Brands also provides databases for wholesalers other than drop shippers. It has addressed the seller's needs for every aspect of their product sourcing and now provides the following databases for online sellers:

- ▶ Drop-ship wholesalers

- ▶ Liquidators

- ▶ Instant import buys

- ▶ Light bulk wholesalers (smaller minimum order requirements)

- ▶ Large volume wholesalers (for the serious eBay seller wanting to buy in bulk)

Note again that you will not order any products through Worldwide Brands. You use the databases only to find the wholesalers you need. From that point forward you will order directly from those wholesalers.

This is a very important distinction from middlemen; with middlemen, you can only select your products from the choices they have. This is the opposite of how product decisions should be made. Sellers should first determine what is profitable on eBay, and then search for the supplier of those products. Worldwide Brands is used strictly to find "reputable" wholesalers for the products after *you* have determined them profitable. *That* is the correct process for product sourcing.

Worldwide Brands also offers software tools that find and analyze niches and products. These tools help sellers determine the potential success for a particular product if selling it online.

Worldwide Brands' product analysis tools include the following:

- ▶ Demand research

- ▶ Competition research

- ▶ Advertising research

- ▶ Pricing research

- ▶ Instant product analysis

◀ *SEE ALSO 7.6, "Product Analysis"* ▶

OneSource

Until recently all of Worldwide Brands' databases and analysis tools were sold separately. It has now bundled all of its databases and analysis products into one bundled offering called OneSource. It offers OneSource for a one-time payment, with lifetime membership. You can even purchase their complete OneSource package at a special discount at www.worldwidebrands.com/studentrate.

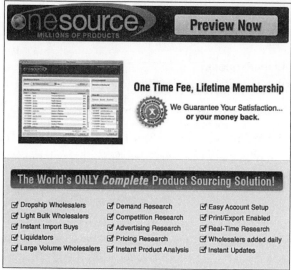

Worldwide Brands' OneSource.

Profit margin is a metric businesses use to determine the relationship of profit to sales. Profit margin is a percentage determined by dividing profit by sales (P/S).

7.6 PRODUCT ANALYSIS

Product Analysis Process

Niche and Product Analysis Tools

Profitability Analysis Tools

Marketplace Research

Terapeak

HammerTap Research

Some of the more difficult problems for eBay sellers are in determining how to find a niche and the right products to sell. This is not an intuitive task, because what is hot in retail stores is not necessarily hot or profitable on eBay.

Many hobbyist and collector eBay sellers approach their product selection with a hunch: an educated guess based on their experience of buying and selling in that marketplace on eBay. They understand the value of the item and what it will most likely bring on eBay.

Amateur sellers, however, have no solid basis for their hunches. They make product sourcing decisions based on whims. Sometimes they guess right and sometimes they guess wrong. A few too many of the wrong guesses, and the eBay seller is out of business.

Serious eBay sellers cannot afford to make product decisions based solely on hunches or guesses. You need to analyze the eBay marketplace first to determine what products are selling, and then conduct in-depth analysis on those products to ensure that they will be profitable on eBay.

Product Analysis Process

Product analysis begins with a reason for you to investigate a particular product or category on eBay. The professional usually starts with eBay itself. He or she may go to eBay's Seller Central to find what is Hot, Very Hot, and Super Hot in the categories he or she is interested in selling.

◁ SEE ALSO 15.1, *"Finding What's Hot"* ▷

Once the ideas for initial products or categories are determined, professional eBay sellers scour eBay to find the demand for the product and the competition from other eBay sellers. When a seller finds that a particular product has high demand yet little competition, he has found an ideal niche. This is where many eBay professionals sell.

The last step of product analysis is to ensure that the products found in the niche will be profitable on eBay. This, in fact, is the most important step; unfortunately, it's usually ignored by beginning eBay sellers. They find what's hot and get in on the action. Only at the end of the month or quarter do they realize that the products are not profitable.

Product analysis is critical to be certain your products will be successful and profitable. Trying to conduct this process manually, however, can be time-consuming and discouraging. In fact, it is impractical to even consider performing Internet and eBay marketplace research manually.

Advanced sellers use product analysis tools to help them with this process. Next we will examine the most popular product analysis tools among experienced eBay sellers.

Niche and Product Analysis Tools

Worldwide Brands (WWB) offers software tools that find and analyze niches and products. Some of the most successful eBay and website sellers use the One-Source tools to analyze potential products that they are thinking of selling.

Worldwide Brands' niche and product analysis tools are as follows:

- ▶ Demand Research
- ▶ Competition Research
- ▶ Advertising Research
- ▶ Pricing Research
- ▶ Instant Product Analysis

The first step in product analysis is to determine if your product or category is a niche. Advanced eBay sellers begin with WWB's Demand, Research, and Instant Product Analysis Tools to quickly make that decision. If they have found a niche, they then use WWB's other tools to perform more in-depth research.

WWB's Instant Product Analysis tool in particular is very popular with professional website owners and serious eBay sellers. The seller simply enters the keywords of the product or category that they are interested in selling. Within seconds this tool scours the Internet searching for relevant marketing, supply, demand, and competitive data. The tool then provides an easy-to-understand product analysis summary score from 0 to 100 percent. This number represents the chance of success for that item if sold online. For example, a score of 15 percent means the item only has a 15 percent chance of being successful online. The seller would immediately pass on that item. An item that has about a 75 percent or greater chance of success has excellent potential and should be investigated further.

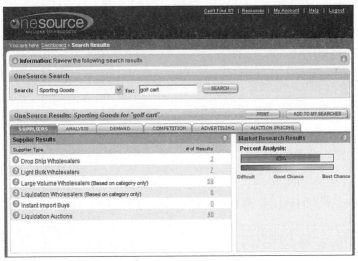

WWB's Instant Product Analysis.

For what would have taken a seller several days to compile manually, this marketing research is provided in summary form in seconds. Sellers can then make informed product decisions quickly. These tools are mandatory for any serious eBay seller and worth the price of membership. You can learn more at www.worldwidebrands.com/studentrate.

SEE ALSO 12.2, *"Competitive Analysis"*

Profitability Analysis Tools

Once a product has been determined to meet the niche or ideal niche requirements for high demand and little competition, the next step is to determine how well the item is currently selling on eBay. During this step, sellers need eBay product-specific analysis tools.

These tools can instantly scour the eBay marketplace and compile and provide the selling and pricing analysis for any particular item. The seller uses this information to perform their most important step, the profitability analysis. The benefits of profitability analysis tools are threefold:

1. To help sellers determine the profitability of an item when making product selection decisions.

2. To enable sellers to quickly determine what components and listing techniques work and do not work in an actual listing, based on real marketplace data.

3. To show buyers what the item has been selling for, and the true marketplace value before placing a bid.

Three eBay research tools are popular among eBay sellers: eBay Marketplace Research, Terapeak, and HammerTap. There are both subtle and considerable differences between the products. You do not need all three of these products, but you should choose the one research tool that best meets your needs and budget.

eBay Marketplace Research

eBay Marketplace Research is an eBay-developed research tool that provides data mining and research information. You can receive up to 90 days of historical research data. There are three levels of Marketplace Research: Fast Pass, Basic, and Pro.

▶ Fast Pass is a pay-as-you-go service with only two days of access. It provides 60 days of historical search history. This is not really an economical option for advanced sellers who conduct multiple searches each month.

▶ Basic is a monthly subscription with 60 days of historical search data and allows unlimited searches.

▶ Pro is a monthly subscription with 90 days of historical data and unlimited searches.

An advantage of Marketplace Research over Terapeak and HammerTap is that it is included in the subscription price for a Premium or Anchor eBay Store. The Basic level is included with a Premium Store subscription and the Pro version is included with an Anchor Store. Premium stores are expensive at $49.95 and Anchor stores $299.95 a month. Make your decision based on the research tool that has the features you require, not because it is included in another package.

Terapeak

Professional eBay sellers must take the time to conduct their eBay research. If they do it manually, each item they research can take 20 to 30 minutes. Terapeak's analysis tool "Research Advantage" can conduct complete marketplace research analysis in seconds. You simply enter the keywords for the item you want to research and Terapeak will provide a summary analysis that includes the following:

- ▶ Average selling price

- ▶ Average number of bids

- ▶ Average sell-thru rate*

- ▶ Best days to sell

- ▶ Best durations

- ▶ Best keywords to use

- ▶ Success of enhancements and listing upgrades

- ▶ Find the hottest products

- ▶ Find the current trends

- ▶ Research other eBay sellers

If there were 100 of a particular item listed and 73 sold, that is a 73 percent sell-thru rate.

There are a few advantages of Terapeak over HammerTap. Terapeak is a web-based product and is open to both PC and Mac users. HammerTap is a PC-based product only. Terapeak also provides data for International eBay websites and also eBay Motors Parts and Accessories. HammerTap provides data only for eBay.com (the U.S. eBay website) and doesn't include any eBay Motors categories. Be sure to compare these advantages with eBay Marketplace Research features and HammerTap advantages before making your selection.

Terapeak, can provide a history of either 30 or 90 days of eBay data depending on the monthly subscription pricing model chosen. You can receive a free two-week trial membership for Terapeak at www.terapeak.com/signup/studenttrial.

HammerTap

HammerTap tends to be the research tool of choice among more advanced eBay sellers. On a basic level, HammerTap can perform the same type of data searches as Terapeak and eBay Marketplace Research and also requires a monthly subscription. However, HammerTap Research has some distinct advantages over the other two.

HammerTap is a desktop application rather than web-based. This allows you to download, sort, group, save, and analyze thousands of listings instantly with your own custom filter criteria. The only limit to this feature is the available space on your computer's hard drive. Note that HammerTap also provides a web product, PowerWeb, but it has much less functionality than the desktop version.

Results		Listing Success Rate (LSR)
Total Listings	140	57.14 %
Listings with Sale	80	
Listing Success Rate (LSR)	57.14%	
Average Sales Price (ASP)	$21.18	
Total Sales	$2,456.60	
Sellers with Sale	49	42.86 %
Average Sales Per Seller	2.37	☐ Listings With Sale
Average Revenue Per Seller	$50.13	☐ Listings W/Out Sale

What do I want answered?
What Category should I list my product in?
Which day should I end my listing?
Which enhancements should I use?
Should I sell my product on eBay?
What title keywords should I use?

eBay item search results using HammerTap.

The HammerTap research tool is very easy to use, even when conducting complex and deep data searches. This is an advantage over eBay Marketplace Research where if you wanted to dig down deep through five levels of data, you would have to perform five separate searches. With HammerTap Research, you set the deep analysis criteria and perform only one search.

HammerTap Research provides significantly more data and provides a deeper, more thorough analysis than its competitors. This is because of the desktop platform. Since the application resides on your own computer's hard drive, you can save the data into a database, then scroll through the spreadsheet to view the information any way you require. You can sort, group, and sub-group the data into multiple views—by price, category, number of bids, and so on. You can also gather, save, and study data about your competitors in order to conduct competitive analysis.

HammerTap also allows you to easily exclude irrelevant listings that may skew your analysis results. This means your reports can be specifically trimmed to analyze only the particular type of item you are selling.

A tool is of no use if you don't know how to use it, and user training is where HammerTap shines over the other two providers. They provide extensive free training to teach their users not only how to use their eBay research tools but how these tools can directly and immediately improve business. Their software training includes a free one-hour live introductory **webinar.** Then free monthly webinars are offered on a variety of subjects. Forums are also ongoing and provide videos and training for how to use their product.

Finally, the biggest advantage and newest feature of HammerTap is that it is able to provide not only 90 days of historical data from "today," but 90 days of historical data from the same time period one year ago. This is most significant as it allows users to analyze seasonal selling.

You can learn more about HammerTap Research features, and receive a 10-day free trial plus a special discount rate at www.hammertap.com/studentrate.

WORDS TO GO . . .WORDS TO GO . . .WORDS TO GO

A **webinar** is a web-connected conference, meeting, or seminar where each attendee can view the presentation and communicate with the other participants from his or her own computer.

8

SELLING INTERNATIONALLY

8.1 WHY SELL INTERNATIONALLY?

eBay never sleeps and boasts sales of over $100,000 per minute. Those sales are occurring 24/7 all around the globe. In fact, 51 percent of all eBay sales are international.

If you choose not to sell internationally, you eliminate half the sales activity on eBay and probably 15 to 30 percent of your potential customers. Stated differently, you can increase your sales 15 to 30 percent—immediately—just by selling internationally.

To appeal to more buyers around the world, eBay maintains separate websites for 27 countries. For example, the eBay website for the U.S. is www.ebay.com, for Canada it is www.ebay.ca, the United Kingdom is www.ebay.co.uk, and for Australia it is www.ebay.com.au.

Sellers can have listings posted on all 27 sites or specific sites by selecting the "international site visibility" upgrade option within the Sell Your Item form when they create their listings. The specific steps to list an item internationally are covered in Chapter 4.

◀ *SEE ALSO 4.2, "Listing Creation"* ▶

There is another significant reason sellers should consider selling globally. When a seller indicates that they will ship worldwide, it encourages international customers to bid on their item, increasing the number of bidders, which in turn will increase the final price. The winning bidder may live in Ohio, but the bidders from the United Kingdom, Germany, France, and Greece helped to run up the bidding price. Therefore, sellers who sell internationally receive more bids and higher prices on their auction items than those who limit their sales to the United States only.

Many sellers don't ship internationally because they have concerns about filling out customs forms, determining shipping prices, finding a carrier, shipping the items, having e-mail communication with foreign customers, getting paid, and dealing with fraud. None of these concerns should hinder you from selling internationally.

This chapter clearly outlines why you should be encouraged to open a new sales channel using eBay's global marketplace. Don't let international shipping concerns hinder you from worldwide exposure. If you want to increase sales and receive higher bids immediately, then sell internationally!

8.2 WHICH CARRIER TO USE

USPS International Shipping Options

USPS Express Mail International (EMI)

USPS Priority Mail International (PMI)

USPS First-Class Mail International (FCMI)

USPS M-Bag

Experienced eBay sellers use the United States Postal Service (USPS) for most international shipments. This is especially true if a customer desires express delivery. The main reason is cost. The USPS rates can be substantially lower than UPS, FedEx, and DHL. Additionally, these carriers do not ship to as many countries or cities as does the USPS.

The table below compares rates for a 4-pound package sent from Chicago to different countries, using different carriers. Rates do change, and the price listed for a particular service may no longer be current. However, the comparison between different carriers relevant to eBay sellers will still be valid.

8.2

4-lb package	FedEx Priority	FedEx Economy	FedEx Ground	DHL	UPS	USPS PMI	USPS FCMI Counter
Australia	$111.63	$107.22	NA	$93.21	$118.16	$32.06	$27.50
Canada	$76.31	$68.15	$12.92	$61.00	$16.43	$18.91	$15.46
Greece	$117.37	$106.89	NA	$96.84	$115.54	$35.15	$29.60
Japan	$103.39	$97.57	NA	$85.32	$103.51	$32.06	$27.50
UK	$103.39	$96.70	NA	$86.81	$104.46	$30.40	$29.60

A quick comparison reveals that shipping to Canada is competitive among FedEx Ground, UPS, and USPS FCMI. For all other countries, USPS is clearly the best choice. It is for this reason that the discussion in the remainder of this chapter assumes you will use USPS for all international shipments of individual packages. If you intend to ship freight internationally, see 8.4, "International Shipping Services."

USPS International Shipping Options

There are four popular international shipping options provided by the USPS for eBay sellers: Express Mail International, Priority Mail International, First-Class Mail International, and M-Bags.

All USPS shipping options and their associated features are described in this chapter. For further questions about international rates, size limits, customs forms, or other details, go to the USPS International Mail Manual link at http://pe.usps.gov/text/imm/welcome.htm, ask your local postmaster, or call 1-800-ASK-USPS.

USPS Express Mail International (EMI)

Express Mail International (EMI) is a fast way to ship overseas. EMI offers day certain service with a money-back guarantee and online tracking to 190 countries. Automatic tracking and $100 of insurance is included. The weight limit for EMI is dependent on the destination country.

If you ship items by EMI, you will need to complete an Express mailing label 11-B as well as Customs Form 2976-A. These forms are available at any post office or can be printed automatically from the USPS website when purchasing shipping labels online. You can also print them when paying for your shipping labels through PayPal.

◄ SEE ALSO 8.5, *"Customs Forms and Duty"* ►

USPS Priority Mail International (PMI)

Priority Mail International (PMI) is an accelerated airmail service to over 190 countries and territories worldwide for packages up to 70 pounds. It also provides customers with a reliable and economical means of sending correspondence, business documents, advertising messages, printed matter, and lightweight merchandise. PMI delivery is now available in most European countries and others will have this service soon.

PMI is cheaper than EMI and is the way many eBay sellers ship lighter-weight international packages. It is also interesting to note that PMI packages often arrive just a few days later than Express. Therefore, PMI provides the best value for you and your customer for packages that qualify.

The same Priority Mail boxes you use for domestic shipping are used for Priority Mail International (any of the sizes, whether eBay co-branded or not). In addition, you may use Flat Rate Priority Mail boxes for shipments under 20 pounds to most countries. The flat-rate fee varies by the destination country. Currently Canada and Mexico are $23, and all other countries are $37. These boxes are available from your local post office or can be ordered from www.usps.com. When shipping items under 4 pounds with these boxes, you should use Customs Form PS 2976. For packages over 4 pounds, use 2976-A.

◄ SEE ALSO 8.5, *"Customs Forms and Duty"* ►

USPS First-Class Mail International (FCMI)

First-Class Mail International services provide convenient and economical ways to ship light-weight items 4 pounds and under, to virtually every country in the world. Shippers that use FCMI will need to provide their own corrugated shipping box.

◀ *SEE ALSO 6.7, "Packing Materials and Corrugated Boxes"* ▶

USPS M-Bags

A discounted method for shipping printed material internationally is with the use of sacks called M-Bags. Printed material would include books, magazines, newspapers, journals, directories, sheet music, commercial advertising, and promotional material.

The materials are all placed into an M-Bag and shipped to one address by airmail. The total weight limit for M-Bags must not exceed 66 pounds. M-Bags also cannot be insured.

The materials in the M-Bag cannot be loose, but must be placed in one or more padded envelopes or corrugated boxes, then placed inside the M-Bag. Each package in the M-Bag must be marked "Postage Paid—M-Bag." The M-Bag must have PS tag 158 attached. Both the required tags and the M-Bags are free and available from your local post office.

8.2

8.3 INTERNATIONAL USPS SHIPPING RATES

Determine a Rate Estimate

Include the Rate in Your Listing

International USPS Discounts with PayPal

USPS offers the easiest method for determining international shipping rates compared with the other carriers. Addresses and postal codes are not needed. USPS charges the same rate for delivery anywhere within a particular country.

Determine a Rate Estimate

To determine an international shipping rate estimate that can be included in your eBay listing, go to www.usps.com and click on Calculate International Postage. You then choose the destination country and package type and enter the weight. The different mailing service rates are provided along with any desired extra services.

You can also use the Research Rates link on the Sell Your Item Form to get international rates while you are creating your listing. This can save you time and effort.

Include the Rate in Your Listing

Some sellers provide only the shipping cost within the United States in their listings and have a statement asking that international bidders e-mail them for the shipping rate to their country. This not only discourages many potential bidders, it is also time-consuming for you to respond to all of those individual e-mails.

This is especially true if the item you are listing on eBay is a commodity item. Make it simple for you and your customers. In your description, state the international rates to the countries where packages are most often sent by eBay sellers.

Most international buyers will be from Canada, the UK, Europe, Australia, Hong Kong, and Japan. In the following rate table, note that you can group rates to most European countries, as you will discover that the shipping rates for PMI are about the same. Therefore, state the shipping rates for these key countries in your description as follows:

SHIPPING & HANDLING RATES FOR OUR INTERNATIONAL CUSTOMERS

Country	Shipping Service	S&H Cost
Australia	USPS Priority Mail International	$_____ U.S.
Canada	USPS Priority Mail International	$_____ U.S.
Europe	USPS Priority Mail International	$_____ U.S.
Hong Kong	USPS Priority Mail International	$_____ U.S.
Japan	USPS Priority Mail International	$_____ U.S.
UK	USPS Priority Mail International	$_____ U.S.

For all other countries, please e-mail us for the shipping method and cost.

You can also choose to use eBay's shipping calculator for international shipments the same way as for domestic. When you create your listing using the Sell Your Item Form or Turbo Lister, choose the "Calculated" rate and enter the package size, weight, and UPS or USPS shipping service. eBay will then provide the rates to your international customers automatically if they are logged in to their eBay account.

◀ *SEE ALSO 6.8, "Determine the Shipping Rate"* ▶

International USPS Discounts with PayPal

8.3

Shippers who purchase their shipping labels online can save 5 percent on USPS PMI rates and 8 percent on EMI rates. Additionally, these discounts can be paid for using PayPal.

You can do this directly from your My eBay page. Simply click on the Ship button next to the name of your customer and you will be taken to PayPal. All of your "ship from" and "ship to" addresses will be automatically filled in for both the shipping label and customs form. You simply pay for the discounted shipping and then print the label and customs form.

◀ *SEE ALSO 6.11, "eBay's Shipping Center"* ▶

◀ *SEE ALSO 8.5, "Customs Forms and Duty"* ▶

8.4 INTERNATIONAL SHIPPING SERVICES

Tracking International Packages

Insuring International Packages

Home Pickup for International Packages

APO/FPO Addresses

Shipping Freight Internationally

There are additional services available to eBay sellers when shipping internationally. Using the USPS website, you can print shipping labels, postage, customs forms, and even request home pickup for international shipments.

Tracking International Packages

EMI offers full, en-route tracking to the major cities in most countries. PMI and FCMI do not have a tracking system that can fully track a package throughout each segment of the journey. They do offer delivery confirmation when the package arrives at its destination. Note that this is no different than the USPS domestic delivery confirmation. USPS does not track Priority and First Class domestic mail during transit, but reports only the delivery confirmation.

Insuring International Packages

EMI, PMI, and FCMI offer optional insurance for damage or loss on packages shipped to most countries. A few samples of international insurance rates are $1.95 for $50, $2.75 for $100, $3.80 for $200, and $6.95 for $500 of insurance.

In order to save money on insurance, or if you cannot obtain insurance for the destination country, you can use a private insurance company. The two private insurers most popular with eBay sellers are U-Pic and DSI.

◀ *SEE ALSO 6.11, "eBay's Shipping Center"* ▶

Home Pickup for International Packages

USPS offers free home pickup for international packages using its Carrier Pickup service. This is available for all types of packages up to 70 pounds each, as long as at least one Priority Mail (or Express Mail) package is included.

You can schedule carrier pickups online until 2:00 A.M. (the morning of the requested pickup day), at www.usps.com. Prepaid postage must be applied to each package, and all packages must be ready to go before the carrier arrives.

◀ *SEE ALSO 6.11, "eBay's Shipping Center"* ▶

APO/FPO Addresses

An Army or Air Force Post Office (APO) or the Navy's Fleet Post Office (FPO) address means that the buyer is a service member stationed overseas or in U.S. territories such as Guam. This mail service is another reason to use the USPS, as no other carrier ships APO/FPO packages.

USPS delivers APO/FPO mail to a large Military Post Office (MPO) on either coast. The military then transports the mail by military air cargo to wherever the recipient is stationed or deployed.

When shipping to an APO/FPO address, you can still use the USPS Priority Mail boxes and pay standard domestic rates (since an APO/FPO is technically a U.S. address). This includes flat-rate services. In addition, you get a $2 discount on the new Large Flat Rate Priority Mail box (12" × 12" × 5½") if shipping to an APO/FPO address. The standard domestic fee is $12.95, APO/FPO is $10.95. All other Flat Rate Priority Mail boxes will cost the same as domestic shipping (currently $8.95).

The delivery time specified by the USPS is only to get it to the MPO on whichever coast is closest. From that point, it is the military's responsibility to deliver it to your customer. They will wait until a pallet is full before shipping it out, so it could take from a few days (if your package is one of the last on the pallet) to over a week (if it's one of the first and has to sit a while) to even leave the country.

The Military Postal Service Agency estimates delivery times to your recipient are 10 to 14 days for Priority Mail and 24 days for Parcel Post (which can be used for APO/FPO addresses), but the actual time will vary based on where your customer is actually located. Military service members and their families understand how APO/FPO works and know that the delivery time is variable. So don't worry about getting negative feedback or low shipping-time ratings because of this system. Even if you don't offer international shipping, you may be asked to ship to an APO or FPO box. Really, the only difference for you between domestic and APO/FPO is that you will need to complete the larger Customs Form 2976-A. If supplying your own box, restrictions are 70 pounds and 130 inches in length and girth (L + 2W + 2H).

Alcohol, firearms, certain food, hazardous materials, and other items may be restricted based on the zip code of the recipient. A helpful site for determining restrictions for APO/FPO packages is www.oconus.com/ZipCodes.asp.

Shipping Freight Internationally

This chapter has assumed that you will be shipping individual international packages. This is the method that nearly all small business eBay sellers use to ship international packages. If you own or run a larger organization, however, there may be times when you are shipping larger or more expensive items or freight.

Carriers

FedEx, DHL, and UPS now rejoin USPS in our international shipping equation. Each carrier has different terms, policies, and procedures. Visit each carrier's website and search for "international freight" or use their provided links for international shipping. It is best if you call and speak with a customer service representative.

Export Packing List

An export packing list is required for all freight shipments. This will be more detailed than the simple customs forms used for individual packages. The list must cover all individual packages sent on a pallet or in a crate or container and will be used by U.S. and foreign customs agents to assess the freight contents.

The packing list should contain the following:

- ▶ The contents and type (box, crate, and so on) of each individual package included.

- ▶ The tare, net, legal, and gross weights of each package. This is used to determine the total weight.

- ▶ The size measurements of each package in both U.S. and metric.

Shippers Export Declaration

All shipments with a value over $2,500 require a Shippers Export Declaration (SED) Form 7525-V to be completed. The exemption country to this rule is Canada. The form and instructions can be found from www.census.gov/foreign-trade/regulations/forms.

Certificate of Origin

In some cases, because of free trade agreements such as NAFTA, certificates of origin can be used to avoid paying import tariffs. U.S. free trade agreements exist with Canada, Mexico, Israel, Australia, Singapore, Chile, and Jordan. Other countries are in negotiation with the United States now and may be added. Use the links below for more information.

List of FTAs: http://ustr.gov/Trade_Agreements/Section_Index.html

Visit www.export.gov for further instructions on completing a NAFTA certificate.

Insurance Certificate

Freight shippers will most likely require a certificate of insurance for loss or damage during transit. Talk to your carrier about this insurance.

Packing

All individual packages must be carefully packed to ensure a safe journey whether by truck, rail, or ship. In some cases, certain shipping markings are required on the packages that list the country of origin and possibly the contents. If you need help packing a freight shipment, or would like a local professional export packing company to do the packing for you, contact your carrier for recommendations.

If you will be sending international freight shipments as part of your business plan, begin with a professional export packing company. Use them several times until you fully understand how to pack and ship international freight. Mistakes made during this process result in lost time and money because of customs problems and delays.

8.4

For Further Export Information

Shipping international freight is more complex than shipping individual packages. Before you attempt this process, learn all you can from your carrier or a professional export packing company. Other beneficial information about exporting is available from a few U.S. government websites provided below.

▶ Visit the site www.export.gov and review the "Export Basics Guide" as well as other relevant links.

▶ Visit the Small Business Administration's export website below, click on "Export Library," and download the PDF document "Breaking into the Trade Game: A Small Business Guide for Exporting":

www.sba.gov/aboutsba/sbaprograms/internationaltrade

▶ To speak with an export authority, call your local U.S. Export Assistance Center. It will be listed in your phone book.

8.5 CUSTOMS FORMS AND DUTY

Customs Forms

Customs Form Fraud

Packages Held Up in Customs

Avoiding Customs Problems

Items shipped internationally must pass through that particular country's customs authorities before delivery. During assessment, the customs officer makes a determination based on the information provided by the shipper on the customs declaration form or the package may be opened for inspection.

The customs officer may determine that duty or administrative fees are due depending on the value of the item declared on the customs form. Each country has different thresholds of duty. If duty is assessed, the package is usually held in a customs office or local post office branch where the recipient pays the duty and picks up the package.

The seller is responsible only for accurately completing the customs declaration form and paying the required postage. The seller is not involved in collecting or paying duty. This is strictly between the recipient and their country's customs authorities.

Packages now tend to move faster through customs than they did a few years ago. This is partly due to the elimination of surface shipments (literally by ship) for individual packages sent by the USPS. EMI, PMI, and FCMI packages are now all sent by air, tend to move faster through customs, and have fewer problems than did surface shipments.

Custom backups and delays can occur during slow delivery times of the year such as the Christmas holidays. Other uncontrollable factors can also increase delays. For example, a quick devaluation of the U.S. dollar can cause a huge influx of foreign buyers taking advantage of the strength of their currency. Additional buyers from their country produce more packages through their customs branch offices. Severe weather may also affect delivery times.

Customs Forms

Every internationally bound item (including APO/FPO) must have a customs declaration form completed and attached to the package. The forms are easy to understand and complete. The required information is merely the sender's name and address, the recipient's name and address, a very brief description of the item, and the U.S. dollar value of the item.

If you ship items internationally by EMI, you will need to complete an Express mailing label 11-B as well as Customs Form 2976-A. These forms are shown here and available at your local post office or online if you print prepaid shipping labels.

Express Label 11-B.

Customs Form 2976-A.

Be sure to check "Return to Sender" on the bottom right of the 2976-A form in case the item is not deliverable to the address provided. If that box is not checked, there is no guarantee it will be returned to you.

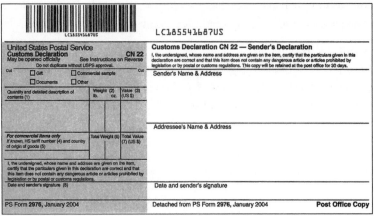

Customs Form 2976.

Items shipped by Priority Mail International and using a Priority Mail box should use Customs Form PS 2976 (the small one with a green color section). This is the simplest form and can usually be completed quite quickly.

Customs Form Fraud

Sometimes an international customer will ask you to change the information on the customs form in order to lower or avoid paying duty. They may ask you to mark the item as a "gift" or lower the total value of the item. Don't be tempted to do this.

Providing false information on a customs form is fraud. It is your name that is on the signature line of the customs form, not the buyer's. You have a legitimate eBay business and do not want to commit fraud. If you sell many items to a particular country and are caught committing fraud on a customs form, you can be banned from shipping to that country.

It is certainly not worth the risk. Respond with a friendly e-mail to the buyer and decline their suggestion. If you receive several of these types of e-mails, you should add a polite disclaimer to your listings.

Packages Held Up in Customs

A package that arrives in a foreign customs office is assessed and either approved for delivery or held in detention because the item violates an import rule, regulation, or law. Most customs mail branches will inform the recipient that their item is being held and provide a detention number.

Contacting the customs branch without the detention number will do little good. Most customs mail branches do not even track the packages through their facility. The packages are either approved and sent on or held in detention.

If your customer contacts you wondering where the package is, there is little you can do to help once the item is in a foreign country. While USPS EMI mail will track a package throughout its journey, it is of no benefit until the package clears customs. If your package is held in detention, the customer should work with his or her own country's customs authorities to resolve the problem. The notice he or she receives will give the detention number and contact instructions.

Avoiding Customs Problems

It is your responsibility as a seller not to sell or ship items that may be prohibited in a particular country. Just because an item is allowed in the United States does not mean it is permitted in other countries. These items typically are alcohol, tobacco, firearms, other weapons, pharmaceuticals, narcotics, certain foods, and other items that are prohibited or quota restricted in that particular country.

Going to http://pe.usps.gov/text/imm/immctry.htm and clicking on the particular country brings up the specific prohibited items for that country. General information is sometimes found on the World Customs Organization website www.wcoomd.org. A good site to learn the basics of exporting is www.export.gov/exportbasics.

8.5

You can also conduct an Internet search for a particular country's Customs website (i.e., Canada Customs). If their restrictions are not obvious from their site, contact them through e-mail and ask for a list of restricted or prohibited items. Many times, it is a PDF document that you can download and print.

8.6 GLOBAL COMMUNICATION AND PAYMENTS

Communication

Payments

The popularity of eBay worldwide has attracted a large number of international buyers and sellers. In fact, sales from international buyers now account for over half of eBay's total annual sales. eBay and PayPal have developed a streamlined method for purchasing and paying for items between international trading partners who use different languages and currencies.

Communication

Your international customers will receive communications from eBay and PayPal in their native language. However, eBay does not translate any of your listing descriptions or e-mails into their language. If international buyers are viewing your listing on eBay, then they most likely can read and write at least some limited English.

If they have a question, they will send an e-mail through eBay. The e-mail will most likely be in English, as they understand that you live in the United States, but it may sometimes be a bit difficult to interpret. A lengthy response from you will usually confuse a foreign buyer even more, so keep your e-mails brief and to the point.

If you receive e-mails or phrases in a foreign language, you can try using language translation software. These applications are available for purchase. A free language translation tool is available at www.freetranslation.com.

For short phrases used in Feedback, go to Google and click on their language link. Be aware that a translated message using language software can be cryptic and is never as good as asking someone who speaks the language to translate for you.

Payments

PayPal is now available in over 190 countries and most likely in the country where you will be selling. With PayPal, foreign buyers can pay for items just as easily as a customer in your hometown.

Buyers will receive an invoice from eBay (in their native language) with the equivalent currency in U.S. dollars required from your listing. Your customer will then pay for your item with U.S. dollars. If a customer instead pays you with another currency, you will be sent an e-mail from PayPal with the option to accept or decline the currency.

Never accept MoneyGram or Western Union payments from any buyer (domestic or international). These can be a source of fraud and are specifically banned by eBay (as are many other payment services). Just state plainly in your policies that you only accept PayPal payments from international customers.

◀ *SEE ALSO 8.7, "International Fraud"* ▶

8.6

8.7 INTERNATIONAL FRAUD

Avoiding International Fraud

International fraud on eBay tends to come more from foreign sellers rather than buyers. After all, a buyer must pay you and the money be deposited in your Pay-Pal account before you even ship the item. There are other fraud concerns if you accept another payment method, but you should specify PayPal only for international shipments to easily avoid these potential problems.

Unfortunately, any country and any transaction may be a source for unethical or fraudulent activity. Use the information provided to learn what "might" happen. Train yourself to watch for the slightest irregularity in any transaction, and your observations will help protect you and your business.

Avoiding International Fraud

There are a few rules to international selling and shipping that, if followed, should minimize your risk.

Rule 1. Only accept PayPal as your method of payment from international buyers. Western Union payments, personal and bank checks, or MoneyGrams can be a source of fraud. The more that an international buyer insists on using an alternative form of payment, the more you should suspect fraud.

Be sure to make it clear in your description that you will only accept PayPal payments from international buyers. This way, if a buyer insists on sending you a check, you can cancel the transaction because the buyer hasn't followed your payment selling terms. You can cancel transactions using the Unpaid Item (UPI) process.

◀ SEE ALSO 9.2, *"Unpaid Items and Non-Paying Bidders"* ▶

Rule 2. Never ship any item until you have received the PayPal payment. Note that there sometimes is a slight delay in international payments through the PayPal process. Don't be alarmed or let your international buyer panic if she e-mails you to say she sent a payment, but it has not yet posted to your account. It should arrive within a few hours. Still, do not ship the item until the payment is shown in your account.

Rule 3. Be sure to check to see if the buyer lives in a country that is known for mail fraud and/or phishing e-mails. In the past, eBay has reported that those countries have been Nigeria, Indonesia, and Romania. Sellers can avoid these problems by setting their Buyer Requirement preferences in their My eBay page.

Check for the latest scams against eBay buyers and sellers by visiting www.millersmiles.co.uk/search/eBay.

◀ *SEE ALSO 10.2, "My eBay Special Features"* ▶

◀ *SEE ALSO 14.1, "eBay Fraud"* ▶

8.7

9

ADVANCED SELLING

9.1 SECOND CHANCE OFFERS

A Second Chance Offer (SCO) is an efficient method sellers use to remarket to the non-winning bidders of their auction. This strategy can only be used in an auction-style format, since Fixed Price listings end with only one bidder.

◀ *SEE ALSO 3.3, "Listing Formats and Bidding"* ▶

When the winning bidder does not pay for the item, an SCO can be used to sell the item to the second highest bidder. This is the preferred method to quickly move the item rather than having to relist it. A SCO can also be used if the auction did not meet the Reserve price. If the highest bidder was close enough for you, you could send him a SCO for the price he bid.

An advanced strategy is to use SCO to sell commodity items to multiple non-winning bidders. Once the auction ends, the seller can click on the Second Chance Offer link in the listing to view every bidder's highest bid during the auction. The seller can then choose all the bidders whose highest bid was at an acceptable price. An SCO invoice is then automatically e-mailed from eBay to the selected bidders. If these bidders choose to accept the offer, they will then pay the highest bid they made during the auction.

This strategy is beneficial both to the non-winning bidders, who may be able to pay several dollars less than the winning bidder did, and to the seller, who can quickly move quantities of product. Sellers who choose this advanced SCO method have reported success rates of 50 percent or more.

When making an SCO, you have the option to leave the offer open for 1, 3, 5, or 7 days. You can also make multiple SCOs even if they exceed your inventory. eBay will track your SCO sales and cancel all outstanding SCOs once your inventory quantity has been depleted. For example, if you have three items in stock, you can still make 10 SCOs. After the third SCO is accepted, eBay will cancel all the other offers you made.

Additionally, there are no insertion fees or fees associated with sending the SCO e-mailed invoices through eBay. If the bidder chooses to accept the offer, the seller would only pay the associated Final Value fee.

◀ *SEE ALSO 3.4, "eBay Fees"* ▶

If you have received a Second Chance Offer and want to ensure that it is legitimate, first go to ebay.com and sign in to your eBay account (do not use a link in the SCO e-mail you received). Go to your My eBay page and check your My Messages inbox. Any SCOs for you will appear there.

9.1

9.2 UNPAID ITEMS AND NON-PAYING BIDDERS

Filing a UPI Dispute

Mutual Withdrawal from Transaction

Strikes

Items that are won at auction or purchased with Buy It Now but then never paid for are defined as Unpaid Items (UPIs). The buyers who have not paid for these items are called non-paying bidders or buyers (NPBs).

Sellers should make all attempts to contact a buyer before taking action against him or her. Many times the buyer has not paid for the item simply because she forgot, has been out of town, or hasn't checked her e-mails and didn't even realize she won the item. Don't immediately assume that the buyer is intentionally delinquent.

If, however, the buyer has not responded within seven days of the listing end date, send a reminder e-mail. If all attempts to contact the buyer have failed and the buyer remains unresponsive, you should file a UPI dispute form. This is done primarily to have the eBay fees associated with the item credited back to your account. You must wait a minimum of seven days, then you have up to 60 days from the listing end date to file a UPI dispute.

Filing a UPI Dispute

When a seller completes eBay's UPI dispute form online (found under Site Map, Dispute Console or from your My eBay page), the buyer receives an "alert" e-mail from eBay declaring the dispute. If the NPB logs into his eBay account, a pop-up alert message also appears, reminding him to pay for the item.

If the NPB then pays for the item, you can close the dispute using the "We've completed the transaction and we're both satisfied" option. An NPB who chooses to dispute the seller's claim of non-payment must provide eBay with proof of payment.

If the NPB ignores the e-mail from eBay and does not pay for the item within seven days, the seller can then close the dispute using the "I no longer wish to communicate with or wait for the buyer" option. The buyer will get an Unpaid

Item Strike and the seller will get the Final Value Fees automatically credited back to his account (usually within 10 days).

◄ *SEE ALSO 3.4, "eBay Fees"* ▶

The seller also receives a free insertion fee if he relists the item. Many sellers choose not to relist auction listings. Instead they offer the item to the highest non-winning bidder from the original auction, using eBay's Second Chance Offer feature.

◄ *SEE ALSO 9.1, "Second Chance Offers"* ▶

Mutual Withdrawal from Transaction

Some winning bidders have buyer's remorse after winning an item and may contact the seller asking to cancel the transaction. Other buyers may have made a mistake such as clicking a Buy It Now button twice and then needing the seller to cancel one of the purchases.

If the seller disagrees, he should communicate with the buyer to try to resolve the dispute. If the dispute cannot be resolved, eBay recommends using their third-party mediator SquareTrade at www.squaretrade.com.

If the seller agrees to cancel the transaction, he will still need to complete eBay's UPI form, stating that both parties have agreed to cancel the transaction (the seller is not required to wait seven days, and can file immediately after the listing ends). eBay will then send an e-mail notification of the cancellation form to the buyer asking for confirmation. If the buyer confirms, the transaction is cancelled. The buyer will not receive a strike and the seller will receive the Final Value Fee credit.

Note that the notice to the buyer also will generate a full-page pop-up alert when the buyer logs in to their eBay account. They are given the choice to accept or decline the offer. Many times, without even reading it or realizing what it is, they decline. Therefore, before you cancel the transaction, send an e-mail to the buyer to let them know what to expect.

Strikes

Buyers who do not pay for their items even after a UPI dispute has been filed will receive a strike on their account. If they receive three separate UPI strikes, their account will be suspended. UPI strikes do not change a member's Feedback score.

◄ *SEE ALSO 10.3, "Feedback"* ▶

Removing Strikes

Buyers can appeal a UPI Strike if they can provide eBay with proof of payment. The seller can also choose to remove the strike if the buyer eventually pays for the item (this is completed through the Dispute Console in My eBay).

9.3 ACCOUNT PROBLEMS OR LISTING CANCELLATION

Delisted Items

Suspended Account

Appeals and Account Reinstatement

Delisted Items

Active listings are sometimes removed from eBay for a variety of reasons. This can happen if an item is not in accordance with eBay policies; an item is potentially fraudulent, prohibited, or restricted, if a **VeRO** violation occurs, or if the seller is keyword spamming. Another member may have actually reported the item to eBay. Many times, however, the item is flagged by proprietary eBay software developed to search for potential listing violations.

If your listing is cancelled and you feel it is unwarranted, you can appeal the decision by following the instructions in the e-mail notification. If the cancellation is then ruled a mistake, your eBay fees will be credited to your account and you are free to relist the item.

◀ *SEE ALSO 14.5, "Prohibited and Restricted Items"* ▶

◀ *SEE ALSO 4.2, "Listing Creation"* ▶

Suspended Account

Reasons for a suspended seller account usually involve a violation of eBay's rules and policies, not paying eBay's monthly fees, or three separate item UPI strikes. A member with a suspended account cannot buy, sell, or leave feedback. This applies not only to their suspended account, but any other accounts that they may still have access to. In addition, these members, their family members, and even their eBay associates cannot open a new account.

eBay notifies members of a suspended account with an e-mail and also in their My Messages page within My eBay. If you receive an e-mail about any account problem, be sure first of all that it is not a spoof e-mail sent from a scam artist.

◀ *SEE ALSO 14.1, "eBay Fraud"* ▶

Limited Account

An account is sometimes not suspended but may be limited from certain selling options due to the type of items being sold. The most common reasons are items that are routinely counterfeited or categories habitually known for fraud.

◄ SEE ALSO *Chapter 14, "Fraud Prevention"* ►

Blocked Account

Account access can also be blocked due to an invalid e-mail address. You may also be blocked for unauthorized use of your account due to account theft or a particular concern over questionable selling transactions.

Appeals and Account Reinstatement

If an account was suspended due to non-payment of monthly account fees, the account can be reinstated after the fees are paid. Many times this problem occurs because the credit card used for the automatic payment is outdated or declined, or the checking account is too low in funds.

If, after payment of the funds, your account remains suspended, limited, or blocked, contact eBay to resolve the problem. Accounts suspended due to more serious reasons such as three UPI strikes can possibly be reinstated through an appeals process. The e-mail notification from eBay announcing the suspension will contain the instructions for reinstating your account. You can check your account status under the View Invoices link on the Account Status menu in My eBay.

WORDS TO GO . . .WORDS TO GO . . .WORDS TO GO

Verified Rights Owner (VeRO) is eBay's policy to protect intellectual property such as copyrights and trademarks.

9.4   ADVANCED SELLING TECHNIQUES

Revising an Active Listing

Canceling an Active Listing

Blocking Bidders

Your eBay Preferences

There are certain techniques that are more rare but sometimes needed for the more experienced seller. You can perform most of the following techniques by choosing the appropriate link on your My eBay page.

Revising an Active Listing

Nearly any information in a Fixed Price listing can be revised except for the format. If it is a multiple item Fixed Price listing and one of the items has sold, you can only add (amend) to the description or add listing upgrades that increase visibility such as gallery, bold, and highlight.

An Auction-Style listing that is active on eBay can also be revised, as long as there have been no bids and there are more than 12 hours left before the auction ends. If bids have occurred but more than 12 hours still remain, you are only allowed to add to the description or add visibility listing upgrades.

If bids have not occurred and less than 12 hours remain, you can add visibility features, more item details, item specifics, or add new payment methods. If bids have occurred and less than 12 hours are remaining, you can only add visibility features.

You can revise a single item in your eBay Store inventory at any time. If it is a multiple store item listing and one of the items has already sold, you can revise the description, price, quantity, store category, and listing upgrade features.

Canceling an Active Listing

You can cancel an active listing, but it should never be because the auction is not going well. However, if your item is no longer for sale—for example, if it's lost or broken—you can cancel the listing. If you choose to do this you will forfeit all insertion and listing upgrade fees.

Canceling auctions once they are underway is not in the spirit of eBay. Remember that eBay tracks this type of activity. If you do this too often, you may be contacted by eBay about your questionable selling practices.

9.4

Blocking Bidders

Occasionally there will be a buyer who causes unjustified trouble for you, creates additional work, makes negative feedback threats, or is the cause of some type of trying experience. Once the transaction is completed, you may choose to not ever sell to them again.

You can block these troublemakers from becoming a future customer by going to Site Map and choosing the Block Bidder/Buyer List link under Selling. You simply enter their User ID and they can no longer bid on any of your items. You can update the list at any time.

If a seller has blocked you from bidding on their items, you can e-mail them asking to be pre-approved, but it is the sole discretion of the seller to allow you to bid.

Your eBay Preferences

You should take the time to set up your preferences so eBay will know how you want them to handle different situations. Using the "Preferences" link under My eBay, then My Account, you can set up preferences for listings, communication, alerts, or even filtering potential buyers. The details for setting your preferences are found in Chapter 10.

◀ *SEE ALSO 10.2, "My eBay Special Features"* ▶

9.5   EBAY SPEAK, ACRONYMS

Because eBay only allows 55 characters in a listing title, many sellers use acronyms to save precious character space. Acronyms that are relevant only to eBay have been given the nickname "eBay Speak."

A review of eBay listings shows that sellers in certain categories may use several acronyms while sellers in other categories rarely use them. If the top sellers in your category include acronyms in their title, it usually means the buyers expect them, so you should probably use them as well.

A few of the more commonly used acronyms follow. A complete list can be found using eBay Help and typing "eBay acronyms," then selecting "eBay acronyms" from the results page.

Common Acronyms
Auto: autograph
B&W: black and white
BC: back cover
BIN: Buy It Now
DOA: dead on arrival
FB: feedback
GBP: Great Britain Pounds
HB: hardback (book)
HTF: hard to find
LTD: limited edition
NC: no cover
NR: no reserve price for an auction-style listing
OEM: original equipment manufacturer
OOP: out of print
PM: Priority Mail
RET: retired
SC: soft cover (book)
S/O: sold out
Sig: signature
USPS: United States Postal Service
VHTF: very hard to find
XL: extra large

9.5

Item Condition Acronyms

E or EC: excellent condition

EUC: excellent used condition

FC: fine condition

G or GC: good condition

GU: gently used

GUC: good used condition

MNT: mint, perfect condition

MIB: mint in box

MIMB: mint in mint box

MIMP: mint in mint package

MIP: mint in package

MNB: mint no box

MOC: mint on card

MOMC: mint on mint card

MONMC: mint on near mint card

MWBT: mint with both tags

MWMT: mint with mint tags

NBW: never been worn

NIB: new in box

NM: near mint

NOS: new old stock

NRFB: never removed from box

NWT: new with tags

NWOT: new without original tags

SCR: scratch

VF or VFC: very fine condition

VGC: very good condition

VGUC: very good used condition

9.6 AUTHENTICATION AND GRADING

Counterfeit items cannot be sold on eBay. Some replica items can be sold if the listing clearly states that the item is a replica.

◁ *SEE ALSO 14.5, "Prohibited and Restricted Items"* ▷

If you are selling genuine items that are frequently counterfeited or replicated, it is a good idea to have your item authenticated. For more expensive or collectible items, you should view authentication as simply part of your selling cost.

eBay does not provide authentication or grading for sellers' items. There are, however, a few eBay-approved authentication service providers.

Usually it is best to use an authentication service that specializes in the item you are selling. The common specialties are items such as autographs, sports or political memorabilia, trading cards, jewelry, comic books, rare coins, stamps, Beanie Babies, or Native American artifacts.

Buyers can also use authentication or grading services to have an item's physical condition evaluated before they bid. The seller would need to approve of and cooperate with this process.

You can contact authentication and grading service providers first for initial opinions on your item. Their professional grading and authentication services are available for a fee.

9.6

eBay provides a list of professional and independent authenticators and grading evaluators. These service providers are not allowed to buy or sell on eBay to prevent any potential conflict of interest. To find eBay's list of authentication and grading service providers, go to eBay Help, type "authentication" in the search box, and click on "View a list of companies."

9.7 EBAY EXPRESS

Advantages of eBay Express

Qualifications for eBay Express

eBay Express (EE) is a separate, specialty-selling website. Buyers will find eBay Express by either going to eBay.com and clicking on the eBay Express tab, or by going directly to www.ebayexpress.com.

The purpose of EE is to target customers looking mostly for new, fixed-price goods from a variety of experienced sellers who offer buyer protection and sell in a more conventional e-commerce method (at a fixed price as opposed to auctions).

Advantages of eBay Express

One of the main advantages of EE is that buyers can shop among many sellers, adding items to their shopping cart along the way. When they finish shopping, they can check out with PayPal and pay for all their items, to all the sellers, at once. Additionally, if they don't have a PayPal account, they can pay with their credit card through PayPal. eBay Express, then, is marketed to buyers who want items instantly and don't want to muddle through all listings that include auctions. They also want the assurance that the sellers are experienced, in good standing, and offer buyer protection. Essentially the thought will be "Shopping on eBay Express eliminates the bad sellers, and the products can be purchased immediately from a number of sellers—all at once."

With eBay Express, buyers will ...

- ▶ Get it new: Most items are new, or refurbished and factory sealed. Used items can also be purchased and are just one click away. But the condition must be stated for all items. Some categories are excluded, including most antique items.

- ▶ Get it now: Everything is sold at a Fixed Price.

- ▶ Fill a shopping cart: Buyers can purchase items from multiple eBay Express merchants and pay for everything, including shipping, in a single, secure transaction using PayPal or a credit card.

- ▶ Buy with confidence: Every transaction is safe, secure, and fully backed by eBay Express Purchase Protection.

Qualifications for eBay Express

For your items to appear on eBay Express, you need to meet certain qualifications that are listed below.

- ► You need a feedback score of 100 and a 98 percent positive rating.

- ► You must be registered on eBay US or eBay Canada and ship the item from a U.S. address (the item must also be listed on eBay.com).

- ► You must be a Premier or Business PayPal member.

- ► Your PayPal account must be set to ship to unconfirmed addresses as well as confirmed.

- ► You need to allow buyers to pay with "combined payments" (this setting is in your Selling Preferences within My eBay).

- ► You must list items in Fixed Price, Store Inventory, or "Auction-Style with Buy It Now" formats.

- ► Fill in the Item Condition field if one appears during your listing creation.

- ► Use Pre-Filled Information for media items (books, DVDs, music, video games, etc.).

- ► Include shipping costs in your listing.

- ► Provide an item photo.

- ► Use eBay checkout (one of your My eBay preferences).

- ► Have your feedback profile set to Public (i.e., not Private).

9.7

Sellers need to do nothing more than fulfill the qualifications above and their Fixed Price items will automatically appear on eBay Express. To learn more about selling on eBay Express, select the Help link on eBay.com and type "eBay Express" in the search box.

9.8 POWERSELLERS

eBay's Marketplace Policies

PowerSeller Benefits

Loss of PowerSeller Status

Sellers on eBay.com, half.com, eBay Motors, or eBay Express who attain a minimum level of gross sales or volume for a three-month running average are called PowerSellers. This membership is free and automatic to qualified sellers.

The minimum PowerSeller level is Bronze and requires a minimum of $1,000 in gross sales, or 100 items per month, have a minimum of 100 feedbacks along with a 98 percent or better positive feedback rating, and have an average 4.5 rating on each of the four Detailed Seller Ratings. Sellers who meet the PowerSeller levels  listed in the table below, comply with all eBay marketplace policies, and maintain an eBay account in good standing will receive the PowerSeller icon next to their User ID signifying that they are an experienced seller.

eBay PowerSeller Levels

Bronze: $1,000 or 100 items

Silver: $3,000 or 300 items

Gold: $10,000 or 1,000 items

Platinum: $25,000 or 2,500 items

Titanium: $150,000 or 15,000 items

There are also alternative annual requirements so seasonal eBay sellers can still qualify as a PowerSeller. They must have sold at least two items per month for the last 12 months (24 items). They must have also achieved sales of $12,000 or sold 1200 items within the last 12 months.

eBay's Marketplace Policies

PowerSellers (in fact, all sellers) must also comply with the following eBay Marketplace Policies:

▶ **Excessive shipping and handling:** Sellers should charge standard rates and never gouge buyers for shipping charges.

▶ **Shill bidding:** You or your friends are not allowed to bid on your own item. This unscrupulous practice is sometimes done to run up the price on an auction item. It is a serious offense resulting in immediate suspension.

▶ **Site interference:** Blocking, obscuring, or modifying content on an eBay page is not permitted.

▶ **Accepted payments:** You must use eBay-approved forms of payment.

▶ **Transaction interference:** Buyers cannot contact the seller asking to purchase the item outside of eBay or contact any bidders warning them about the seller. Sellers cannot contact bidders asking them to purchase the item outside of eBay.

▶ **Keyword spamming:** All keywords used in the listing title must be relevant to the item sold.

▶ **Links policy:** Sellers cannot place a static or clickable link on their listings to a website outside of eBay unless the site is strictly informational. No links or references are allowed to sites that solicit eBay User IDs, passwords, or e-mail addresses.

▶ **Choice listings:** Sellers cannot list an item on eBay and then in their description mention they have other sizes or colors available and ask the buyer to let them know which product they want upon checkout.

▶ **Misleading titles:** Titles must accurately reflect the actual item that is for sale.

▶ **Payment surcharges:** Additional fees for a standard method of payment (including PayPal) are not permitted.

▶ **Spam:** Sellers may not send unwanted e-mails to any member.

▶ **No item listings:** eBay listings should be used to sell items or services, not for advertisement or personal and political statements.

▶ **Categorization of listings:** Items must be listed in categories appropriate to the item.

▶ **User agreement violations:** Seller must comply with all of the user agreement policies signed during registration.

◀ *SEE ALSO 1.3, "Register as a Seller"* ▷

PowerSeller Benefits

There are some distinct benefits to becoming a PowerSeller, including the ability to purchase health insurance at a group rate. Other advantages include access to the PowerSeller Newsgroup and discussion boards, prioritized e-mail or phone customer support based on PowerSeller level, special promotion mailings, discounts on eBay fees, credit for feature fees as well as Final Value Fees for UPI transactions, priority placement of their items over other sellers in buyer search results, and additional services not available to other sellers.

Loss of PowerSeller Status

eBay evaluates a PowerSeller's status every month and the seller must qualify based on a rolling three-month average. If sellers are in jeopardy of losing their status, they are notified by eBay of the problem at least a month in advance.

If they fail to meet the minimum requirements, sellers lose the PowerSeller logo next to their User ID and all the associated benefits (except for health coverage). Sellers can be automatically reinstated to PowerSeller status by meeting the minimum requirements once again.

10

MY EBAY

10.1 MY EBAY OVERVIEW

My eBay Views

Located on the Primary Navigation toolbar at the top of each page is a tab called My eBay. All important buying and selling activities between you and eBay are tracked and available for review by clicking on this tab. My eBay is also where you can update your personal preferences and account information.

This chapter will discuss the various views, features, and benefits of My eBay. Screenshots are provided as visual aids to the text, but it is best if you examine this chapter while online, logged into eBay, and following along in your own My eBay page.

My eBay Views

There are several different views of My eBay. Each view is available by scrolling down the left-hand column of the page and clicking the desired view.

My eBay Views.

My Summary: All recent activities are available at a glance, including My Messages, Items Won, Items Currently Selling, and Items Sold. Note that if you do not have activity in a specific area, it will not show on My Summary.

All Buying: Shows Buying Reminders, items you are watching, your buying totals (bid or won) in the last 31 days, items you are currently bidding on or have made Best Offers on, items you have won, and items you didn't win.

This link also provides a Bid Assistant to help you bid on multiple listings for the same product. This tool allows you to bid on several listings concurrently but protects you from winning more than one (when one auction ends, if you did not win, the Bid Assistant automatically places your specified bid on the auction in your list that ends next, and so on).

All Selling: All items scheduled to list at a later time, items you are currently selling, items you have recently sold, and items that went unsold.

Want It Now: Use this tab to post a request for items you desire but may be currently unavailable on eBay.

My Messages: Important messages about your account from eBay and PayPal and e-mails from your customers are posted here. If you think you have received a possible spoof e-mail, check here to see if eBay has a message for you. If there is no message from eBay about the problem stated in the e-mail, it was a spoof.

◀ *SEE ALSO 14.1, "eBay Fraud"* ▶

My Neighborhoods: You can connect with other members who have similar eBay interests. Hobbyists, collectors, clubs, or sellers that share an interest in particular items or categories on eBay can find each other and communicate using this link.

All Favorites: Sometimes a buyer has an interest in a more rare item. Rather than having to constantly search eBay every few days, buyers can set up favorite keyword searches that constantly monitor eBay looking for matching items. If an item appears on eBay with those keywords, you are automatically notified by e-mail. You can also save your favorite sellers and categories here in order to easily locate them at a later date.

My Account: Use this link when you need to change your personal information or selling preferences. This also includes the links for leaving feedback, viewing your selling account fees, or subscribe to other eBay services such as eBay Stores or sales reports.

10.1

◀ *SEE ALSO 10.3, "Feedback"* ▶

◀ *SEE ALSO 11.1, "eBay Stores Overview"* ▶

10.2 MY EBAY SPECIAL FEATURES

Relist an Item

Seller Preferences

Customize Your Display View

Sorting Your Sold Page

My eBay is packed with multiple features and optional views of an eBay Buyer's and Seller's activities. Sellers in particular should take the time to set up their preferences in order to better streamline and automate their selling process. The most popular and useful features of My eBay are described here.

Relist an Item

Not all of your items on eBay will sell the first time you list them. However, you don't have to duplicate the time you spent creating and listing your item to relist it. You can view all of your items that did not sell during the last 90 days under All Selling, then the "Unsold" link. Use this link to begin the relisting process.

eBay also wants your item to sell, so if you relist the item within 90 days from you're My eBay page, you are usually eligible for the Relist Credit. Although you will pay a second insertion fee (for the relisted auction), if it sells, you will get this fee credited back. But be aware: if the item does not sell the second time, you do not get the fee credit. Also, the Relist Credit only applies to the Insertion Fee, not to any listing upgrades or featuring fees.

◀ *SEE ALSO 3.5, "Listing Upgrades and Fees"* ▶

A mistake many new sellers make is to immediately relist an item that did not sell. Keep in mind that if you list an item immediately, it is most likely being viewed by the same buyers who rejected it last week.

You have up to 90 days to relist the item. It may be best to wait a few weeks before relisting, so you can try selling it to a fresh group of buyers. Other strategies would be to change the date/time, title, price, or listing format to attract other bidders.

Seller Preferences

Use the Seller Preferences link to let eBay know how you want it to handle certain situations with transactions, e-mails, and payments. It is important to take the time to set your preferences, as these can eliminate or streamline many manual tasks. You can find your Preferences link under My eBay, then My Account.

There are four major categories of eBay preferences:

Notification Preferences

Notification preferences determine how and when you receive automatic eBay alerts or notifications. These include alerts for buying, such as e-mail reminders when an item is about to close. Alerts for selling are available to notify you when your item was listed, sold, or ended unsold.

Seller Preferences

Sellers should set their seller preferences when creating listings so eBay will know their choice for picture services, listing previews, or combined shipping discounts. You can also set PayPal checkout to automatically send invoices to your buyers, or to set buyer requirements to block certain buyers from bidding on your item.

Setting your buyer requirements gives eBay permission to block buyers you consider potential trouble from bidding on your items. A particular buyer can be blocked or a group of buyers can be blocked based on conditions such as their country of registration (if it's a country you don't ship to), UPI strikes, or if they do not have a PayPal account.

You can block buyers who have caused trouble for you from bidding on your items. Simply use the Block Buyer link to make an exemption list based on their user ID. If the buyer later tries to bid on one of your items, he will receive a notice that he must be preapproved by you before he can bid.

10.2

You can also use buyer requirement preferences to block bids from buyers who live in countries that you do not ship to. When creating your listings, use the checkboxes in the shipping section to select all countries you will ship to. eBay will then block buyers who live outside of your accepted country list from bidding on your item.

Using this buyer requirement is particularly useful if you don't ship internationally. That way you cannot get an international bidder (who didn't read your shipping terms) winning your item and then have to decide if you want to make an exception to your rule, or deal with canceling the bid and sending a Second Chance Offer to the next highest bidder.

Member-to-Member Communication Preferences

These settings inform eBay as to how you want to communicate with your buyers and sellers through either e-mail or eBay's Internet phone service, **Skype.**

General Preferences

Use this link to determine how you want eBay to display your searched items and your different My eBay views. You can also review or revoke authorizations from third-party companies that perform actions on your behalf such as eBay's **Accounting Assistant.**

Customize Your Display View

On the top right section of your default My eBay page (the My Summary view) is a Customize Summary link. Use this to add or remove the columns of information for each view of My eBay. Be sure to click the Save button once you have your new preferences chosen.

Sorting Your Sold Page

You can quickly sort all the activity on your Sold Page by selecting any of the icons shown near the top. Simply click one of the icons, and all sales activity will be sorted to your requested view as described below.

My eBay Sort Bar.

Envelope: Sort by e-mails sent

Cart: Sort by Checkout status

$: Sort by Payment status (non-payment is indicated by a transparent dollar sign)

Box: Sort by Shipping status

Star: Sort by Feedback left for others

Cloud: Sort by Feedback received

Arrow: Sort by Items that have been relisted

People: Sort by Second Chance Offers sent

Note that when viewing your My eBay page, some icons have an up or down arrow. Clicking once will perform the sort and clicking again will give the opposite sort. For example, clicking on the Payment status will show all items sold that *have* been paid for. Clicking the icon again will show all items sold that *have not* yet been paid for.

WORDS TO GO . . . *WORDS TO GO* . . . *WORDS TO GO*

Skype is an instant messaging and communication software application eBay members can use to chat over the Internet for free. Each member would need the Skype application software and a headset in order to speak to other members. Sellers who offer this feature can insert their Skype name into their listings so buyers can find and communicate with them.

Accounting Assistant is an eBay-developed tool to easily and efficiently load all eBay and PayPal transaction information into QuickBooks and Quick-Books Pro. This feature is used for business accounting and tax purposes.

10.2

10.3 FEEDBACK

Leaving Feedback

Feedback Ratings

Feedback Comments

Evaluating Feedback Profiles

Feedback Stars

Improving Feedback Ratings

Resolving Feedback Disputes

Feedback Profiles offer a measured overview of a member's past performance with their trading partners. Buyers can examine a seller's feedback score to help predict the possible experience of a future transaction with a particular seller.

Buyers should always check the Feedback Profile of a potential seller before they bid. This will help them determine if the seller has a good profile or if previous buyers have reported particular problems through their ratings and comments.

It is expected that every sale on eBay will have a comment and rating made from both the buyer and seller about the quality of the transaction. It is not mandatory that feedback occurs, but it is expected in order to be a good eBay citizen. In reality, though, as a seller you should expect about 70 percent of buyers to actually leave feedback for you. However, you should always leave feedback for all of your buyers.

Leaving Feedback

Who should leave feedback first, the buyer or seller? It can be debated, but usually if a buyer has paid for an item, the seller should leave positive feedback at that point. The buyer should wait until they have received the item before they leave their feedback.

Members can leave feedback for their trading partner up to 90 days after the listing ends. To leave feedback, click on the Feedback link under the My Account section of your My eBay page. Then choose the Leave Feedback link.

Members can view their own Feedback Profile under their Account, Feedback Profile link or by clicking on the Feedback Score next to their User ID. Members can also view other members' Feedback Profiles by clicking on the Feedback Score next to their User ID.

Feedback Ratings

eBay allows members to leave a feedback rating for every transaction. Feedback comments can be positive, negative, or neutral. Every positive rating will raise a Feedback Score one point. Each negative rating will decrease the overall score by one. A neutral rating is not counted in the score. All feedback from unique buyers will count in the seller's score. For returning buyers, one feedback per week is allowed.

Detailed Seller Ratings (since May 2007)		
Criteria	Average rating	Number of ratings
Item as described	★★★★★	35
Communication	★★★★★	35
Shipping time	★★★★★	35
Shipping and handling charges	★★★★★	35

Detailed Seller Ratings (DSRs).

Detailed Seller Ratings

Buyers can also rate the seller on detailed factors such as the accuracy of the item's description, communication, shipping time, and the shipping and handling charges. The **Detailed Seller Rating** system is based on a five-star scale (one is the lowest to five, the highest) for each criteria.

Detailed Seller Ratings (DSRs) do not affect the overall feedback score but are available in order to provide a more complete review of the seller's performance. Multiple Detailed Seller Ratings from a single buyer will be averaged when calculating the Detailed Seller Rating. All DSRs are anonymous and sellers cannot change or appeal them.

Maintaining a good DSR score is of utmost importance to PowerSellers, since it is the best way to determine customer satisfaction. In order to maintain Power-Seller status, a 4.5 DSR score must be maintained in all four criteria: "Item as described," "Communication," "Shipping time," and "Shipping and handling charges." Sellers who maintain an overall DSR of 4.6 and above for the past 30 days will receive priority placement in buyer search results over sellers with lower scores. By contrast, sellers that have a poor DSR score (dissatisfaction rates greater than 5 percent) or a poor score for excessive shipping and handling fees will receive low priority placement in search results. While this will affect few sellers, it will greatly affect the bad ones—and hopefully weed them out of eBay.

PowerSellers with all four DSRs rated at 4.6 or higher for the past 30 days will receive a 5 percent discount on their Final Value Fees. PowerSellers with a 4.8 or above rating qualify for a 15 percent discount on their Final Value Fees.

10.3

Feedback Comments

Along with a rating system, members can leave a brief comment about the transaction. Comments are permanent and can rarely be removed later, so do not leave unduly critical or mean-spirited comments for the purpose of retribution. Future sellers can see the comments you have left for other sellers, and if your comments have been unreasonable, they may choose to block you from bidding on their items. Comments should always be fair and objective.

Before you leave poor or negative feedback for a seller, remember that sometimes things can go wrong in a transaction. Packages may get lost or the item damaged in transit. Give the seller the benefit of the doubt and judge them by how they handle the problem.

Sellers cannot leave negative or neutral feedback for buyers. eBay changed to this new rating system because too many sellers were withholding their feedback until the buyer left them positive feedback. It was a form of feedback extortion as buyers felt they could not give honest feedback due to the fear of retaliation. While this is limiting, sellers can still respond to the comments and feedback scores they receive, and they can certainly report deadbeat buyers.

A seller's feedback percentage is now based on all feedback received during the last 12 months. Therefore, any negative or neutral feedback will be removed after one year and no longer affect your feedback percentage. eBay suggests that a good overall score is a 98-percent positive feedback rating.

◀ *SEE ALSO 9.2, "Unpaid Items and Non-paying Bidders"* ▶

Evaluating Feedback Profiles

The top of a member's Feedback Profile page (under the User ID) shows the Lifetime Summary of the user's Feedback. It includes the total number of Positive Feedback, Negative Feedback, and the Positive Feedback Percentage (often known as the Feedback Rating).

Recent Feedback Ratings are found in a summary box on the left of the page. It shows the number of positive, neutral, and negative feedback ratings in the last 1, 6, and 12 months.

Detailed Seller Ratings are in a summary box on the right side of the page. These are given in a one-star (lowest) to five-star rating.

Below these summary ratings are four tabs that show feedback comments. Clicking on each tab will reveal a different view of feedback for each member.

The tabs are Feedback as a seller, Feedback as a buyer, All Feedback, and Feedback left for others.

Sometimes buyers will leave a positive score but with negative comments. Therefore, when evaluating a potential seller, you should take the time to click on these comment tabs and read a few pages of comments rather than glancing only at the overall Feedback Score. For help in determining whether a seller is reputable, check the "eBay Seller Evaluation Checklist" link at www.trainingu4auctions.com.

Feedback Stars

Once your feedback score reaches 10 points, you will receive a yellow Feedback star. The points are your accumulated total from both buying and selling. As you progress and gain eBay experience, you will earn different star ratings. Listed below are all of the star ratings associated with the required feedback numbers:

EBAY FEEDBACK STAR RATING

Star Color	Required Points
Yellow	10–49
Blue	50–99
Turquoise	100–499
Purple	500–999
Red	1,000–4,999
Green	5,000–9,999
Yellow shooting star	10,000–24,999
Turquoise shooting star	25,000–49,999
Purple shooting star	50,000–99,999
Red shooting star	100,000 +

10.3

Improving Feedback Ratings

There are certain factors that eBay buyers tend to use to measure their satisfaction with a seller. If a seller provides great service in these areas and there are no disappointing surprises when the buyer receives the item, the buyer will tend to give a good detailed DSR feedback rating.

Shipping time and costs tend to be a particularly volatile area for eBay buyers. Never try to make money on shipping by listing an item for a few cents and then charging an exorbitant amount for shipping. Some dishonest sellers do this in order to avoid eBay fees. Not only is this against eBay policy, it is the quickest way to make your buyer angry.

Always include your shipping rate in your listing and only charge an accurate, reasonable amount. Then ship promptly after you have received payment.

◀ *SEE ALSO 6.8, "Determine the Shipping Rate"* ▶

Never mislead a buyer about the condition of your item. Give a complete explanation about your item including a factual description of the item's condition. Never call an item new if it is not. If there are flaws, mention them and take a picture of the flaw and include the picture in your listing.

Check and respond to e-mails within 24 hours. If practical, provide shipping dates and tracking information to your buyers. You can resolve most problems and complaints by contacting your buyer promptly and working with them in a reasonable manner to determine the solution.

Resolving Feedback Disputes

If you believe you have received negative feedback unfairly or if you regret leaving poor feedback for another member, you have a few options.

You can leave a comment in response to a comment left for you. Keep your comments fair and professional. How you handle negative feedback reflects directly on your professionalism and may influence your future potential buyers.

You may want to leave a follow-up to an earlier comment you left. This can be done once, and is usually done after the dispute is resolved.

If a buyer does not respond to an **Unpaid Item (UPI)** dispute, eBay will penalize them with a UPI strike. Once the buyer receives a UPI strike, their feedback comment and rating for the seller, if any, is removed automatically by eBay. If a buyer receives three UPI strikes, their account is suspended. If a buyer is suspended, any negative or neutral comments he left will be automatically removed by eBay. You can access the UPI forms from the Dispute Console link located near the bottom of the left-hand column, under your All Summary page on My eBay.

◀ *SEE ALSO 9.2, "Unpaid Items and Non-paying Bidders"* ▶

If you cannot resolve the dispute without the help of a third party, eBay recommends using SquareTrade's professional mediators at www.squaretrade.com.

◀ *SEE ALSO 14.3, "SquareTrade"* ▶

> ***WORDS TO GO*** *. . .WORDS TO GO . . .WORDS TO GO*
>
> **Detailed Seller Rating (DSR)** is the portion of a seller's feedback profile where buyers can leave a more specific and complete review (such as item description or shipping) of the seller's performance and their customer's satisfaction.
>
> An **Unpaid Item (UPI)** strike occurs when a seller reports a buyer that has not paid for an item won from the seller. The buyer is given a clear warning and enough time to pay. If they do not comply, they receive an Unpaid Item (UPI) strike. After three UPI strikes, they are banned from eBay.

10.3

11

EBAY STORES

11.1 EBAY STORES OVERVIEW

Advantages of an eBay Store

When to Open an eBay Store

eBay Store Inventory

How Buyers Find Your Store

How Buyers Search Your Store

Store Referral Credit Program

eBay stores are an effective and economical way to open a new sales channel, promote your merchandise, and market your business. Stores are a unique area of eBay where individual sellers can display all of their listings in their own customized online storefront. Owning an eBay store is similar to having your own personal website on eBay.

Stores are used mostly in conjunction with standard eBay listings. Storeowners list only their most popular items on eBay and then cross-promote them with related items in their store. Typical store items are add-on products like accessories or different sizes, colors, or models. This **upselling** strategy also has lower listing fees and longer time periods of exposure for store listings compared to standard eBay listings; however, these items do not show up in standard eBay search results.

Advantages of an eBay Store

As an eBay storeowner, you will have more visibility on eBay as well as an improved image to buyers. A store allows you to market more products at a reduced cost. Many sellers who have an eBay store have reported that their sales increased after opening their online store.

You can custom design your store and have complete control over the way it looks to your buyers. Custom designing can include your own color schemes, graphics, banners, and more. You can create a design theme that is recognizable and specific to your listings, business correspondence, and promotional materials. You will also own your own store web address (URL) that you can promote to all your buyers both on and off eBay. You should print your store URL on all promotional and marketing materials that you use.

eBay Stores Design Center.

Stores are arranged by categories, which gives a more complete and organized display. eBay has developed management tools that will help you to manage your store, market your business, create promotional campaigns, and send e-mail newsletters to your customers.

Traffic reports are provided free of charge and allow you to closely monitor and control your store. You can use these reports to study the traffic patterns and activities of your customers and store visitors. Storeowners also have privileged access to phone support with a live eBay representative.

◀ SEE ALSO 11.5, *"Manage Your Store"* ▶

When to Open an eBay Store

Sellers who just want to get rid of stuff around the house do not need an eBay store. Store benefits such as custom-themed displays, marketing, and cross promotions are negligible when listing unrelated, low-value, used items.

Consider opening an eBay store only after you determine your primary products and then the accessories and add-on products you will sell. Once you have accomplished this and have several items to sell, you are ready to open your store.

eBay Store Inventory

All of your listings will be displayed in your store, including your standard Auction-Style or Fixed Price listings. Within 24 hours of opening a new eBay store, all of your current eBay listings can be seen. Any new listings that you then create will appear in your store almost immediately.

You can create store listings that will be viewable only within your store. These will not appear in a standard eBay keyword search except under certain conditions that we'll detail shortly. All items created specifically for store inventory are in the Fixed Price format. The advantage of a store listing compared to a standard listing is the significantly reduced eBay insertion fee (3, 5, or 10 cents) and much longer durations (30 days compared to 7 or 10 days).

How Buyers Find Your Store

Whenever a member conducts a keyword item search on eBay, store listings do not usually appear in the search results. However, if fewer than 30 listings were produced during the search, eBay will include a section after all of the results for items from eBay stores that have matching keywords. Buyers can also find store items by one of the following methods:

- ▶ Linking from one of your standard listings to "View Seller's Store Items" or to a direct link you provide in the auction description. This is the most common method.

- ▶ Clicking the Stores tab from any eBay page and performing a search that will only return store inventory listings.

- ▶ Store inventory listings can appear in a standard search if the buyer chooses to view Buy It Now listings.

- ▶ On the search results page, a buyer can also choose to "See additional Buy It Now items from eBay Store sellers." This search will display the store name, a link to the store, a description of the store, and the number of matching items within that store.

- ▶ Buyers are also able to search for a specific eBay store by its name. If a store name is found that is an exact match, that store name and description is returned in the results list. If stores have part of the name within their title, they will be displayed below the exact match.

How Buyers Search Your Store

When a buyer visits your store, they are able to search for items using the Store Search box. This allows buyers to type the keywords of the product they're interested in and the tool will search for that item only within your store.

Buyers can search by keywords alone or also search for matching keywords in the descriptions of the items (by checking the "in titles & descriptions" box). This tool is a useful feature for stores that have numerous items in multiple categories, as a buyer does not have to scroll page-by-page looking for a specific item.

Store Referral Credit Program

Storeowners can receive a credit to their eBay fees when they direct Internet buyers to their store. The reason is that the website owner is sending business to eBay.

If a storeowner has a website, they can place links on their site with a special code that directs these buyers to their eBay store. eBay is then able to track where the traffic to the store originated and can determine when a visitor has come from that storeowner's website. If the visitor purchases an item from their store, eBay will credit 75 percent of the Final Value Fee charged for that sale to the storeowner's account.

WORDS TO GO . . .WORDS TO GO . . .WORDS TO GO

Retailers use **upselling** to encourage a customer to either upgrade a product they are interested in buying or purchase an accessory for the item. An example would be promoting a camera bag or memory card when selling cameras.

11.1

11.2 STORE SUBSCRIPTION LEVELS

Store Item Insertion Fees

eBay storeowners pay a monthly fee based on their store's subscription level. There are three levels to choose from: Basic, Premium, and Anchor. Most eBay sellers should start with a Basic store and can easily upgrade to a Premium store when business grows. Note that an Anchor store is for true eBay professionals running a sizable and full-time business. The cost is not practical for part-time sellers.

At $15.95 per month, the Basic store subscription is an inexpensive way for sellers to expand their business. This package offers an unlimited number of product pages (store inventory listings), five customizable catalog pages, and up to 300 custom store categories. The Basic level also provides a store web address, promotion boxes to highlight specific items in your store, 1MB free storage using Picture Manager, and the ability to send 5,000 e-mails as store newsletters each month to their subscribers.

Priced at $49.95 per month, the Premium store package offers everything in the Basic package. It also provides 10 catalog pages as well as the ability to send 7,500 monthly newsletter e-mails. Also included in the Premium subscription is Selling Manager Pro, eBay Marketplace Research, 1MB free and $5 off the subscription to Picture Manager, and access to more advanced store traffic reports.

The Anchor professional subscription level is priced at $299.95 per month. In addition to all that is included with the Basic and Premium stores, the Anchor store package provides 15 catalog pages; 10,000 newsletter e-mails; and a free 1GB subscription to eBay's Picture Manager.

Store Item Insertion Fees

In addition to the monthly subscription fees, storeowners pay an Insertion fee to list an item in their store and a Final Value fee, only if the item sells. Insertion fees are only 3 cents for store items priced under $24.99, 5 cents for $25 to $199.99 and 10 cents for items $200 and above. These items are listed in the store for 30 days. When creating a store listing, the seller can choose to have the item end after 30 days or to automatically renew it again every 30 days until it is sold. This option is called Good 'Til Cancelled (GTC). A complete description of all fees associated with store items is provided in Chapter 3.5.

◄ SEE ALSO 3.5, *"Listing Upgrades and Fees"* ▷

11.3 SET UP AND BUILD YOUR STORE

Quick Setup

Create Store Categories

Customize Your Store

Promotion Boxes

Search Engine Optimization

Create a store that will grab attention and also be buyer-friendly. These two factors are important to your store's success. Making an excellent first impression when a buyer enters your store is essential. Study other eBay stores to learn creative and practical design concepts and discover attractive layout possibilities.

Make sure that you always have enough listings in each category to make the overall appearance more attractive to your buyers. If you only have a few listings in each category, you may have too many categories. Bare store shelves do not give a positive impression. Buyers want to see stores that are fully stocked just like they would when browsing a catalog or visiting a retail store. A fully stocked eBay store encourages buyers to stay and browse.

Quick Setup

By using the store design tools developed by eBay, you can set up a store in minutes. Store layout and design decisions are made with simple menu and template selections. You can use the basic layout or the advanced layout eBay offers.

You will also have access to a selection of template store logos that will help the customer identify what goods you sell. You can also replace the template logo with your own. You can use inexpensive and simple-to-use logo design software such as Logo Creator or Logo Design to create your own distinct logo.

11.3

Create Store Categories

Your store layout will include categories that act as virtual aisles and shelves. You can have up to 300 custom categories to organize, display, and draw attention to your items. Your store categories do not need to match eBay's categories but should be specific to the items you sell.

Each category name can consist of up to 29 characters. Whenever you create any new eBay listing, you then assign it to one of your store categories. This allows eBay to cross-promote your store items with your standard eBay listings.

◀ *SEE ALSO 12.5, "Marketing Your Business"* ▶

You can add, rename, edit, move, or delete store categories at any time. Categories will not appear in your store if no listings are there. You can also easily move items from one category to another at any time.

The goal is to create a group of categories that make it easy for the buyer to quickly find the different items you have without being overwhelmed or confused. You want to make a visitor's shopping experience simple and pleasant. Organize your categories by brand, type of item, price levels, or other factors. Visit other eBay stores or professional online websites that sell similar products and study their category layout and store design strategies.

Customize Your Store

An eBay store subscription includes useful, easy tools for creating and designing the type of appearance your store will need. Keep in mind how your store will contribute to your overall business marketing and promotion strategy.

Design your store to be visually unique from any other competing stores. Create an enjoyable shopping environment for your buyers. Be creative with your color schemes and graphics and create a store theme. Developing your own store logo is another way to create brand recognition when used in the store's listing header.

Avoid a cluttered or disorganized store. The buyer must be able to quickly find and learn about your products. Use gallery pictures and promotion boxes, and place items on sale using Markdown Manager whenever appropriate. The key is for you to customize your store and build brand recognition as well as credibility, in a fashion that is buyer-friendly, appealing to the eye, and unique from all the other stores.

◀ *SEE ALSO 11.5, "Manage Your Store"* ▶

Promotion Boxes

You can include promotion boxes on different pages throughout your store to promote and advertise your items. You can use these flexible, customized displays for a variety of purposes such as highlighting featured items, announcing specials, or providing alternative ways for buyers to browse in your store.

There are basically two ways to create and then manage promotion boxes in your store. You can use the pre-designed promotion boxes that will appear on all of your store category pages, or you can create your own custom promotion box.

Search Engine Optimization

Make sure you design your store so Internet search engines can find it and list your store in their user's search results. This process is known as **Search Engine Optimization (SEO).** Match the text used in your title, descriptions, and categories with the most likely keywords you feel Internet users will use when searching for the items you sell. This increases the chance of your store appearing in their search results.

Listed below are a few keyword finding tools that will help you find popular searches and appropriate keywords on eBay and the Internet. Include these keywords in your store name, category names, store description, and in the content of your store's custom pages. Use your store traffic reports to monitor what your visitors are viewing and buying and possibly change your keywords accordingly. Some sellers even open a separate website that auto-directs the Internet user to their eBay store.

◀ *SEE ALSO 11.5, "Manage Your Store"* ▶

Here are some helpful keyword-finding tools:

- ▶ pulse.ebay.com
- ▶ keyword.ebay.com
- ▶ adwords.google.com/select/KeywordToolExternal
- ▶ www.wordtracker.com
- ▶ Enter the phrase "Yahoo keyword finder" into a search engine, such as Google.
- ▶ Search for other keyword finders by entering the phrase "keyword finder" into a search engine.

11.3

WORDS TO GO . . .WORDS TO GO . . .WORDS TO GO

Search Engine Optimization (SEO) the development of web page and keywords to receive a priority ranking placement in the results page of an Internet search engine.

11.4 STORE PROMOTIONS AND STRATEGIES

Selling Strategies

If you simply list items in your store and provide no further marketing or promotion, the results will be disappointing. Store items do not appear in a buyer's standard search results. You must promote your items in either your standard listings, other areas of eBay, or off-eBay to drive traffic to your store.

Selling Strategies

Make the most of your Auction-Style and Fixed Price listings by selling your most popular items in these selling formats. These standard listings will receive the most exposure on eBay through either standard keyword searches or buyers who browse through categories where the items are listed. Next, when writing the descriptions for these listings, include links to related items in your store.

The best store selling strategy is to first grab the buyer's attention with your most popular items using standard listings. Offer combined shipping discounts for multiple-item purchases. You then send them to your store with embedded "click here" links in your descriptions, to additional models, sizes, colors, or products.

Cross-Promotion with Auction Listings

Cross-promoting your items is a powerful way to display more items to your buyers. You can use it to either sell additional items or upsell the buyer a more expensive item. It's an opportunity to introduce your buyers to even more of your items that are related to their search and therefore may be of interest.

Cross-promotion is automatically performed by eBay for all storeowners. Once you open a store, the standard listings you create will also include cross-promotion pictures and links to your store products. When a buyer views one of your standard listings, pictures of four additional items from your store are displayed. This cross-promotion will occur each time a buyer bids on your item, wins your item, or simply views your listing.

You can choose to let eBay randomly select the store items to be displayed in your listings or you can manually control the items you want promoted. Two separate groups of products can be shown to better match your store items to the buyer's activity. For example, you can show one group of products when a buyer simply views your listing (for upsell purposes) and another group displayed during check-out to sell related accessories.

◀ SEE ALSO 12.5, *"Marketing Your Business"* ▶

Think Like a Buyer

When building, custom designing, or promoting your eBay store, think like a buyer. Create special categories that will quickly attract a buyer's attention. Use Markdown Manager to display a discount sales tag on certain items. Create a category called "Bargain Bin." Any buyer who is interested enough in your items to visit your store will certainly want to check your bargain bin. Place items there that are not selling; mark them down and move them out.

Create E-mail Newsletters

eBay allows storeowners to create an e-mail list for their customers only if they use the eBay-developed e-mail marketing tool. This restriction is to avoid unwanted spam to eBay members.

Customers subscribe to a seller's newsletter by clicking the "Sign Up to Store News-letter" link located in the store. The seller can then send periodic e-mails and newsletters advertising sales, promotional discounts, and newly arrived products.

You should also place reminders in your listings, flyers, and business correspon-dence to encourage your buyers to sign up for your mailing list. Use a phrase in your standard listings such as, "To be notified of our upcoming specials, sign up for our store newsletter." Then provide a link to your newsletter signup page.

You can easily build newsletter signup links using the "Newsletter Signup" pro-motion box as well as the "page link builders" in your store's **HTML Builder.** Links to the promotion boxes as well as the HTML Builder are available by selecting the "Seller, manage store" link at the bottom of the page, and then in the left-hand navigation area under Store Design. For additional information, select the Help link and type "html tags stores" in the search box.

◀ SEE ALSO 12.5, *"Marketing Your Business"* ▶

11.4

WORDS TO GO . . . WORDS TO GO . . . WORDS TO GO

HTML Builder is a tool storeowners can use to insert Hyper Text Markup Language (HTML) code into their store design in order to create special design features.

11.5 MANAGE YOUR STORE

Markdown Manager

Vacation Settings

Store Traffic Reports

Proper management is also crucial for your store's success. eBay has developed special tools to help storeowners track, monitor, and manage their store.

Markdown Manager

With Markdown Manager, you can easily create and promote attractive sale campaigns for your store items. The items can be discounted by a percentage amount or a specific dollar amount. These items will display a "strikethrough" of the regular price and then display the sale price. This provides an eye-catching highlight to your sale items. The prices will also be in red with a sales tag telling the buyer what the discount percentage is.

You can also schedule when your markdown campaign should start and when it should end. Once it is active, use your e-mail newsletter tools to announce to your subscribers that you are having a sale. As the sale is coming to a close it will say on the listing page how many more days are left of the sale to entice the buyer to purchase now before the sale ends.

◀ SEE ALSO 11.4, "Store Promotions and Strategies" ▶

◀ SEE ALSO 12.5, "Marketing Your Store" ▶

Vacation Settings

The Vacation Settings are useful tools that make it possible for you to set up your store so you can be away for a few days' or even longer vacation. This feature protects you from an unexpected store sale while you are away. You have three vacation setup options, which can be used individually or in combination:

Inventory Listings Unavailable: This makes your inventory listings unavailable and displays a "vacation" message in your store. Using this option hides all of your items so that buyers simply do not see them in your store, in the search results, in cross-promotions, or on any of the other eBay pages. Keep in mind that only your store inventory listings will be hidden; all standard Auction-Style and Fixed Price eBay listings will continue to appear to your buyers. Therefore, make sure all of these listings have ended (and items have been shipped) before you leave.

Once you return, turning off this option will restore all of your items to normal. Note that all eBay Insertion fees and store subscription fees will continue while you are away.

Vacation Message in Your Listings: You can display a vacation message in your listings. Your buyers will see this message above the item descriptions of all of your active listings. You can also select a date when you expect to return from your vacation that will appear in the message. Because of eBay policy restrictions, you will only be able to use the standard vacation message offered by eBay. Buyers can still buy items from your store under this option. The message is mostly to inform them their shipments will be delayed. This is a particularly useful option if you have to go out of town on short notice.

Vacation Message in Your Store: Choosing this option will allow you to place a banner message in your store pages informing buyers that you will be away for a certain period of time. This message will appear below your custom header without affecting any text you have saved in that area. Buyers can also still purchase from you with this option.

Store Traffic Reports

With your eBay store, you will have access to a number of free, valuable traffic reports that will enable you to monitor, track, and analyze the activities of your store visitors. Study your traffic reports to determine where your visitors are coming from and what pages in your store they are visiting. This information is invaluable and will assist you with determining your market strategies for your store's future:

Unique Visitor Report: This report will show the number of **unique visitors** who visited your store during the last month.

Page Views Report: This report tracks the number of times visitors have viewed certain pages. This includes pages from all of your listings, pages within your store, your Feedback Profile, as well as your Seller's Other Items page.

11.5

Visits Report: This helps identify how and where buyers are accessing your store and listings. It provides insight about which sites and search engines your visitors are coming from. You'll also discover which keywords they are using to find you. You can also use this report to identify the impact of any changes or modifications that you have made to your store or listings.

Referring Domains Reports: This reveals the websites that your visitors were visiting immediately before accessing your store or listings. You can then determine how visitors are finding your store.

Search Engine Report: This report identifies which search engines your buyers are using to locate your store and listings. This information is invaluable because it identifies which search engines are sending the most buyers to your store.

Search Keywords Report: This lists each keyword used to find your store and standard listings. These reports will help you to quickly identify which keywords are most effective for use in your listing titles.

Most Popular Pages Report: This report identifies which products and pages your buyers are viewing. These reports will enlighten you as to which items and pages are of most interest to your buyers.

Popular Listings Report: This displays the number of times your listings have been viewed. This report identifies which items are the most popular.

Store Home Page Views Report: This reveals the number of times your store's homepage has been viewed. You can monitor how many people have viewed your store's homepage each day. This tool will enable you to assess the success of your marketing strategies, special sales and promotions, and their effectiveness to drive traffic to your store.

Store Search Keywords Report: This report counts how many times a keyword was searched within your store. This report helps identify which keywords are most frequently used to search for items within your store.

Note also that Premium and Anchor stores will also receive two additional reports: Path, and Bidding and Buying. The Path report reveals the complete path visitors used as they clicked through your store. The Bidding and Buying report not only shows the websites that sent you visitors but if these visitors actually purchased an item. This identifies which websites are sending you visitors

WORDS TO GO . . .WORDS TO GO . . .WORDS TO GO

Unique visitors are only counted once, no matter how many times they return to the site within the month.

who buy.

11.6 PROSTORES

ProStore Features

ProStore Subscription Levels

ProStores enables users to create their own website. It is a solution for individuals or businesses that wish to reach new customers, increase their online sales, and grow their business at a faster rate than with just an eBay store alone.

ProStore Features

ProStores provide small and medium-size businesses the opportunity to sell products and services with a virtual storefront website. You will be able to extend your theme, open a new **sales channel,** and cross-promote your website with your eBay store. The goal of a ProStore website is to attract new customers to your business who shop online but rarely on eBay.

Create a Website

It is easy to create a website using ProStore's template-based setup and design wizard. With most subscription levels, you can create unlimited web pages, sell an unlimited number of products, and cross-reference your product catalog by category, product name, or manufacturer.

A powerful search engine enables your customers to search by price, keyword, **SKU,** category, subcategory, price range, or product name. You'll also have the ability to submit listings to other popular shopping search engines including Yahoo!, Shopping.com, Shopzilla, and Froogle.

Buyers can store their shopping cart if they aren't ready to complete a purchase and then come back later to add to their cart or pay for their order. They can also save frequent shopping cart orders to make repeat purchases quick and easy. This is an ideal feature if you sell consumable goods and have a high rate of returning customers.

11.6

Sell Different Products

Higher subscription level sites can provide the ability to sell downloadable products such as software, e-books, and music. You will also be able to reach new customers by creating e-mail promotions, newsletters, and announcements.

Sales Management

A robust sales-management system allows for updating orders, issuing credit, and creating reports. You can add invoices for orders taken by phone, in person, or by e-mail. You can also set up recurring billing for member subscriptions, services, and installment payment options. Additionally, you can download and share your product, order, and customer information with QuickBooks, Access, and Excel.

Automate Drop-Ship Orders

The highest subscription level, ProStores Enterprise, can automatically notify drop shippers of orders for direct "hands-free" fulfillment. A secure area on your site is also available for drop shippers to update shipping status for you and for your buyers.

Create an Affiliate Program

An affiliate program pays other website owners to send buying customers to your site. You would pay a commission only if their customer purchases one of your products. You can build, track, and manage your own affiliate program with full reporting, variable commissions, and online signups. You can also create buyer groups that display different prices after login, such as loyalty and wholesale programs, or for negotiated discounts with special affiliates.

Marketing Campaigns

Access is available for advanced promotional capabilities, including storewide sales, quantity discounts, and promotion codes. A ProStore can also easily link to your eBay store for cross-promotion. Note that you can only drive traffic from a website to an eBay store. It is against eBay policy to drive traffic from an eBay store to your ProStore.

However, all traffic that is sent to your eBay store qualifies for eBay's Store Referral Credit Program provided you set up the link with the correct referral code. With this program, eBay tracks where a buyer originates. If they came from your site and they purchased from your store, you would then receive 75 percent off your Final Value Fee for that sale.

◀ SEE ALSO 11.1, *"eBay Stores Overview"* ▶

ProStore Subscription Levels

Currently there are four different subscription levels for ProStores: Express, Business, Advanced, and Enterprise. Each is described here along with their associated monthly subscription price. Note that an eBay storeowner will receive

30 percent off the monthly subscription prices once they link their eBay Store with their ProStore (it is verified every month before your ProStore subscription is billed). For further information about ProStores, visit www.prostores.com.

ProStores Express (Starter): $6.95 per month plus 1.5 percent transaction fee This is the basic package for online sellers who normally stock 10 or fewer products but would like a website. This level includes two pages plus a shopping cart for checkout using PayPal. This subscription level is for low-volume sellers.

ProStores Business: $29.95 per month plus .5 percent transaction fee This is the customizable ProStore version. It includes everything in the Express level plus an unlimited number of products, 5GB of storage space for page content, 24/7 customer service technical support, the ability to download all transaction details into QuickBooks for tax and accounting purposes, and the capability to also submit listings to other popular Internet shopping websites besides eBay.

ProStores Advanced: $74.95 per month plus .5 percent transaction fee This level is designed for small to medium-size online sellers. Features include the ability to sell services with scheduled billing cycles or products that have multiple choices such as different colors or sizes.

The ProStores Enterprise: $249.95 per month plus .5 percent transaction fee This level is for medium to large online sellers. Enterprise allows the ability to link to third-party backend computer systems to automate ordering and package tracking from drop shippers. You can also develop affiliate programs. You can also create customer groups that allow special discount pricing when the buyer uses a special login you provide.

WORDS TO GO . . .WORDS TO GO . . .WORDS TO GO

A **sales channel** is the method businesses use to sell items to their customers. Examples would be retail store, online store, or direct (in-person) sales.
SKU is an acronym for Stock Keeping Unit. It is more commonly referred to as a product, item, or inventory number.

11.6

12

GROWING AN EBAY BUSINESS

12.1 DEVELOP YOUR HIGH-LEVEL BUSINESS PLAN

The eBay Business Plan

Get Help and Professional Advice

eBay selling can be an enjoyable hobby, but for the serious seller it should be, first and foremost, a business.

There can be many forms of an eBay business, each with a different style and different requirements. An eBay service business would have quite different constraints and demands than an eBay product retailing business.

The best way to start a new eBay business, grow an existing one, or revive a sluggish one is to treat it like a "real" business. Get a business license. Invest your profits in new products. Market yourself and your business. Find reputable, professional suppliers to be the source for your products. Sell in new niches and markets with different types of products. Watch your costs. Pay yourself a salary. Become profitable. It is time to get serious and develop a plan for your business.

The eBay Business Plan

Think of your business plan as the road map to success. Without it, how do you know where you're going and how will you get there? How will you know when to correct your course, and how will you know when you have arrived? Without the business plan road map, sellers tend to wander in the eBay wilderness.

First, you need to determine what type of business you want, why you want it, and what you expect to accomplish with it. If you are already a successful seller, determine how your business should now evolve and grow. The plan should remain fluid as you move through your selling experiences and progression phases. You may need to correct the course or even chart a new course.

An eBay business plan should be developed before startup. If your business is already underway and without a plan, put it on autopilot for a few days and devote time and serious thought to completing one. Consider some of the following important questions during your eBay business plan development.

Type of business:

▶ What business are you in? Manufacturing, wholesaling, importing, retailing, liquidation, antiques, collectibles, services, other?

▶ Why do you want to sell on eBay? Financial reasons or constraints, easy entry to the online world, low startup costs, easy procedures and requirements?

▶ Where will you sell? Only eBay or multiple sales channels? Trade shows, other online sites such as Yahoo! and Craigslist, rental space at an outlet mall? Open your own website and cross-promote to eBay?

▶ What are your facilities? Home-based, rental space, mini warehouse, office, or industrial park?

Customers, sales, products, and services:

▶ What will you sell? Products, services, both?

▶ Who are your customers? Consumers or businesses? What are the demographics? Why would they want your products?

▶ Will you be in general sales (selling unrelated items) or niche sales (specializing in related items)?

▶ Have you conducted a profitability study and competitive analysis to ensure these products will be profitable if sold on eBay?

Product sourcing:

▶ Will you become a reseller of new products, refurbished products, or used products?

▶ Where will you get your products? Wholesalers, liquidators, manufacturers, importers, government surplus, local auctions, online auctions, estate sales, or other sources?

▶ How can you ensure that the sources above will be reputable product suppliers?

▶ Are these products easy to procure, pack, and ship?

▶ Will you use drop shippers or stock inventory?

▶ Where will you store the inventory?

Selling strategies:

▶ How will you sell your products or services on eBay? Auction-Style, Fixed Price, Store Inventory, or a combination? Will you list your primary products and cross-promote additional products or services?

▶ Will you open an eBay store? If yes, what subscription level: Basic, Premium, or Anchor?

◀ *SEE ALSO 11.2, "Store Subscription Levels"* ▷

12.1

▶ How will you market your business? Promotional flyers, newsletters, e-mails, eBay discussion boards and blogs, attend trade shows?

◀ SEE ALSO 12.5, *"Marketing Your Business"* ▶

Goals:

▶ What is business success and how will you measure it?

▶ What are your annual, quarterly, and monthly goals?

▶ What will be your business and sales progression? What are the goals, products, and selling strategies for business phases 1, 2, and 3?

◀ SEE ALSO 12.9, *"Strategies for eBay Business Phases"* ▶

▶ At what scheduled interval will you reassess your business plan?

Financials:

▶ What are your projected monthly and quarterly revenues?

▶ What will be your costs? Fixed overhead costs such as rental space. Equipment costs. Variable costs such eBay and PayPal fees. Product cost of goods sold (COGS).

▶ How will you pay for your products?

▶ When will you become profitable? Will you be profitable enough to make the effort worthwhile? Will you be profitable at all with the specific products you want to sell on eBay?

Get Help and Professional Advice

An eBay business plan development may seem daunting, but it does not have to be. Unless additional capital is your goal, you do not need to develop a detailed business plan that you would submit to a lending institution complete with a **financial pro forma.** You do, however, need to give careful consideration to the previous questions, then determine the best answers and develop your plan.

You can get professional help from retired, experienced businesspersons at www. score.org. Find a local chapter and set up an appointment.

The Internet has many useful websites for entrepreneurs that can help with business plan development. Google "business plan help" and you will receive many links. Two popular sites are Startup Nation at www.startupnation.com and Entrepreneur Magazine at www.entrepreneur.com. The Small Business Administration www.sba.gov also has considerable helpful information. These sites not only have information about business planning but other information useful to small business owners such as business loans and private health insurance.

> **WORDS TO GO . . .** WORDS TO GO . . . WORDS TO GO
>
> **Financial pro formas** are financial documents used during business plan development to project potential cash flow and income statements.

12.1

12.2 COMPETITIVE ANALYSIS

Conduct Product Marketplace Research

Conduct eBay Marketplace Research

Before deciding on the products you will sell, you should conduct a competitive analysis. Do you have a large number of competitors? Who are the top sellers in your category? Are they selling the same products that you want to sell? What is the sell-thru rate and demand for these products? Can you make an acceptable profit if selling these products online? These questions and more will all be answered after you have completed a product and marketplace analysis.

Conduct Product Marketplace Research

Before buying their products to sell on eBay, advanced sellers conduct historical research on the Internet and on eBay to ensure a particular product will be viable if sold online. In fact, conducting product market research prior to procuring products is a major difference between professional and amateur eBay sellers.

Serious eBay sellers should conduct a competitive product marketing analysis for any product, niche, or category they are interested in selling. Completing this analysis manually is nearly impossible for a busy eBay seller. Instead, use market and product analysis tools.

An Instant Product Analysis Tool

One of the most popular tools used by many successful eBay sellers is Worldwide Brands' Instant Product Analysis. While other tools are made for data-mining eBay, Instant Product Analysis conducts marketplace research of the entire Internet and provides the results sometimes within seconds. Sellers can then use this information to make quick product decisions.

Simply enter the keywords of your product, niche, or category. The tool explores the Internet searching for relevant product demand and competitive data. The tool examines the data, scrubs it to eliminate the outlying and irrelevant data, and presents an easy-to-understand mini product-analysis summary report.

The mini report provides a percentage score bar that is segmented from 0 to 100 percent. This number represents the chance of success for that product, niche, or category if sold online. The lower the percentage, the lower your chances for success. A higher percentage score tells the seller that the online demand is high and the competition is low, identifying a favorable marketplace.

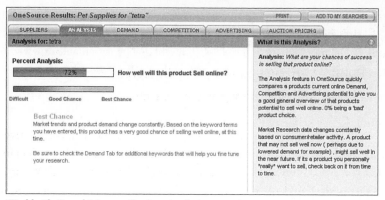

Worldwide Brands' Instant Product Analysis.

In your research, if you receive a score above 75 percent, that's an excellent indication that you have possibly found a winning category, niche, or product to begin selling. A score that is about 90 percent and above has identified an **ideal niche.** In that case, you have most likely discovered a winner.

◀ *SEE ALSO 7.2, "Niche Markets"* ▶

WWB's Product Analysis Tools are part of its OneSource package offered for a one-time payment, with lifetime membership. Learn more and receive a special discount at www.worldwidebrands.com/studentrate.

Conduct eBay Marketplace Research

No seller can be an expert in all areas of the eBay marketplace. Sellers often create listings for items they've never sold on eBay before. Without research, they would create their listings by guessing at the most important elements of the listing. How should they sell it? What keywords, format, and starting price should they use? Should they add a Buy It Now button or a Reserve price? If so, what should these prices be? What should they write in their description?

These are all important questions you have to answer in order to create the listing. It does not make sense to guess when you can answer them all with proper research. It does make sense to find the top sellers of that item on eBay and study how they sell it to have similar results.

The eBay Marketplace Research methodology involves finding the top sellers of that particular item on eBay, studying how they list their items while looking for particular characteristics, and then mimicking their methods. In particular, you should study the keywords, categories, starting price, listing format, and other significant elements used by the top sellers.

12.2

It is very important for a serious seller to understand how to conduct proper eBay research. Listed below are the elements of proper manual research as viewed from a higher level. A more detailed, step-by-step methodology is available at www. trainingu4auctions.com under the How to Conduct eBay Research link.

The eBay research methodology steps are …

1. **Find the top sellers:** Use the Advanced Search link and Completed Listings check box to find all sellers for that item. Arrange the prices from highest to lowest to find the top sellers. Narrow the search by only viewing the items that are shown with a green price, denoting that the item sold.

2. **Study the top listings:** For only the listings that were the top sellers, study and note the following information:

   ▶ What keywords were used?

   ▶ In what category did they list the item?

   ▶ What was their starting bid?

   ▶ Did they use a reserve?

   ▶ Was it an Auction-Style or Fixed Price listing?

   ▶ Did they use a Buy It Now price?

   ▶ How detailed was their description?

   ▶ How many photos did they use?

   ▶ How many days did they run their auction?

   ▶ How many hits did their auction attract? (Look at the bottom of the listing for the hit counter. Note that sometimes the counter is hidden by the seller.)

3. **Merge and purge the information:** Not all sellers will use the same keywords, starting price, etc. You need to compare all of the above factors and determine the best choice for each.

4. **Create the listing:** Now as you create the listing for your specific item, you have the answers to all of the critical selling elements. Best of all, these answers are based on solid research information, not guesswork. You have created the best possible scenario for the item to be successful.

Note that steps 1 and 2 in particular are where the HammerTap, Terapeak, and eBay Marketplace Research tools are invaluable. These tools provide 90 days of search data while a manual search only provides two weeks of data. Their data and analysis is deeper, more informational, more substantial, and much quicker to retrieve and analyze than a manual search. These tools are reviewed in Chapter 7.

◄ SEE ALSO 7.6, *"Product Analysis"* ►

WORDS TO GO . . .WORDS TO GO . . .WORDS TO GO

An **ideal niche** is a market where there is very high demand but little competition for a particular product or group of products within a niche.

12.2

12.3 BUSINESS AND INDUSTRIAL CATEGORIES

Advantages of B2B Selling

B2B Product Sourcing

Purchase Business and Industrial Products

Many sellers ignore the Business and Industrial (B&I) categories on eBay. This is because of the often mistaken mindset that the eBay marketplace is for selling items, one at a time, to individual buyers. Many times, however, the large profits that are made on eBay are from **B2B** transactions in the Business and Industrial categories.

From eBay's homepage, on the left side of the screen is the link to the Business and Industrial categories. The top-level categories are as follows:

- ▶ Agriculture and Forestry
- ▶ Construction
- ▶ Food Service and Retail
- ▶ Healthcare, Lab, and Life Science
- ▶ Industrial Electrical and Test
- ▶ Industrial Supply, MRO
- ▶ Manufacturing and Metalworking
- ▶ Office, Printing, and Shipping
- ▶ Other Industries

Spend time scrolling through the numerous B&I categories and their associated products to discover a large variety of potential selling opportunities. Sellers in many of these categories sell to small businesses. For example, if a large corporation needs new copiers, it will most likely purchase new freestanding copiers from a copier salesman. Small businesses with tighter budgets, however, may want to purchase their copiers at a significant discount on eBay. If you are able to purchase liquidated, overstock, or factory-refurbished copy machines, you have a niche in eBay's Office, Printing & Shipping category.

Advantages of B2B Selling

One of the biggest advantages of selling B2B is the potential revenue. Units are not usually sold for $10 here, but several hundred to several thousand dollars. As a seller, it takes about the same time to list, sell, pack, and ship a $1,000 item as it does a $20 item. This makes the **effort-benefit ratio** of selling much higher in many B&I categories than standard eBay categories.

Compare a B2B sale with a typical eBay sale. A small businessperson is not wasting time surfing eBay for fun. Industrial customers have the money to spend and are highly motivated. They want to solve a problem in their business and need to do it quickly. They are searching eBay for the solution. For example, an expanding small business may need new desks. A restaurant needs a new overhead industrial fan. A commercial electrician needs a refurbished industrial motor. A hair stylist needs new chairs. Compare those sales with selling a $20 trinket, and you can see why many eBay professionals choose to sell in B&I categories.

B2B Product Sourcing

Most of the time, products for B2B sales are acquired the same way as products for other categories. This includes wholesalers, liquidators, surplus, government surplus, closeouts, and importers. While the procedures and sources are usually the same, the cost for the B&I items are higher than those for standard eBay categories.

◀ *SEE ALSO Chapter 7, "Product Sourcing"* ▶

Somewhere near where you live are industrial parks. These buildings are occupied with small to medium manufacturers. Many specialize in a few niche products. Visit them and discover what they sell and whether they have products that need liquidating. Conduct your research on eBay for those products to determine the market potential. Start with one or two, and if sold successfully, consider purchasing the entire lot.

◀ *SEE ALSO 12.2, "Competitive Analysis"* ▶

Most capital equipment items sold in the Business and Industrial category has a $20 insertion fee. The Final Value Fee is one percent of the final value (maximum $250).

Purchase Business and Industrial Products

This section of B&I would not be complete without mentioning that, as a small business owner, you should always consider purchasing your business equipment, furnishings, and office supplies from eBay. You can save precious capital, especially critical during a startup, and still receive quality items from reputable sellers. Check for great deals on these items in the Office, Printing, and Shipping category.

WORDS TO GO . . .WORDS TO GO . . .WORDS TO GO

B2B refers to business-to-business sales as opposed to business-to-consumer.

An **effort-benefit ratio** measures how much effort is required to achieve a desired result. It is used to help determine whether a product is worth selling or a task is worth continuing.

12.4 OBTAIN A BUSINESS LICENSE

Advantages of a Business License

Local Business License

Comparing Business Entities

Choosing the Right Business License

Incorporation Service Providers

Sellers do not need a business license to sell on eBay. However, you cannot build a serious business until you have a business license. Some individuals don't want a business license because of the tax-filing requirements, but the simple fact is, taxes are required for your eBay sales whether you have a business license or not. Surprisingly, a business license may actually lower your taxes. In fact, there are many advantages to having a business license.

Advantages of a Business License

There are many good reasons for an eBay seller to become an official business and obtain a business license. Legitimate tax deductions can be used when running a licensed business. These include all costs associated with the business from shipping and product costs to business equipment and room rental in your home. Utility bills, car mileage, and trips to trade shows are also legitimate tax deductions for a profitable eBay business.

A primary reason to obtain a business license, however, is so you can order your products at wholesale prices from product suppliers. When you ask for a dealer application form from wholesalers, one of the first questions they will ask is, "What's your tax number?" If you do not have a tax ID number, they will not sell to you, period. Without a business license, you have significant constraints on your potential source of products. Stated another way, a business license opens the door to a multitude of other product sources while unlicensed businesses have only a limited access.

12.4

A business license is now fairly easy and inexpensive to obtain. In most states, you can get a business license online in just a few minutes. However, remember that this is an important step. Before you jump immediately into getting a business license from your state, there are some differences you should understand and questions you need to answer first.

Local Business License

Nearly all businesses need a local city or county business license or permit. The license allows the businessperson the legal right to own and operate his or her business within the city or county.

The rules and regulations vary depending on where you live. Note that some communities have strict rules for home-based businesses, such as not allowing tractor-trailer trucks to deliver merchandise to private homes. Call your local city hall with any questions and to request an application.

If you already have a business license, you don't need another one for your eBay business. You can simply file a Doing Business As (DBA) form with your state. Filing a DBA makes your new eBay business legal and places your new business under the umbrella of your already established business.

Comparing Business Entities

A business can be formed as a sole proprietorship, partnership, C corporation (C-corp.), S-corporation (S-corp.), or a limited liability company (LLC). Most small businesses are sole proprietorships, partnerships, or the increasingly popular limited liability company. Many professional eBay sellers are registering as LLCs.

Sole Proprietorship

A sole proprietorship is a type of business that is owned by one person. In most states it requires minimal paperwork. All liability of the business is assumed by the owner. Sole proprietorships usually have less regulation but sometimes a higher tax rate than a corporation or LLC.

Partnerships (General and Limited)

A partnership is a business agreement between two or more individuals. It is more formal than a sole proprietorship in that a partnership agreement defining each partner's role, responsibility, and boundary should be documented. An advantage is that income and expenses pass through to each partner according to the details outlined. A general partnership shares all debt and liabilities equally among the partners. A limited partnership assigns the liability and debt only to the general partner.

C and S Corporations

The C corporation, also referred to simply as a corporation, is the most formal type of business entity. The corporation has certain liabilities, rights, and privileges that individuals do not. The owners are treated as employees and all corporate tax reporting is separate from the owners rather than passed through to the owner's personal tax. While this formation protects the owner's personal assets, it has the disadvantage of requiring the most record keeping and regulation. A second disadvantage is double taxation, once for the corporation and again for the individual owners.

A subchapter-S corporation is similar to a C-corp. in asset protection and record keeping. It also has the advantage of passing taxes through to the individual owner(s), thereby eliminating double taxation.

Limited Liability Company

The key to making the decision as to which type of business is right for you is based primarily on minimizing your taxes while offering maximum asset protection. This is why most new eBay businesses choose the LLC.

A limited liability company is considered a hybrid between a corporation and a partnership (or sole proprietorship). It offers protection similar to that of a corporation in that the owner's risk is limited only to their investment in the LLC. It does not require the rigid structure and reporting requirements of a C-corp. or even S-corp. Taxes pass through an LLC much like a partnership or a sole proprietorship and in most cases, taxes are less. The LLC has become the business type of choice for most serious eBay sellers. It offers maximum protection while minimizing regulation and taxes.

Choosing the Right Business License

If you have an attorney, you should talk to him or her before making your decision. However, you do not need an attorney to obtain a business license. You can get a business license free or at a substantially reduced cost by following these steps:

1. Search the web for your state's Department of Licensing and select the Business License division. Read all the questions you will need to answer in order to apply for a business license. Note any questions you have.

2. Talk to your CPA (or other certified tax advisor) and ask what type of business you should form for your eBay business. You want to minimize taxes and maximize protection.

3. Contact SCORE at www.score.org and talk to one of its licensed retired attorneys. Ask him or her all of your remaining legal questions, free of charge.

12.4

4. Return to your state's Department of Licensing website and complete the proper application forms, or use Incorporation Service Providers (ISP) to complete and file all of the required paperwork for you. The cost, if using an ISP, is substantially reduced when compared to what an attorney would charge. *Note in this case ISP refers to Incorporation Service Provider and not the more commonly known Internet Service Provider.*

Incorporation Service Providers

If you feel unsure or uneasy about tackling all the steps required to get a corporate business license, yet want to avoid a costly attorney's fee, an Incorporation Service Provider (ISP) is the solution. An ISP will act on your behalf and file all the required forms for a corporate business license (including LLCs) in your state. It replaces the need for an attorney during the license process and acts as your registered agent.

It can file the required paperwork for your state on your behalf and pay your state's required fees. Also, you can easily obtain additional services such as the tax identification number and your reseller's certificate that many product suppliers will require.

ISPs charge a very reasonable service fee plus the state filing fees. This is a safe and inexpensive way to get a license and ensure that all the proper steps are taken and forms completed.

There are several ISPs now listed on the Internet. Two of the more popular ones that many eBay sellers use are Biz Filings at www.bizfilings.com/studentrate and Legal Zoom at www.legalzoom.com/studentrate.

12.5 MARKETING YOUR BUSINESS

Newsletters and E-mail Marketing

Cross-Promotion

Promotional Flyers

Market Your eBay Store

Market Your Business

In order for an eBay business to grow to its full potential, it needs to be properly marketed. There are many ways to market a business besides just listing products on eBay. Marketing can occur on eBay, but for a business to truly reach the point of critical mass, significant strategic-marketing efforts must also occur off-eBay.

Newsletters and E-mail Marketing

eBay storeowners can create targeted e-mail lists using an eBay-developed, web-based marketing tool to produce promotional and informational e-mails and newsletters for their subscribers. These are ideal methods to announce special sales, discounts, and new products.

Storeowners have the Sign Up to Store Newsletter link on all of their listings. By selecting this link, the member has subscribed to the seller's newsletter e-mail list. Note that because of anti-spamming rules, this must be the only method used to add e-mail addresses to your list. You are not allowed to add any e-mail address to your list without the member's opt-in consent.

The e-mail tool provides simple-to-use templates you can choose and then customize with pictures of your products and provide links to your store. Buyers can choose from five separate subject categories when they select the signup link. You can then create e-mail campaigns targeted to your buyers' specific areas of interest.

Newsletter Metrics

eBay also provides metrics for you to measure the success of your e-mail campaign. You can track each promotional e-mail by specific factors such as number of e-mails opened, item link clicks, number of bids, and resulting sales. To learn more, select the Help link at the top right of any page and type "e-mail marketing overview" in the search box.

Cross-Promotion

eBay storeowners benefit from having their listings cross-promoted with other items in their store. When buyers view a listing, they will see additional items from the seller. The items displayed can be either randomly selected by eBay or manually selected by the seller.

Cross-promotion from eBay store.

Cross-promotion is an upselling strategy used to promote additional items that are related to the listing. It is a clever way to sell add-on accessories. Two completely different groups of cross-promotion items can be developed. One group of items can be presented during the auction and a different group shown during the checkout process. For example, if you sell digital cameras, cross-promote them with other cameras to present a larger selection to the buyer (group one). Once your camera auction ends, show camera bags, tripods, and memory cards during the buyer's checkout process (group two).

Promotional Flyers

Free promotional flyers are available to eBay storeowners, and these can be used to market their store and promote their products. The flyers can be customized so the seller can announce sales, shipping discounts on future purchases, or other promotions such as "Upcoming Mother's Day Specials." This encourages return customers who will, in turn, recommend your store to their friends.

You can print promotional flyers and place them in shipments to buyers. You can also use the flyers as a thank-you letter, to provide special product instructions, or for selling related accessories. You can include a reminder about feedback as well as information regarding return policies and product-related instructions. Retail storefront owners can print the flyers, place them on their counters, and include them with each purchase to advertise their eBay Store, promote their items, and announce upcoming events.

Market Your eBay Store

You can't just open an eBay store, sit back, and expect sales to roll in. Since eBay store items do not usually appear in standard searches on eBay, you have to make potential buyers aware of your eBay Store and its products. Below are some additional ways to promote your eBay Store and market your business both inside and outside of eBay.

▶ **Promote your store in your listings:** In your listing descriptions, include links to pages or specific items in your store.

▶ **Develop a color or design theme:** Use Listing Designer when you create eBay listings to incorporate your store colors, logo, banner, and theme. Use the same design elements and theme on business cards and promotional advertising flyers.

▶ **Create an About Me (also called About the Seller) page:** That describes your business, policies, and customer service. Members can then click the "About Me" icon next to your User ID to learn more about your business and why they would want to purchase from you. This page is also the only place you are allowed to put a link to your off-eBay retail website.

▶ **Promote outside of eBay:** Promote your store in e-mails, newsletters, and printed materials. Always include your store's name and URL (web address).

▶ **Make your eBay store your website:** Secure a web domain name from a domain hosting service provider and redirect it to your store URL (a direct website URL looks more professional than an eBay Store URL). Print the web address on all business correspondence.

▶ **Check your store traffic reports:** Find out where your visitors originate, what products they are attracted to, and which ones they buy.

▶ **Optimize your store for SEO:** Internet search engines can find your items on eBay if you have properly optimized your store. Search engine optimization (SEO) allows Internet shoppers to discover your items on eBay.

◀ *SEE ALSO 11.3, "Set Up and Build Your Store"* ▶

12.5

Market Your Business

You can market your business outside of your listings. Use eBay blogs and discussion boards to create an interest in you and drive readers to your listings and store.

▶ Create an eBay My World page to inform potential buyers about your business, products, and policies.

▶ Start an eBay blog to help you find new customers from the Internet that could be interested in your products.

◀ *SEE ALSO 16.4, "eBay Connect"* ▶

► Use chat rooms and discussion boards to meet and communicate with other members. Always include your eBay User ID, store name, and URL with your signature.

◀ *SEE ALSO 16.3, "Chat Rooms and Discussion Boards"* ▶

► Attend trade shows and conferences. Visit the vendors at smaller booths and speak with the owners of the company. They are usually more eager to network and negotiate a deal. The first time, you should attend as a buyer. The next time you may want to be there to sell and have your own booth. Find trade shows at www.tsnn.com.

12.6 SUCCESS IS PROFIT, NOT SALES OR FEEDBACK

Profit Margin

What Is a Good Profit Margin?

The most important metric for any business is profit. Without profit, your eBay sales activities are just a shipping hobby. Many sellers never fully understand this.

eBay sellers talk about their gross monthly sales revenue as though it were profit. "I sold over $3,000 in the last three months. I am now a Silver PowerSeller!" Few stop to ask, "How much money did I make?"

Other sellers never even bother to determine how much they make. It seems their primary goal is to gather a mountain of 100 percent positive feedback. These are the attitudes of an eBay beginner. The advanced, professional seller must understand that the primary goal of any business is profit.

Profit Margin

Businesses measure their profitability with the metric of profit margin. Markup is sometimes confused with margin, but they're quite different. Markup is when a seller adds a certain percentage of their cost to determine the item's price. Profit margin is a percentage determined by dividing profit by sales (P/S).

For example, a seller sells a particular gadget on eBay. His cost is $10. If he wants a 150 percent markup, then the price is $15 ($10 × 150 percent). However, his profit is $5 ($15 – $10), so his profit margin is 33 percent (5/15). He has a 150 percent markup and a 33 percent margin.

What Is a Good Profit Margin?

An acceptable profit margin is entirely your decision and should vary based on the products you sell. Most retailers with storefronts would like to at least double their money. This is commonly referred to as **keystone.** If keystone is your goal, the gadget procured for $10 should be sold for $20. This is a 200 percent markup and 50 percent margin. If you purchase your products from wholesalers, then keystone is a good goal. You can't expect much better than keystone on eBay because then your prices would be higher than competing retailers.

12.6

255

If you source your products in **lots** from liquidators, surplus, and closeout suppliers, or the item's cost is very low, then you should consider a much higher margin. You may need six, seven, eight, or even more times your cost to make the effort-benefit ratio of the quantity purchase worthwhile.

◀ SEE ALSO 7.4, *"Wholesalers, Liquidators, Importers"* ▶

For items that are **drop-shipped,** the margins can be (and usually are) much less. The reason is that there is no charge for the item until it sells. Plus there is no money tied up in inventory. Therefore, sellers who drop-ship are often more interested in how much money they can make on that item rather than its expected margin. It may be well worth the effort to sell an item for less than a 15 percent margin if you can still make $150, as long as the manufacturer allows this amount to be discounted off the **MSRP.**

◀ SEE ALSO 7.5, *"Drop Shippers"* ▶

In summary, you should have different profit-margin goals depending on how you procured the product. A simple question you should ask yourself when considering any product is, "Will this item be financially rewarding enough to make the effort of listing, selling, and shipping worthwhile?" If not, move on to items that are.

WORDS TO GO . . .WORDS TO GO . . .WORDS TO GO

Keystone pricing is used by retailers to determine the price of an item. It is determined by doubling their cost.

A **lot** refers to items sold by suppliers in bulk and in a certain quantity.

Drop-shipped items are sent from a wholesaler directly to the end customers, for an online retailer. The seller doesn't stock, pack, or ship the product.

MSRP is the manufacturer's suggested retail price.

12.7 CONSIGNMENT AND TRADING ASSISTANTS

Advantages of Using a Trading Assistant

Find a Trading Assistant

Become a Trading Assistant

Become a Registered eBay Drop-Off Location (REDOL)

Trading assistants (TAs) are experienced eBay sellers who sell items for other individuals on a consignment basis. TAs handle every step required to sell the item, including conducting the research, taking the pictures, writing the description, and creating the listing. They will also answer questions from buyers, collect the payment, and ship the item to the buyer. If the item does not sell, it is returned to the individual.

A fee is charged for the consignment sale. Fees vary among TAs, but in most cases they range from 30 to 40 percent and include all expenses, including the eBay and PayPal fees that alone can be 10 percent or more.

Advantages of Using a Trading Assistant

TAs are used by individuals who don't have the time, the eBay knowledge, or the interest to sell the item themselves. An individual with little eBay experience may decide to benefit from a TA's selling experience and reputation on eBay. Many TAs specialize in particular categories on eBay and have the knowledge to sell those items for maximum value.

TAs can assess the value of items and help their clients sort through items. They can quickly identify items of value (around $50+), what should not be sold on eBay (because it has little value), and what cannot be sold because eBay prohibits it.

Find a Trading Assistant

12.7

To find an eBay Trading Assistant near you, go to www.ebaytradingassistant.com. All TAs listed in this directory have a Feedback Score of at least 100 and a 98 percent or better positive feedback percentage.

Trading Assistants are not employees or even independent contractors for eBay. TAs own their consignment business independent of eBay. There is no endorsement or approval process from eBay other than that they have met the feedback requirements in order to be included in the directory.

When deciding between TAs, be sure to ask about their experience, specialties, fees, drop-off procedure, and schedule. Check their Feedback Profile and ask how you will be paid or what the procedure is if the item doesn't sell. You should also ask them to provide references from former clients. You want an experienced professional, not someone who does this as a hobby.

Become a Trading Assistant

Experienced eBay sellers can expand and augment their business by becoming a TA. If you meet the Trading Assistant requirements, you can begin consignment selling.

You control how you run your consignment business, such as the types of items you accept, the fees you charge your clients, and the hours you keep. You will need to determine if your state requires an auctioneer's license to become a Trading Assistant. The Trading Assistant program at eBay can help you determine if your state's Department of Licensing requires the license. Also, check with your city hall for local zoning laws if you intend to conduct business from your home.

To become a TA you must have a more formal business structure and marketing plan. Marketing flyer templates, press kits, and program logos are all available for download from eBay. You will also have access to the TA Education & Training hub and TA workshops. A popular auction management software tool that also has a component developed for consignment selling is Meridian at www.noblespirit.com.

Trading Assistant Requirements

The requirements to become a TA and be included in eBay's trading assistant directory are as follows:

1. You must have sold 10 items on eBay during the previous three months, and maintain that sales level.

2. Have 100 or more feedbacks.

3. Have a 98 to 100 percent positive feedback.

4. Have an eBay account in good standing.

5. To remain a TA, you must abide by the eBay Trading Assistant Style Guide.

Become a Registered eBay Drop-Off Location (REDOL)

REDOLs are TA storefronts that also meet further eBay requirements. REDOLs receive priority placement in the TA directory search results. Clients can also search the directory specifically for REDOLs.

Any TA who also meets the requirements for a REDOL will be displayed on eBay with a special trading post icon next to their User ID. Trading assistants must meet additional requirements in order to qualify as a REDOL. A full explanation of all requirements can be found at ebaytradingassistant.com, then click the Registered eBay Drop off Location Terms & Conditions link. The primary REDOL requirements are:

1. TA offers a staffed drop-off location or storefront with regular hours.

2. Adhere to certain customer support standards.

3. Procure $1M in liability insurance plus carry a $25,000 bond to protect the checks to your sellers.

4. Must abide by the REDOL agreement and the REDOL style guide.

12.7

12.8 SELLING SPECIALTY SERVICES

Services That Qualify

Specialty Services is a relatively new category on eBay. In this category you can sell a service instead of a product. This is a great way to expand an eBay business if you (or others that you can employ) have particular service skills.

Do you have special talents, skills, or abilities that you could sell as a service? Can these services be performed by you remotely, and then delivered to customers anywhere? If yes to both of these questions, you should consider selling these as services on eBay.

A particular strategy is to cross-promote your products with services. For example, someone who sells violins can cross-promote the fact that they also repair musical instruments. They can list these services in their eBay Store.

◄ *SEE ALSO Chapter 11, "eBay Stores"* ▷

The listing creation process for specialty services on eBay is the same method used for products. The listing formats such as Auction-Style or Fixed Price as well as the fees charged are also the same. The only difference is that the listing must be in the specialty services category.

◄ *SEE ALSO Chapter 4, "Creating Listings"* ▷

Services That Qualify

eBay defines a service as a listing that involves any significant labor post-transaction, which is based on buyer specifications. eBay has provided the following examples:

▶ Custom design of crafts, clothing, or personalized items.

▶ Restoration of collectibles such as art, antiques, pottery and glass, toys, dolls, and stuffed animals.

▶ Repair of computers, consumer electronics, cameras, watches, musical instruments, autos and motorcycles, and test and measurement equipment.

▶ Website design, About Me pages, graphic design, logos, listing templates, signs, and banners.

▶ Personalization of items such as stationery, clothing, signs, and business cards.

▶ Valuation and authentication services, market research and analysis.

Finding detailed information on eBay about selling Specialty Services can be difficult as it is buried a few levels deep in Seller Central. Therefore, use the following link: http://pages.ebay.com/sellercentral/specialtyservices.

12.8

12.9 STRATEGIES FOR EBAY BUSINESS PHASES

Phase 1, Beginner

Phase 2, Advanced

Phase 3, Professional

As eBay sellers progress in their selling experiences, they usually pass through three general phases: Beginner, Advanced, and Professional. Each phase has particular identifiable characteristics, challenges, and selling methods. Following is a summary of the selling strategies and best practices that are used by the more successful eBay sellers during each business phase.

Phase 1, Beginner

▶ Avoid low-priced items. Sell medium-priced items ($20 to $100) to several customers. Think higher volume and medium prices.

▶ Conduct eBay marketplace research before you create your listings. Find the top sellers of the item, mimic how they sell, and expect the same results (see 12.2).

▶ Keywords are the most important factor in your listing. It is how 80 percent of your customers will find you. Think like your buyer (see 4.2).

▶ Get free Priority Mail shipping boxes from the USPS at ebaysupplies.usps. com.

▶ Pack items like a professional does and ship quickly (see 6.7).

▶ Write your description as if you have no photo (see 4.2). Take your photo as if you have no description (see 5.3).

▶ Learn how to take professional-looking photos (see 5.3).

▶ Consider using listing upgrades such as bold, subtitle, and 10-day auctions.

Phase 2, Advanced

▶ Sell medium- to higher-priced items ($50 to $200) to individuals and higher-priced items ($200 to $2,000) to businesses. Think higher-priced items plus higher volume.

▶ Be a contrarian and distinguish yourself from the competition with different gallery photos, subtitles such as "Free Shipping" or "We Ship Worldwide," or better pricing and faster shipping.

▶ Sell in more than one category or niche with a variety of unrelated profitable items.

▶ Extend your eBay presence by selling Fixed Price items in order to have them listed on eBay Express (see 9.7).

▶ Consider using strategically selected, advanced listing upgrades to promote your listings such as highlight, Border, Gallery Featured, Gallery Plus, Featured Plus, Home Page Featured, and listing in Two Categories (see 3.5).

▶ Open an eBay Store to cross-promote and expand your product line with accessories (see 11.4).

▶ Sell internationally and increase your sales immediately by 10 to 30 percent (see Chapter 8).

▶ Turn on your "Baydar" (eBay radar) by always looking for new, profitable products from a variety of sources such as magazines, catalogs, newspapers, malls, online websites, blogs, and your eBay competitors.

▶ Use software tools such as Instant Product Analysis (see 12.2) to conduct Product Marketplace Research. Use eBay research-analysis tools to determine profitability. The tools used would be HammerTap, Terapeak, or eBay Marketplace Research (see 7.6).

▶ Get eBay-developed seller tools to help with time-consuming tasks such as listing creation, bulk e-mails, automating feedback, and tracking sales and inventory. Tools would be Turbo Lister (see 13.1), eBay Accounting Assistant (see 13.2), and Selling Manager Pro (see 13.3).

▶ Source your products from reputable wholesalers, liquidators, drop shippers, and importers. Find reputable sources from product trending analyst companies such as What Do I Sell (see 7.4) and product sourcing companies such as Worldwide Brands (see 7.5).

▶ Drop-ship expensive items to save inventory costs (see 7.5).

12.9

▶ Purchase or use professional-quality photography equipment (see 5.2).

▶ Pull your weeds. If a product isn't selling, have a "fire sale" and move on. Sell only profitable products (see 12.6).

▶ Use your inventory budget wisely. Don't go narrow and deep in inventory, stocking large quantities of a few products; spread your money wide among several profitable, quick-moving products.

Phase 3, Professional

▶ Sell higher-priced items ($100+) to individuals and ($500 to $10,000+) to businesses. Think higher-priced items with lower volume.

▶ Sell "lots" to individuals or businesses (see 7.4).

▶ Sell in the Business and Industrial categories (see 12.3).

▶ Study your competition by scouring their listings for new products and selling strategies. Don't fear them—learn from them and then beat them.

▶ Control your costs by monitoring your eBay and PayPal fees. Purchase in bulk to receive product discounts.

▶ Don't hire employees too soon. Use part-time workers when you need help. Seek someone in your neighborhood. Ask an energetic teenager or college student to work two or three days a week to help with packing and shipping.

▶ Drop-ship as much as possible or expand to storage facilities (see 7.5). Visit office and industrial parks and see whether a business there will rent storage space. Consider outsourcing your shipping to fulfillment centers (see 7.4).

▶ Expand your business to other sites such as Half.com, Amazon, Yahoo!, Craigslist, and many others.

▶ Use affiliates to drive business to you. You will pay only if the customer buys from you. Commission Junction (www.cj.com) and Link Share (www.linkshare.com) are two popular sites to manage affiliate selling.

13

AUCTION MANAGEMENT TOOLS

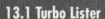

13.1 Turbo Lister

13.2 eBay Accounting Assistant

13.3 Selling Manager Pro and File Exchange

13.4 Sales Reports and Metrics

13.5 Third-Party Software Tools

13.1 TURBO LISTER

Turbo Lister Benefits

Upload Listings to eBay

Solution for Slow Dial-up Connections

System Requirements for PCs

Blackthorne Basic and Pro

Turbo Lister is an eBay listing tool that was developed and is fully maintained and supported by eBay. The tool is essentially a database that helps sellers simply, quickly, and efficiently create professional looking eBay listings. Turbo Lister is free and available for download at http://pages.ebay.com/turbo_lister.

Turbo Lister Benefits

With Turbo Lister, you do not have to be connected to eBay when you are creating your listings like you do when using the **Sell Your Item Form (SYIF)**. Instead, you install Turbo Lister on your hard drive. Then you can create all of your listings offline, directly from your hard drive. Once your listings are complete, only then do you connect to the Internet and upload the listings to eBay.

◀ *SEE ALSO 4.2, "Listing Creation"* ▶

Database Advantages

There is a distinct advantage in having all of your listings saved on your computer's hard drive rather than stored on eBay. Listings are removed from the eBay servers after 90 days. So if you wanted to relist an item that you sold more than 90 days ago, you would need to create the listing again. By comparison, if you created the listing in Turbo Lister, the file will remain on your computer until you delete it.

Duplicate Listings

Once you have a listing created in Turbo Lister, you can easily duplicate that listing and then edit it to create another listing very quickly. An example is if you are selling sweatshirts in different sizes. You create the first listing in size XXL and then make four duplicates of that listing. You then edit each duplicate, make the necessary changes from XXL to XL, large, medium, and small, and then save each size under a new file name. You have now efficiently created a new listing for each sweatshirt size.

Change Listing Formats

Turbo Lister can also quickly change listing formats. An Auction-style listing can be changed to a Fixed Price or Store Inventory with the click of the mouse.

◀ *SEE ALSO 3.3, "Listing Formats and Bidding"* ▶

Upload Listings to eBay

One of the best advantages of Turbo Lister, compared to the Sell Your Item Form, is the simplicity when relisting items. All listings created with Turbo Lister are saved using simple file management. This makes the listings easy to find later for editing or when relisting items.

Once you create a listing, you can upload it to eBay with a few mouse clicks. This is extremely simple and convenient if you have a particular product line and list the same items every week. With Turbo Lister, you can quickly find the listing, then click once to add the item to the Upload List. Continue this process, adding more and more of the items you want to sell for that week to the Upload List. Once the list is complete, another mouse click uploads all of the items to eBay.

Solution for Slow Dial-up Connections

If you are on a slow dial-up connection and cannot upgrade to a high-speed Internet connection, Turbo Lister is most likely your best solution. It is a distinct advantage for sellers on dial-up connections that are too slow for multiple listings to be sent to eBay. You simply create all your listings on your hard drive, then click the Upload to eBay button just before you turn in for the evening and let your listings upload during the night.

If you have multiple listings or an unreliable dial-up connection, you can also solve this problem using Turbo Lister. Download Turbo Lister onto your wireless laptop, create your eBay listings in the laptop, and then visit the local Internet café or library that has free high-speed Internet service. You can then quickly connect to the Internet and upload the listing files.

System Requirements for PCs

The system requirements for Turbo Lister for the PC are as follows:

13.1

- ▶ Microsoft Windows 2000, XP, or Vista
- ▶ Pentium II and above
- ▶ At least 250MB free disk space, more than 500MB recommended
- ▶ RAM: 128MB, more than 256MB recommended
- ▶ Internet Explorer 5.5 or later

Note to Mac users: Many sellers with older Macs use the software tool Virtual PC to run Turbo Lister. New Macs have dual-boot capabilities and sellers can boot to the Windows operating system.

Blackthorne Basic and Pro

Blackthorne is a step up from Turbo Lister. It is also created and supported by eBay, but requires a monthly fee of $9.99 for Basic and $24.99 for the Pro version.

The Basic subscription provides the features of Turbo Lister plus the ability to track sales and manage buyer communication and feedback. The Professional version offers all of the basic features plus the ability to track and manage inventory and sales reporting, and provides login access to multiple users.

The system requirements for Blackthorne Basic and Pro are as follows:

- ▶ Windows Vista, Windows 2000, Windows XP
- ▶ 1.5 GHz Intel Pentium Processor or equivalent
- ▶ 512MB RAM
- ▶ 50MB free hard drive space

WORDS TO GO . . .WORDS TO GO . . .WORDS TO GO

Sell Your Item Form (SYIF) is the step-by-step online form that sellers use to create an eBay listing.

13.2 EBAY ACCOUNTING ASSISTANT

Until recently, eBay sellers had to download their financial information from PayPal using **comma-delimited** files, and then use Excel to open and read them in raw spreadsheet form. This required further data manipulation and formatting in order to have understandable information that could be used for tax and accounting purposes. This all changed with Accounting Assistant.

This program comes with a wizard to help you determine how best to download the transactions and fees from eBay and PayPal. While downloading, the data is automatically entered into a QuickBooks or QuickBooks Pro accounting application. Your data is downloaded in complete form so that you won't have to do any additional data entry or manipulation once it resides in QuickBooks.

The benefits of this tool are enormous because the tedious entry of financial information is eliminated. It also reduces errors as the data is transferred directly into QuickBooks without any need for further manipulation.

You need to have QuickBooks software in order to use this feature. Some sellers choose to have their accountant install Accounting Assistant in order to download the information into their QuickBooks program. You need to also have a subscription to either an eBay store, Selling Manager (or Pro), or Blackthorne (or Pro). Your computer must also meet the following minimum requirements to run eBay's Accounting Assistant:

- ▶ Microsoft Windows 98, ME, 2000, XP, NT
- ▶ 100 MHz processor and at least 30 MB free hard drive space.
- ▶ RAM for Win 98/ME: 64MB (128 recommended)
- ▶ RAM for Win 2000/XP/NT: 128MB (256 recommended)

For more information, select the Help link and type "Accounting Assistant" in the search field.

13.2

WORDS TO GO . . .WORDS TO GO . . .WORDS TO GO

Comma-delimited is a type of data file that uses commas to separate the data fields from each other. This format is used to transfer data files from one application or computer system to another.

13.3 SELLING MANAGER PRO AND FILE EXCHANGE

Selling Manager's Features

Selling Manager Pro's Features

File Exchange

Selling Manager and Selling Manager Pro are both online tools that help medium- to larger-volume eBay sellers track and manage their listings. They are essentially an upgrade to a seller's My eBay page with a more robust offering of features and services.

◀ SEE ALSO 10.1, *"My eBay Overview"* ▶

Selling Manager's Features

Selling Manager's communication features are of particular benefit to higher-volume eBay sellers. Sellers can create custom e-mail messages to be sent automatically to buyers for different occurrences on eBay. For example, you can create a custom "thank you" e-mail and have it positioned for eBay to automatically send to your buyers as soon as they have won an item.

Feedback can become an annoyance to higher-volume eBay sellers. With Selling Manager, you can automate feedback. Most sellers set up their Selling Manager to automatically leave feedback as soon as a buyer has paid for the item with Pay-Pal. About 90 percent of buyers pay with PayPal, so you'll eliminate the need to manually leave 90 percent of your feedback.

Selling Manager also provides "bulk" features. This allows you to list multiple items or send numerous feedbacks with one click of the mouse. For more information on Selling Manager, click on the Site Map, and then look under Selling Tools.

Selling Manager Pro's Features

Selling Manager Pro provides the same features as Selling Manager plus automated listings. This feature benefits the seller who has a product line and lists the same items each week. They can be programmed to automatically list every week, every other week, or whatever schedule you prefer. The Pro version also provides inventory tracking, monthly **P&L reports,** and sales analysis reports for the products you sell.

The price of Selling Manager is $4.99 per month. Selling Manager Pro is $15.99 per month. For more information on Selling Manager Pro, go to Site Map and then look under Selling Tools.

Note that Selling Manager is free for Basic eBay Store subscribers, and the Pro version is free if you own a Premium or Anchor Store. eBay Stores were presented in Chapter 11.

◀ *SEE ALSO 11.3, "Subscription Levels"* ▶

System Requirements

Selling Manager and Selling Manager Pro are web-based services. There are no system requirements other than a PC or Mac running either Internet Explorer 4.0, Netscape, or AOL.

File Exchange

eBay's File Exchange is an "end-to-end" selling tool specifically designed for high-volume sellers. With File Exchange, the seller can use a **flat file** such as an Excel spreadsheet, a database program such as Access, or other inventory software to load all his listings in bulk to/from eBay at once. This can be either a download or upload depending on the function required.

The biggest advantage of File Exchange is that it can interface to any platform or operating system's protocol. This is ideal for high-volume sellers who have their own inventory or sales tracking system. This is a free service to sellers as long as they have been registered for 90 days and have averaged 50 or more active listings per month for the last two months. For more information on File Exchange, see the Site Map and then Selling Tools.

WORDS TO GO . . .WORDS TO GO . . .WORDS TO GO

P&L reports refers to a monthly or quarterly profit-and-loss report for a business.

Flat file refers to a computer file that has had all of its application format protocols removed. This allows the file to be easily shared and understood by other computer applications.

13.3

13.4 SALES REPORTS AND METRICS

Sales Reports Plus

eBay makes it easy to track the key elements and **metrics** for your eBay sales by providing free sales reports. This is of utmost importance for sellers who want more in-depth analysis of their sales. This helps in all aspects of eBay business decision making such as listing creation, timing, the success of certain items or promotions, and identifying trends.

The sales reports include your sales activity trends over a certain period of time. The report includes this information:

▶ Total sales

▶ Ended listings

▶ Successful listings (number and percent)

▶ Average sale price per listing

▶ Net eBay fees

▶ Net PayPal fees

Sales Reports Plus

Sales Reports Plus is the upgrade that provides more in-depth analysis of the key metrics required to monitor your eBay sales. In addition to the information provided in Sales Reports, the Plus version also provides the following:

▶ The number of **unique buyers**

▶ Metrics by category

▶ Metrics by listing format (Auction-Style, Fixed Price, Store Inventory)

▶ Metrics by ending day and time

▶ Detailed and summary eBay fees

The sales reports are free and accessible 24 hours a day from your my eBay page, under My Subscriptions. You can sign up for the sales reports by selecting the Help link, typing "sales reports" in the search field, then selecting Sales Reports, Subscribing and Unsubscribing.

WORDS TO GO . . . WORDS TO GO . . . WORDS TO GO

Metrics are performance measurements used to analyze the effectiveness of different sales marketing techniques.

Unique buyers are only counted once no matter how many times or items they have purchased from a particular seller.

13.5 THIRD-PARTY SOFTWARE TOOLS

Solutions Directory

Certified Providers

Auction Management Software

There are many tools developed and available to eBay sellers from **third-party software vendors.** Most are offered through membership subscriptions. However, not all vendors offer the same quality of product. Therefore, eBay has provided a Solutions Directory where users of these products can leave feedback as to their satisfaction.

eBay also provides a list of providers that they have certified as meeting certain criteria. Again, even though eBay has certified them, this does not always mean their users are pleased. Before you purchase any solution tool, be sure to see what their users are saying about that product first.

Solutions Directory

eBay provides a Solutions Directory to help sellers determine what software tools are available based on the sellers' needs. Included in the directory are selling solution tools, buying solution tools, and other tools such as data analysis. Use the directory's Solutions Finder to help you narrow the field of vendors and pinpoint the specific type of products available based on your selling requirements and business needs.

The directory also provides user ratings and feedback similar to *Consumer Reports* magazine. Be very careful to read the comments that other users have made before you purchase the tool or sign up for any of their services. Even though eBay may list them as a solution, this does not mean they have satisfied users. The eBay Solutions Directory can be found using the Site Map, under Selling Tools.

Certified Providers

The eBay Certified Provider Program recognizes the best companies that supply add-on subscription services to eBay members. These are the top companies that have been certified by eBay as solution providers because of their expertise, experience, and other criteria. All of the companies are considered by eBay to be helpful to sellers wanting to grow their business through services or technology.

Many of the companies listed as Certified Providers are those covered in this book, such as Terapeak and HammerTap for data services and WhatDoISell or Worldwide Brands for product sourcing services. Again, be sure to read what the users of these products are saying first, before your purchase. A complete list of eBay's Certified Providers can be found in the Site Map, under More Community Programs.

◀ *SEE ALSO Appendix B, "Resources"* ▶

Auction Management Software

Finding a complete, end-to-end auction management tool can be a bit difficult from the Solutions Directory. Therefore, following is a discussion of the most popular eBay auction management software. Some are developed entirely by eBay, while others are developed by third-party vendors.

The benefit of a software package that has been completely developed by eBay is that you know eBay will still exist next year. In the past, sellers have expended considerable time and money in third-party auction management software, only to face disappointment later when the company goes out of business. The disadvantage with using eBay software, however, is that third-party vendors usually offer a much more robust and full-featured auction management package.

eBay's Auction Management Software

Sellers may want to consider an eBay-developed auction management package. The complete package would be either Blackthorne (see 13.1), or a combination of other eBay tools that have been described earlier in this chapter and are listed below:

▶ Turbo Lister

▶ Selling Manager Pro

▶ Sales Reports

▶ eBay Marketplace Research (Could be replaced by Terapeak or Hammer-Tap. Refer to 7.6.)

▶ Accounting Assistant

13.5

Third-Party Auction Management Software

Following is a list of the more popular auction management software tools developed by third-party vendors and used by eBay sellers. Note that this list is not exhaustive and is not an endorsement. The vendors listed are for informational purposes and as a starting point for your search. They are listed in alphabetical order, and then identified as either **web-based** or **desktop-based** applications.

Some offer minimal features with lower monthly fees while others are full-featured with fees reaching $100 per month. You should visit each website and compare the features and prices to determine the best tool for your eBay business. Then be sure to check what the actual users are saying about the product from the Solutions and Certified Provider directories before you purchase.

- Auction Hawk: www.auctionhawk.com (web)
- Auction Sage: www.auctionsagesoftware.com (desktop)
- Auction Wizard 2000: www.auctionwizard2000.com (desktop)
- Auctiva: www.auctiva.com (web)
- ChannelAdvisor: www.channeladvisor.com (web)
- DEK Auction Manager: www.dekauctionmanager.com (desktop)
- Infopia: www.infopia.com (web)
- Marketworks (owned by ChannelAdvisor): www.marketworks.com (web)
- Spoonfeeder: www.spoonfeeder.com (web)
- Vendio: www.vendio.com (web)
- Zoovy: www.zoovy.com (web)

WORDS TO GO . . .WORDS TO GO . . .WORDS TO GO

Third-party software vendors are independent software development companies that are not owned or managed by eBay but develop software to be used by eBay buyers or sellers.

A **web-based** application means that the software does not reside on the user's computer but on a web server. The computer must be connected to the Internet in order for the software to function.

A **desktop-based** application is installed and runs on the user's computer. The computer does not need to be connected to the Internet in order for the software to function.

14

FRAUD PREVENTION

14.1 EBAY FRAUD

eBay Scams

Spoof and Phishing E-mails

Avoiding eBay Fraud

If You Are a Victim

eBay's Security and Resolution Center

Fraud still occurs on eBay, but it is much less prevalent and much more difficult to conceal than it was just a few years ago. This is mostly due to over 2,000 dedicated employees in eBay's Trust and Safety division. In addition, several proprietary, automated software programs are constantly scanning eBay listings looking for fraudulent listings, prohibited items, or violations of eBay policies.

eBay has also placed restrictions in certain "high-risk" categories. Some categories (and sellers) are now required to offer only a "safe" method of payment (such as PayPal or other approved method). PayPal now may hold funds for as long as 21 days because of the item type or seller's feedback score.

eBay Scams

A good indicator of potential eBay fraud is when either a buyer or seller suggests bypassing eBay's standard procedures or safe payment methods. Others may insist that the method of payment be taken offline. These deceptive sellers then collect the money and never ship the product.

Buyers may also persist in suggesting that the seller cancel the listing on eBay and that they complete the transaction offline. The pitch is that this will save money on eBay and PayPal fees. However, this also eliminates eBay and PayPal's built-in safety nets for sellers. When the cashier's check arrives, the seller ships the product—then deposits the check in their bank only to discover that it's a counterfeit.

The most common scam among dishonest international sellers is that they list an item with a low starting bid and purposely do not list a shipping charge. Once the item is won, they add an outrageous shipping rate to the invoice. The buyer had no idea about the inflated shipping rate until after they won the item. E-mailed complaints from the buyer are often met with harsh threats from the fraudulent seller. The buyer capitulates and pays the excessive charge.

When a hot new item comes on the market, such as an iPhone, deceitful sellers sometimes list the item on eBay using a picture of the box. All other information in the description indicates they are selling the product, but buried deep in the text is the fact that they are actually selling only the box. Most buyers will over-look the fine print, bid on the item for several hundred dollars—and win a box!

These types of fraudulent activities are what eBay's Trust and Safety department has been reducing. Even law enforcement sometimes becomes involved. Sellers who used to get away with relentless fraudulent activity on eBay are now being prosecuted and imprisoned. To learn more, check the Police Blotter link under eBay's Security and Resolution Center.

You can avoid falling victim to eBay scams by staying current with the latest scams against eBay buyers and sellers. Visit www.millersmiles.co.uk/search/eBay.

Spoof and Phishing E-mails

Unwanted e-mails called spam have been a problem ever since the Internet became popular in the early 1990s. In the late 1990s and early 2000s, spam became such a problem that e-mail-filtering software was developed for individuals to use on their computers.

Unfortunately, spammers and scammers are still around today with new methods and traps. Many times, they masquerade as either eBay or PayPal and try to trick you into giving away your login and password. These are called spoof, hoax, or phishing e-mails, since they impersonate a legitimate company or website.

Most of the fraudulent eBay or PayPal e-mails involve a statement such as "We have noticed some unusual activity in your account," or "We need to update your account," or "Your account has been suspended." Other e-mails may look as though one of your trading partners has a question about your item or is threatening to leave negative feedback because of non-shipment. However, if you look carefully at the title of the item, it is not anything that you are selling or have ever sold.

What these criminals hope is that you don't examine the e-mail carefully and instead have a knee-jerk reaction to quickly resolve the problem. If you click on the active link in their e-mail, you land on a web page that has the same look as the login page to either eBay or PayPal. If you then proceed to enter your login and password, you have just given the criminals access to your account.

14.1

Hijacked Accounts

When sellers inadvertently provide their login and password information to spoof sites, the criminals will sometimes hijack the seller's account. They are usually looking for sellers with great feedback and then they take control of the account, pose as the seller, and list a very expensive item such as a boat trailer. In the listing description, they write not to use PayPal but to use some other method of payment that they recommend as "better than PayPal."

The scam, of course, is that there is no boat trailer. The unsuspecting buyer sees that the seller has great feedback, clicks Buy It Now to win the item, and then makes the payment directly to the criminal, not the legitimate seller. The criminal must do all this quickly, before the seller discovers they have an item for sale on eBay that they did not list. This is one good reason for sellers to set their preferences to e-mail them whenever they list an item.

Identifying a Spoof E-mail

Active eBay members receive several legitimate e-mails from eBay or PayPal every week. Mixed among them occasionally are the scams known as spoof, hoax, or phishing e-mails.

Some e-mails are easily identified as spoof simply by the manner in which they address the recipient. A legitimate e-mail from eBay or PayPal will always address the e-mail directly to you using your first and last name or your registered User ID. Spoof e-mails usually address the e-mail to "Dear eBay Member." That is a big clue. They have no idea who you are. You can immediately conclude: fraud!

Do not rely on the e-mail's "From" address for proof of legitimacy; these can easily be faked. Additionally, any e-mail that asks for personal information should be highly suspect and treated as a spoof.

Avoiding Spoof E-mails

The best way to prevent becoming a victim of spoof e-mails is to simply take no immediate action on any e-mail that makes an unusual statement about your account. Instead, follow the recommendations listed here to ensure that you will not be caught by a spoof e-mail.

Even if the e-mail looks legitimate, never click on any link that is included or embedded in an e-mail. If you don't click on a link, you can't land at a spoof site.

If you think an e-mail that reports an account problem, or that comes from another eBay user, may be legitimate, open your own web browser and log in and check My Messages in your eBay account. This step avoids the link in the e-mail and ensures you are indeed on eBay. If there is any problem with your eBay or PayPal account, or you have a message from an eBay user, there will be a message waiting for you under My eBay, then the My Messages link. If there is no related message, the e-mail is a spoof.

Don't use a common name for passwords. Use a combination of both letters and numbers. Always use a different login and password for every online account you have. This includes using a different password combination for both eBay and PayPal.

The eBay Toolbar is a useful tool that eBay has developed for spoof website identification. This is a free tool that can be downloaded from www.ebay.com/toolbar. The tool will then reside as a thin bar in the top section of your web browser for easy viewing and quick access. The Toolbar has an Account Guard indicator button that will turn green only if you are on a legitimate eBay or Pay-Pal web page. If you click on a spoof website claiming to be eBay or PayPal, the button will turn red. Otherwise, the button is gray for other, non-eBay web searches. Train yourself to look at the button when you are logging in to eBay or PayPal to ensure that the button is green.

If you also enter your eBay and PayPal passwords into the Account Guard, there is an extra level of security. If a member mistakenly enters her eBay or PayPal password into a non-eBay site, a pop-up warning will appear. This is important because the warning will occur *before* the member clicks the "submit" button.

All computer users today who connect in any way to the Internet or receive e-mails should install reputable Internet security and anti-virus software. The general consensus among Internet security consultants is that you need a minimum of three types of security: a firewall, e-mail scanning anti-virus software, and Internet URL security software that will alert you when you land on a phishing or dangerous site (included in Internet Explorer version 7).

Other helpful PC security software includes anti-spam and anti-spyware. However, there are some reasons you may not want to run anti-spam software on your business e-mails. Namely, they tend to filter all unknown e-mails, including those from your new, unknown customers. In short, they may sometimes throw away new business.

◄ SEE ALSO 1.2, *"Preregistration Preparation"* ▶

14.1

Two of the most popular computer security providers are McAfee's Internet Security Suite and Trend Micro's PC-cillin. Another favorite and reputable site to learn more about Internet security as well as problem-solving tips for your computer is www.komando.com.

Reporting Spoof E-mails

If you encounter a spoof e-mail masquerading as eBay or PayPal, forward it by e-mail to eBay at spoof@ebay.com. All e-mails forwarded to eBay will be investigated.

Be sure, however, not to forward the e-mail as an attachment or alter the subject line. This will prevent a proper investigation. Once the e-mail has been forwarded, delete it from your inbox.

Avoiding eBay Fraud

The vast majority of transactions on eBay are legitimate and completed without incident. However, there are criminals who use eBay to prey on both buyers and sellers. Following the rules below will greatly reduce your chance of falling victim.

1. Never go around the standard eBay trading system. eBay and PayPal have carefully developed multilayered safety features in the buying, selling, and payment process. Transactions that bypass the system will forfeit this protection.

2. Never ship your item until you have received payment. Cash must be in your hand or in your PayPal account. Checks must clear the bank before you ship anything.

3. Understand that you may be at risk if the buyer's feedback is zero. To minimize these problems, sellers have the ability to set their **buyer requirement** preferences. Sellers can automatically block any bidders from bidding on their items based on factors such as a feedback score below zero (more **negative feedback** than positive feedback), not having a PayPal account, being registered in a country you don't ship to, or having two **unpaid item (UPI) strikes** in the last 30 days. Properly setting the buyer requirements will also help avoid scams from countries known for eBay fraud.

◀ SEE ALSO 10.2, *"My eBay Special Features"* ▶

4. Never respond to e-mails asking you to cash a check or accept any payment that is worth more than the amount of the item sold. Often these e-mails come with instructions to send the remainder to their "cousin" in the U.S. or elsewhere. Although this seems like an obvious scam, many sellers fall for it. To help avoid this problem, see Rule 6.

5. As a buyer, be cautious when buying items from international sellers in China, Africa, and South America. While many items are legitimate, many scams originate from these areas. The most common are nonshipment of the item after payment or not providing the shipping rate until after the item was won. Only during checkout is the rate finally revealed as an outrageous gouge. To help avoid this problem, see Rule 6.

6. Buyers should carefully investigate the seller before placing a bid on their item. You should review the eBay Seller Evaluation Checklist link at www.trainingu4auctions.com. Be sure your seller passes this checklist test before you place a bid.

For advanced security, PayPal also has a pocket-size device called a Security Key with a digital readout that changes the access numbers to your account every 30 seconds. It works in synch with your PayPal account, so only you could ever know the access number at any time. Learn more by going to PayPal and typing "security key" in the search field.

If You Are a Victim

If you believe you have given your login and password in response to a spoof e-mail or your account has been hijacked, follow these steps:

1. Log in to both your eBay and PayPal accounts and change both passwords immediately. Again, do not use the same password for both accounts. If you can't log in, follow the "forgotten password" procedure.

2. Contact an eBay representative right away to report the incident using the Live Help link at the top right corner of eBay's homepage. You will be given an 800 number to call for their Trust and Safety Division. Work with the representative to ensure that the password has indeed been changed and that there are/were no unauthorized items listed under your account.

3. Contact PayPal immediately by calling 888-221-1161 and speak to a live customer service agent. Inform the agent of the incident and ensure that there have been no unauthorized financial withdrawals.

eBay's Security and Resolution Center

Located under "Marketplace Safety" in the Site Map is a link to the Security & Resolution Center. This is "security central" for resolving security and fraud problems on eBay. If you have a concern involving security or possible fraud, this is where you begin the investigation, reporting, and resolution process.

Before you report any problem, you must make every effort to resolve the dispute with your trading partner first. If you've made this effort but found no resolution, report the problem by going to eBay's Security and Resolution Center and clicking on the Report a Problem link. Problem reports available include the following:

▶ **Item Not Received:** Use this link if you are a buyer and paid for the item but have not received the item, or if the item is different from what was described in the seller's listing.

14.1

▶ **Unpaid Item:** For use when you are a seller and a buyer has not paid for their item. You need to report the problem to receive credit for all eBay fees that were charged to your account when the item sold.

▶ **Spoof E-mail:** Report spoof, hoax, and phishing e-mails using this link.

▶ **Report a Listing Violation:** If you find a listing that is selling prohibited items or violates a listing policy.

▶ **Other Problems:** Use this link to use Live chat, send e-mails, or talk to a live eBay representative (only available to eBay Storeowners) to report other problems or concerns.

The Security and Resolution Center also has marketplace-safe account tips, tutorials, police blotters, and special announcements. eBay's detailed Trading Rules and Policies are also provided, which we will examine next.

WORDS TO GO . . .WORDS TO GO . . .WORDS TO GO

Buyer requirements are preferences set by the seller to limit or block who he will allow to bid on his items.

Negative feedback is an unsatisfactory score left for another member. The negative score is marked −1 for a single transaction.

An **Unpaid Item (UPI) strike** occurs when a seller reports a buyer that has not paid for an item won from the seller. The buyer is given a clear warning and enough time to pay. If they do not comply, they receive an Unpaid Item (UPI) strike. After three UPI strikes, they are banned from eBay.

14.2 EBAY'S TRADING RULES AND POLICIES

Buying Rules

Selling Rules

Feedback Manipulation and Abuse

Profanity

Unsolicited E-mails

Community Board Participation

In order to promote a secure and practical trading environment for buyers and sellers, eBay has developed Trading Rules and Policies. Each trading partner must abide by these rules during eBay transactions. Instructions to report a violation of these rules by another member are detailed in the Security and Resolution Center.

◀ *SEE ALSO 14.1, "eBay's Fraud"* ▶

Buying Rules

Learning and complying with eBay's buyer guidelines will enhance the process for everyone involved in any transaction. It is essential, then, that members follow the buyer trading rules that are summarized below.

1. eBay's trading rules state that buyers cannot bid on items for which they do not actually intend to pay. Payment must also be made for all items won.

   When a seller lists an item on eBay, he is offering an open-ended contract to a potential buyer. When a buyer places a bid on the item, she is agreeing to complete the contract if she wins the item. Therefore, a bidder is under a contractual obligation to pay the seller for the item won.

2. Buyers must not routinely retract their bids. All bids placed on an item are to be submitted in good faith as a serious offer for the item. An occasional retraction is allowed, but it should not be habitual. This is because some buyers place a very high bid to determine the seller's Reserve price and then retract the bid. Now they know what the Reserve is and bid accordingly.

3. Buyers are obligated to follow the seller's payment and shipping terms that were clearly written in the listing. It is the seller's sole discretion whether to allow any exceptions.

14.2

4. Buyers are forbidden to **shill bid** in order to artificially increase the price of an item. Shill bidding occurs when a seller bids on his own item (using another User ID) or has a friend pose as a buyer to bid on his item for the purpose of running up the price. See Seller's Rule 1.

5. Interference with a transaction from a buyer is prohibited. Buyers cannot contact other members currently bidding on an item to harass, question, solicit, inform, or interfere.

   Buyers also cannot contact the seller to ask that the listing be cancelled to purchase the item outside of eBay. If the item was found on an eBay listing, the normal duration, bidding, and transaction process must be allowed to proceed until completion.

Selling Rules

The eBay Seller Trading Rules cover all aspects of selling and have been instituted for clarification and instruction before any transaction even begins. Sellers in particular must understand and adhere to these rules in order to avoid an accidental rule violation during listing creation.

1. Sellers are strictly prohibited from shill bidding or from having a friend shill bid on their items. eBay has developed sophisticated software applications that monitor all transactions for this type of activity. If caught by eBay's software, the seller's account will be immediately suspended.

   This practice is not only strictly forbidden on eBay but is illegal. Continued, deliberate, or organized shilling infractions could involve law enforcement.

2. Counterfeit, prohibited, restricted, or recalled items cannot be sold on eBay. It is the seller's responsibility to ensure that their item does not violate any of these constraints.

SEE ALSO 14.5, *"Prohibited and Restricted Items"*

3. Sellers cannot misrepresent their item in any way. A purposely inaccurate or incomplete description, misleading picture or title, or listing placement in an improper category is not permitted.

   All keywords used in the title must pertain to the item for sale. Sellers cannot **keyword spam** by using irrelevant but popular keywords for the purpose of increased visibility or keyword search diversion.

4. Sellers may not add a surcharge to commonly accepted forms of payment. Therefore, an additional fee cannot be charged in order to accept a buyer's payment by check, money order, electronic transfer, PayPal, or credit card.

5. Restrictions limit any reference to a website that is outside of eBay. Static or clickable embedded links or references in the description that redirect buyers to websites that sell or trade items are not permitted. Additionally, no links or references are allowed to sites that solicit eBay User IDs, passwords, or e-mail addresses.

   Clickable links that connect to a seller's eBay store or to their own items listed on eBay are permitted. Links are also permitted to websites that are strictly informational and relevant to the item. A link to a seller's retail website is allowed only on his About Me page.

6. Infringement on intellectual property rights such as copyrights and trademarks is strictly forbidden. Specifically, under eBay's Verified Rights Owner (VeRO) policy, sellers cannot sell bootleg copies of movies, software, music, books, and e-books. Sellers also cannot sell warranties without the included product or sell a trademarked product box for use with a counterfeit product.

Feedback Manipulation and Abuse

Members should not purchase items from friends or acquaintances primarily for the purpose of enhancing each other's feedback score. In fact, to avoid even the appearance of this practice or shill bidding, sellers should not sell items to family members or friends and businesses should not sell to their employees.

Members cannot leave feedback that contains vulgar, racist, or personal information comments such as a member's name, address, or contact information. A violation of this rule should be immediately reported to eBay's Security and Resolution Center. The offensive feedback will then be removed and any negative feedback score deleted from the member's Feedback Profile.

◀ *SEE ALSO 14.1, "eBay's Fraud"* ▶

◀ *SEE ALSO 10.3, "Feedback"* ▶

Profanity

Sellers cannot use profanity in a public area on eBay. This includes feedback comments, listing descriptions, discussion boards, blogs, and keyword titles. However, product titles that contain profanity in the title are sometimes allowed.

Sellers can use vulgar, profane, or offensive words and phrases in the title and description of their listings only if these words are part of the actual printed title. These exemptions would apply in the categories of books, movies (DVDs, VHS tapes), and music (CDs, tapes, LPs).

14.2

Unsolicited E-mails

Unsolicited e-mails to other eBay members are not allowed. This applies even if the recipient was a former trading partner. Additionally, members are not allowed to copy the e-mail address of a trading partner to create or add to an e-mail-based mailing list.

Instead, if you are an eBay storeowner, you can have your customers sign up for your newsletter e-mail list. The Sign up for Store Newsletter link is automatically placed within the listings of eBay storeowners. eBay provides this service in order to comply with anti-spamming rules for unsolicited e-mails.

Community Board Participation

Members are encouraged to take part in posting to eBay community forums, blogs, discussion boards, and chat rooms. There are multiple forums, each related to specific categories on eBay. This provides a unique opportunity to connect with, learn from, and teach other members who have similar buying or selling interests.

Anyone can read the information available from the forums. However, you must be a registered eBay member in order to post comments and questions. Note that each forum may have slightly different participation rules. Members must understand and abide by the posting and communication rules of each forum.

WORDS TO GO . . . WORDS TO GO . . . WORDS TO GO

Shill bidding occurs when a seller bids on his own item, or has a friend bid on his item for the purpose of running up the price. This practice is strictly forbidden and if caught by eBay's software, the seller's account will be suspended.

Keyword spamming is when the seller uses popular keywords in her title (that are not relevant to the item they are selling) to receive more search hits. All keywords in a title must be related to the item for sale.

14.3 SQUARETRADE

SquareTrade's Online Dispute Resolution (ODR) Process

Occasionally a problem may arise between trading partners such as an unpaid item (UPI), non-delivery of an item, or negative feedback. In every case, eBay does not want to get involved but pushes the problem back to the buyer and seller for resolution. Although frustrating, this is usually the best way to handle the problem.

If you remember the golden rule and treat the offending partner fairly, many times the issue can be resolved. However, sometimes the offending partner will not listen to reason and the only way to solve the problem is by using a third-party mediator. eBay recommends Online Dispute Resolution (ODR) from SquareTrade at www.squaretrade.com.

SquareTrade's Online Dispute Resolution (ODR) Process

The automated, web-based, dispute resolution process at SquareTrade is summarized as follows:

1. File a case: One of the parties files an online form that highlights the problem and gives possible optional resolutions.

2. E-mail notification: SquareTrade notifies the other party of the case by e-mail, along with instructions for resolution.

3. Direct negotiation: Both parties use SquareTrade's proprietary Direct Negotiation tool to communicate directly with each other and resolve the case.

4. Mediator: If the parties still cannot resolve the case, they can choose to have a professional SquareTrade mediator become involved to guide the case to final resolution.

Most cases that are filed and resolved without a mediator using the Direct Negotiation tool are free. If a mediator becomes involved, there is a fee that is determined at the time of the request. Visit www.squaretrade.com for further details or quotes for services.

14.3

14.4 PAYPAL BUYER AND SELLER PROTECTION

Buyer Protection

Seller Protection

Almost everyone has a friend who has some version of an eBay buying or selling "horror story" involving an unscrupulous member. Sometimes, the story is true. Much of the time it is exaggerated. Regardless, instead of resolving the problem, the friend chooses to bad-mouth eBay. Most of the time the problem actually could have been resolved had the buyer/seller known what to do.

Recently, eBay and PayPal have dedicated tremendous resources to developing processes and procedures that provide protection from fraudulent members. Because of this effort, PayPal offers Buyer and Seller Protection policies that can significantly reduce fraud liabilities for eBay members.

Buyer Protection

PayPal's Buyer Protection Policy protects paying buyers from item description fraud or from non-shipment after payment has been made. Depending on several factors, including the type of item sold, PayPal may refund payments from $0 to $2,000.

In order to qualify for this protection, buyers should only buy from sellers who offer Buyer Protection, and pay for the item with PayPal. This protection, if offered, will be indicated clearly in the Buy Safely section of the seller's eBay listing.

Seller Protection

Sellers who have either a Premier or Business PayPal account may qualify for Seller Protection under certain conditions. Seller Protection includes claims of non-delivery or payment chargeback or reversals up to $5,000 annually. Power-Sellers have no annual limit.

The seller qualifications are detailed in Chapter 2, but the primary qualifiers are these:

1. Payment must be made through PayPal. Personal checks, money orders, and cashier checks are outside of the PayPal system and are not covered. Credit cards qualify as long as the transaction was made through PayPal.

Credit cards accepted by the seller using a procedure or merchant account outside of PayPal do not qualify.

2. Sellers must have trackable proof (online tracking) of delivery to a PayPal confirmed buyer address. Note that PowerSellers do not have to ship to a confirmed address. All tracking purchased online from major shipping carriers such as FedEx, DHL, and UPS qualifies, as does USPS delivery confirmation. However, for items sold for over $250, the seller must send the package with Signature Confirmation.

For more detailed information, go to either PayPal or eBay Help and type "Buyer Protection" or "Seller Protection."

◀ *SEE ALSO 2.1, "What Is PayPal?"* ▶

14.4

14.5 PROHIBITED AND RESTRICTED ITEMS

Recalled Items

eBay's Prohibited and Restricted Items

Not everything can be sold on eBay. In fact, eBay has very strict rules against selling certain items and has proprietary software constantly scanning the listings looking for violations.

If your item has been flagged as prohibited, eBay may cancel your listing and send you an e-mail explaining why. Included in the e-mail are instructions for appealing the decision. Serious offenses may result in account suspension.

◀ SEE ALSO 9.3, *"Account Problems or Listing Cancellation"* ▶

Sellers that ship internationally are responsible for ensuring that the item is not restricted or prohibited in the customer's country. Just because an item is legal in the United States does not mean it is legal in all countries.

◀ SEE ALSO 8.5, *"Custom Forms and Duty"* ▶

Recalled Items

Recalled items are strictly prohibited on eBay. It is the seller's responsibility to ensure that their item has not been recalled by the U.S. Consumer Product Safety Commission. You can check the commission's recalled product list at www.cpsc.gov/cpscpub/prerel/prerel.html.

eBay's Prohibited and Restricted Items

Some of the more common items either prohibited or restricted by eBay include tobacco, firearms, alcohol, live animals, credit cards, food, fireworks, and weapons. However, while these items are prohibited, not every associated item is excluded. For example, you cannot sell a rifle, but you can sell rifle stocks, scopes, and trigger guards. You cannot sell tobacco, but you can sell tobacco accessories such as lighters, cigar cutters, and humidors.

The following is an abbreviated list of items that eBay has listed on their site as either prohibited or restricted. You should study eBay's Prohibited and Restricted Item policies carefully to determine whether your particular item is allowed, restricted, or outright prohibited. eBay's complete policy list along with examples and detailed explanations can be found using the Help link and typing "Prohib-ited and Restricted Items" in the search box. If you have any doubt, click the Live help link from eBay's homepage and chat with a live eBay representative.

▶ Adult material: No pornography on eBay's main site. See *mature audiences*.

▶ Alcohol: No alcohol. May allow collectible containers with wine.

▶ Animals and wildlife products: No live animals, mounted specimens, or ivory. Tropical fish and some pelts are allowed.

▶ Art: No unauthorized reproductions.

▶ Artifacts: Native American crafts restricted to members of a recognized tribe. Cave formations and grave-related items are forbidden.

▶ Catalytic converters and test pipes.

▶ Cell phone (wireless) service contracts.

▶ Charity or fundraising listings: Must sell using eBay's Giving Works.

▶ Clothing: No underwear. Used clothing allowed as long as it has been laundered.

▶ Contracts: No contracts that prohibit a third-party sale such as airline tickets.

▶ Cosmetics: No used cosmetics.

▶ Counterfeit coins, currency, and stamps: No counterfeits. Replica coins may be listed if clearly marked "reproduction," "replica," or "copy."

▶ Credit cards: Inactive cards more than 10 years old are allowed.

▶ Drugs, drug-like substances, and drug paraphernalia: Not allowed.

▶ Electronic equipment: No cable TV descramblers, radar scanners, or traffic signal control devices.

▶ Electronic surveillance equipment: No wiretapping devices or telephone bugging devices.

▶ Embargoed goods and prohibited countries: No items from Cuba and other non-U.S.-trading countries.

▶ Event tickets: See eBay's Event Ticket Resale Policy.

▶ Firearms, weapons, and knives: No pepper spray, replicas, stun guns, or other weapons.

▶ Food: Must be sealed and within expiration dates. Perishable foods restricted.

▶ Gift cards: Not to exceed $500, other restrictions apply.

14.5

▶ Government and transit documents.

▶ Government and transit uniforms.

▶ Government IDs and licenses.

▶ Hazardous, restricted, and perishable items: No batteries, Freon, fireworks, other restrictions.

▶ Human parts and remains.

▶ Importation of certain goods into the United States: No CDs, DVDs, videos that were intended only for distribution in a certain country.

▶ International trading: Sellers must comply with the laws of the buyer's country.

▶ Items encouraging illegal activity.

▶ Lock-picking devices.

▶ Lottery tickets.

▶ Mailing lists and personal information.

▶ Manufacturers' coupons: Several restrictions apply.

▶ Mature audiences: Not allowed on eBay's main site but may be allowed on eBay's Mature Audiences category.

▶ Medical devices: No contact lenses, pacemakers, or surgical instruments.

▶ Multilevel marketing, pyramid, and matrix programs.

▶ Offensive material: No racially offensive material or Nazi memorabilia. Many other restrictions.

▶ Pesticides.

▶ Plants: See *weeds and seeds*.

▶ Police-related items: No badges, uniforms, or law enforcement equipment.

▶ Political memorabilia: No reproduction memorabilia.

▶ Postage meters.

▶ Prescription drugs.

▶ Prohibited services: No illegal or mature services such as massages.

▶ Real estate: Multiple restrictions.

▶ Recalled items: Seller responsible not to sell recalled items, including toys.

▶ Slot machines.

▶ Stamps: No counterfeit stamps.

- ▶ Stocks and other securities: No stocks, bonds, or investment solicitations.

- ▶ Stolen property and property with removed serial numbers.

- ▶ Surveillance equipment: No bugs, wiretap devices, miniature transmitters, or surveillance microphones.

- ▶ Teacher's edition textbooks.

- ▶ Tobacco: No tobacco. Related collectibles and accessories may be allowed.

- ▶ Transit- and shipping-related items: No blueprints of transit facilities, airplane operations manuals, or flight attendants' uniforms.

- ▶ Travel: Multiple restrictions.

- ▶ Weeds and seeds: No noxious seeds. Multiple restrictions.

- ▶ Wine: See *alcohol*.

14.5

15

SELLER CENTRAL

15.1 What's Hot on eBay

15.2 Category Tips

15.3 News and Updates

15.4 Additional eBay Resources

15.1 WHAT'S HOT ON EBAY

Finding What's Hot

Seller Central is the primary resource center for eBay sellers. It provides answers to questions that may arise and the knowledge necessary to become and remain a successful seller. Even for the seasoned seller, frequent visits to Seller Central at www.ebay.com/sellercentral provide current and seasonal trends, hot items, and research information for the specific categories in which they sell.

Seller Central is a free service to all eBay members. Most sections are updated at least weekly and some even more often. As new information becomes available, updates and changes are provided to help the seller stay as informed as possible. Checking Seller Central often is necessary for any seller who wants to stay current and well informed.

Finding What's Hot

To discover the best-selling items on eBay, you should first become familiar with the categories that are offered. This in itself can be a daunting task. There are 34 main categories of products listed and each of those has numerous subcategories.

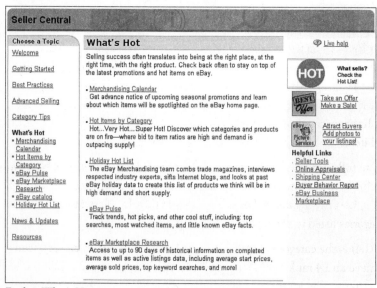

Finding What's Hot.

If you click on the category tab on the left side of eBay's homepage, the categories and subcategories will appear on the screen. The number of items currently listed in each area is shown next to the category listing. This gives you an idea of how many items are currently listed in a particular category and helps you locate the ones with the most items for sale.

Seller Central provides a link on the left column to help sellers find What's Hot. This section provides detailed information about the overall best-selling items on eBay as well as the hottest-selling items in specific categories. Sellers should visit this section often to study what is hot in the categories specific to what they sell.

Merchandising Calendar

The first section under the What's Hot link is eBay's Merchandising Calendar. It provides the dates, events, and categories that will be featured on eBay's homepage. This allows the seller to know in advance if and when their categories will be featured, making it an excellent marketing tool.

Categories featured on eBay's homepage will be seen by potential buyers that otherwise might never have been interested in a seller's products. This is a prime marketing opportunity. Be sure to have all your items listed and eBay stores fully stocked when your categories are featured on eBay's homepage.

◄ *SEE ALSO Chapter 11, "eBay Stores"* ▶

Hot Items by Category

The Hot Items by Category link provides a free, detailed, and informative monthly report of all the hottest categories compared with all eBay categories. The items are ranked Hot, Very Hot, and Super Hot. Sellers should review this report at least monthly to stay current with fads and trends. The report can reveal a hot new category where they may want to sell or alert them when fad or seasonal items are fading out.

In order to fully understand the report, a seller should first understand how categories achieve their Hot, Very Hot, or Super Hot rank. Categories are first ranked as Level 2, Level 3, or Level 4. Level 4 consists of the Hot, Very Hot, and Super Hot categories listed in the report.

Level 4 (L4) is the category of specific interest to eBay sellers. A category can only achieve an L4 rank after meeting an **algorithm-based** comparison using specific criteria. The L4 criteria are summarized as follows:

15.1

▶ The category generates a minimum of 100 bids per week.

▶ Collectively, this category achieves a 50 percent **Sell-Through Rate,** meaning that at least 50 percent of the items listed in that category are actually sold.

▶ The number of bids on the category's items has increased by at least 1 percent from the previous month, for the same type of item.

▶ The number of bids per item in a subcategory is greater than the average for that item's L3 category. For example, Men's Athletic Footwear may register as an L3, while Basketball Shoes may register as an L4.

Once a category achieves an L4 status, it is then labeled Hot, Very Hot, or Super Hot as described:

▶ **Super Hot:** The category has had over 35 percent more bid growth than listing growth compared to the previous month.

▶ **Very Hot:** The category has had between 15 percent and 35 percent more bid growth over listing growth compared to the previous month.

▶ **Hot:** The item has had up to 15 percent more bid growth over listing growth compared to the previous month.

Holiday Hot List

The next informational section under What's Hot is the Holiday Hot List. In this section, eBay has gathered a wide net of "demand" information through media and news research that establishes what the general public is looking for during the holidays. This feature makes it easy for sellers to see what items many buyers are looking for and what items are selling the quickest.

Holiday trends and best-selling items in this section are categorized for easy identification and quick access for the seller. The Holiday Hot List will reveal all areas where the best-selling items and items in short supply can be found. The first link shows the top 25 items. Other top holiday items are listed by their category links.

eBay Pulse

Continuing to browse the What's Hot section reveals the link to eBay Pulse. This segment offers a list of particular items that have been the most popular searches by prospective buyers as well as the top five eBay stores (by number of active listings). This verifies what is being perused the most by buyers and generating the most interest.

eBay Marketplace Research

The last section under What's Hot is eBay Marketplace Research. This is eBay's research tool. Up to three months of data for completed listings is available that presents useful information to help sellers analyze previous sales of a particular item. The seller can use eBay Marketplace Research to determine the best starting price, keywords, and selling format for their item by comparing recent sales of the same item.

◀ SEE ALSO 7.6, *"Product Analysis"* ▶

Hot Items vs. Profitable Items

Sellers should keep in mind that hot items do not always mean profitable items. While it is useful to examine what is hot and in demand on eBay, a seller's primary goal should be what is profitable. So while "Hot" is where the action is, keep in mind it is not always where the profit is.

◀ SEE ALSO 12.6, *"Success Is Profit, Not Sales or Feedback"* ▶

◀ SEE ALSO 7.1, *"What to Sell"* ▶

WORDS TO GO . . .WORDS TO GO . . .WORDS TO GO

Algorithm-based refers to a series of carefully developed mathematical analyses and conclusions. In this case, it is automated using proprietary eBay software for marketing analysis.

Sell-through rate is the percentage of items actually sold when compared to the number of items listed over a given period of time. For example, if 50 of a particular item were listed in one month and 20 of the items actually sold, the sell-through rate would be 40 percent.

15.1

15.2 CATEGORY TIPS

Seller's Edge

Seller Profiles

In Demand

Discussion Board

Seller Guide

Category Tips is a very useful section for any level of eBay selling. It offers a broad range of information and ideas for specific categories. Clicking this link in Seller Central provides a vast amount of information in a detailed yet simplified presentation.

There are 26 major categories listed that represent the merchandise available on eBay. Under each of these 26 categories are five links:

▶ Seller's Edge

▶ Seller Profiles

▶ In Demand

▶ Discussion Board

▶ Seller Guide

Each of these subheadings is specific to the particular category of interest such as Art, Antiques, Health and Beauty, and so on. Here, a seller can find detailed suggestions, tips, and advice to help make their selling experience successful.

Seller's Edge

It is much easier to sell to past customers who have had a great experience than it is to find new customers. Every sale on eBay should include excellent communication and provide service to the customer that paves the way for future sales. The Seller's Edge link assists the seller in making the most of their sale with information to set the stage for future sales.

Selling to repeat customers can be a comfortable transaction for the buyer and the seller. If one sale has been smooth and successful for both parties, they should be much more inclined to continue doing business with each other. Also, what a customer buys lets you know his or her interests. This may open the door to future sales of the same type of items, companion items, or accessories.

The Seller's Edge provides creative ideas and tips for attracting buyers and keeping them interested in the items you sell. Some of the information provided in the "edges" includes …

- ▶ Suggestions for upselling (selling multiples of the same product) or add-on selling of companion items such as accessories.

- ▶ Providing third-party appraisals and authentication to verify if the item is an original and the quality of the item.

- ▶ Ideas for adding the Best Offer option on a Fixed Price listing to let the seller know you are willing to negotiate the price.

- ▶ Information on how to provide accurate shipping rates in your listings.

- ▶ Details about cross-promotion tools to sell accompanying products in the same area of interest.

- ▶ The current and anticipated trends for certain items.

- ▶ Recycling and reuse of products and shipping materials to protect the environment.

- ▶ Advantages of combined shipping if additional items are purchased.

- ▶ Access to StubHub, an eBay option available for selling tickets to sporting events year-round.

- ▶ Information about the eBay Toy Finder section that lists toys by age-appropriate range and type of toy.

- ▶ eBay's CARad Express, which assists vehicle sellers with ads using templates to display photos and write professional descriptions of the automobiles.

Seller's Edge provides a considerable amount of information for the seller. Reviewing this section can make your eBay sales much more attractive, effective and profitable.

Seller Profiles

The next link under Category Tips is Seller Profiles. This link provides a personal aspect and puts a face on the eBay world. It shares the personal stories of many sellers who have found a new career with eBay. Some sell as a hobby in their spare time for enjoyment. Others supplement their income and fund a lifestyle. Many earn a full-time living selling on eBay.

Some of the profiles are very detailed and include how the seller started with eBay, and some tell a more general story behind their success. The profiles all add a personal side to the eBay selling story and remind us that real people make real money on eBay. Reading the profiles will show the motivation and determination that is required to make selling on eBay personally and financially rewarding.

15.2

In Demand

In Demand is the next link in Category Tips. It redirects you to the eBay Pulse section under What's Hot. In Demand shows a list of the keywords that buyers have used for item searches and gives the top five eBay Stores with the most active listings.

Also provided are pictures and links to the **Most Watched Items.** This lets sellers know what buyers want by revealing their keyword searches.

Discussion Board

The next link in Category Tips is Discussion Board. This is another opportunity to make contact with experienced sellers who have similar interests.

There is a discussion board link within each category to individualize the discussion. Areas of interest are varied, such as antiques, art, books, collectibles, and so on. Anyone can search these discussion boards and read the information, comments, and questions. However, to participate in the discussion board, a seller must be registered on eBay and signed in to the community discussion board. eBay has Board Usage Policies and Policy Explanations that should be read before becoming a part of a discussion board.

Forums can be very helpful in learning tricks of the trade from eBay sellers or information about items that have been found, bought, or sold. Some members like to chat about the excitement involved in eBay selling.

◀ *SEE ALSO 16.3, "Chat Rooms and Discussion Boards"* ▶

Seller Guide

Seller Guide is the last link under Category Tips and is customized for several specific categories. Each Seller Guide is designed to provide the best practices, selling advice, and available resources for particular categories.

For example, in Health and Beauty, the Seller Guide explains the process of getting started, how best to sell health and beauty items, keeping tabs on your business, and even advanced selling strategies. In the Craft link, advice is provided for getting top dollar from your listings, appropriate shipping techniques, and how to build a great reputation in the craft hobby.

WORDS TO GO . . .WORDS TO GO . . .WORDS TO GO

Most Watched Items list allows sellers to view what items buyers most often add to their Watch Lists. This is a strong indicator of product interest and demand.

15.3 NEWS AND UPDATES

Category Changes

Changes to Item Specifications

Special Seller Promotions

Seller Central also provides a News and Updates link that will keep sellers current. Any changes within categories, item specifications, or updates concerning upcoming discounts and promotions are reported here.

New tips and creative ideas for selling are also available for the advanced seller. Taking the time to read the information available in News and Updates may mean the difference between just a sale and a great sale.

Category Changes

eBay processes thousands of transactions every day. Each year there are multiple changes, modifications, and updates to eBay's features and services. Therefore, it is necessary to keep members informed of process changes.

The Category Changes section is designed to keep sellers informed of the changes that affect the categories in which they sell. Information is listed by categories to allow individuals to check for changes in their area of interest rather than wading through numerous modifications and changes that will not impact their selling.

Changes to Item Specifics

Item Specifics is a free service offered by eBay that enables the seller to create a clear, concise, and accurate listing. Item Specifics is provided during listing creation and includes selections a seller can make from a drop-down menu for condition, size, color, make, model, or technical specifications. The seller may choose to list their own custom specifics for their item or may choose from the eBay-provided item specification list.

Many buyers search by item specifics when searching for an item. Therefore, it is very important to use them in your description if they are available for the item you are selling. Note that eBay does not make item specifics available for all items. If item specifics are available for your item, additional fields or drop-down menus will appear when you create your listing.

The link Changes to Item Specifics announces any changes that eBay will be making in their Item Specifics list and when those changes will go into effect.

15.3

This allows the seller to stay informed about the Item Specifics options for their category.

◀ *SEE ALSO 4.2, "Listing Creation"* ▶

Special Seller Promotions

It is vital that eBay offers varying promotions that inspire and motivate their sellers. These promotions are designed to keep a seller's interest high, determined to continue on to even greater success.

Some promotions assist the seller with organizing their eBay information. Others provide services that can be helpful in saving time and money, such as getting free eBay co-branded Priority Mail shipping boxes from the United States Postal Service. Special Seller Promotions provide information about additional services offered and supplies the links to access those services.

Finally, the General Announcement Board is where you can receive announcements for new features, promotions, site changes, and news. You can also sign up for announcements concerning a variety of eBay topics.

15.4 ADDITIONAL EBAY RESOURCES

Getting Started

Seller Community

Advanced Selling

Selling Supplies

Best Practices

Selling Solutions

Building Your Business

Seller News

Third-Party Services

Years of providing services to buyers and sellers has equipped eBay with a wealth of collective knowledge. The seller who wants to make top money and run an efficient eBay business should tap this information. It is available from the Resources section in Seller Central.

Getting Started

The Getting Started section of Resources is a step-by-step guide that walks new members through the process of becoming an eBay seller. The first step helps you to decide what to sell just by walking through your own home. Each room contains items that will generate ideas about products to research for possible selling opportunities.

eBay offers tutorials through Getting Started to help new sellers master the details of listing preparation and creation. This includes photography, writing descriptions, and determining shipping rates. There are also seller checklists and workshops available.

Seller Community

eBay's Seller Community provides access to reviews, guides, blogs, and wikis in order for the seller to stay informed. These resources keep sellers in touch with other members and provide one more way to share the successful and newest selling methods.

You can also learn how eBay allows sellers to donate part or all of their sales proceeds to charitable organizations using the eBay Giving Works program. With

15.4

307

this program, individual sellers or a group of sellers can raise money for approved charities and receive tax credit receipts.

◀ SEE ALSO 16.4, *"eBay Connect"* ▶

Advanced Selling

The Advanced Selling link under Resources offers a variety of tools, programs, and reports for the serious seller to stay informed about the selling process. This link is used mostly by PowerSellers looking for advanced strategies and techniques.

Selling Supplies

A sold item is a loss if it arrives broken because of poor packing materials or techniques. Part of the seller's commitment to the buyer is to use proper packing and shipping supplies so the item will arrive at its destination safely.

Supplies are a big part of the selling process. These may be boxes, labels, tape, or packing peanuts, with some or all necessary for the successful completion of the transaction. Products and information for all types of shipping are offered through the Selling Supplies link.

◀ SEE ALSO 6.7, *"Packing Materials and Corrugated Boxes"* ▶

◀ SEE ALSO 6.11, *"eBay's Shipping Center"* ▶

Best Practices

This section of Resources has been developed and continues to be updated to provide the best practices that the most successful eBay sellers use. Key information, tips, strategies, and some of the best selling advice to be found on eBay is presented. The information is concentrated in the following areas of eBay selling:

▶ **Research:** The best prospect for creating a successful sale is to first conduct marketplace research before listing the item. Marketplace research provides the answers to the questions sellers have for how to list a particular product.

◀ SEE ALSO 12.2, *"Competitive Analysis"* ▶

▶ **Pricing:** Information is provided on how to set the correct starting price. If you start an auction too low, it may end in a disappointing final price. Starting it too high may be discouraging to bidders and may result in no bids. Generating a lot of bids usually results in a better final sale price. You need to be able to determine what starting price will kick-start the bidding frenzy for your item.

▶ **Selling formats:** An Auction-Style listing is a completely different way to sell than Fixed Price. One format may create tremendous interest in your item and one may fall flat. Learn how to determine which selling format is best for your item.

▶ **Merchandise:** Provides tips for creating a great listing. The **friction points** of a listing that can either turn potential customers away or turn them into buyers are discussed. Topics covered include keywords, descriptions, photos, and more.

▶ **Promotional tools:** This section provides a list of all enhancements, listing upgrades, and tools that help promote your items and make them stand apart from the competition. Some of these options have a minimal charge, such as adding a border or a bold font or highlighting the description. There are also options for featuring the item to make it more visible so a potential buyer will notice it. These cost more but may be well worth it, especially when displaying a rare, unique or expensive item.

▶ **Packing and shipping:** This area is a major concern and area of confusion for sellers. eBay provides information and assistance to make the shipping process less confusing and more cost-effective. Included are packing tips and suggestions for printing shipping labels.

▶ **Customer-friendly policies:** Confidence on both sides of the sale makes for a more satisfactory transaction. In their policies and descriptions, a seller should provide the answers to common questions that buyers have. This helps to eliminate questions or confusion and also influences the buyer as to the seller's reliability.

▶ **Feedback:** Tips are provided for how to use feedback. Detailed descriptions, professional packing, and prompt shipping provide the best incentive for your buyer to leave you positive feedback.

Selling Solutions

Selling Solutions has information and resources for individual sellers, business merchants, and selling on eBay Motors. Also included is eBay's Trading Assistant program. This program provides an assistant for hire that will do all the work for the seller, from listing the item to receiving payment and shipping the item to the buyer. Trading Assistants work on a consignment basis. Experienced sellers may want to consider becoming a Trading Assistant.

◀ *SEE ALSO 12.7, "Consignment and Trading Assistants"* ▶

Building Your Business

If you already own a business, eBay may be a quick and easy way to expand and increase sales. Selling from a retail storefront is limited to walk-in customers.

15.4

Adding a website may increase sales a bit—eventually. Adding an eBay sales channel can fuel new sales almost overnight. With eBay, the retailer's market has been increased from a local store to a worldwide opportunity.

Seller OnRamp

Advanced information and even live help is available in the Building Your Business section for the seller who wants to sell wholesale or internationally. eBay has staff experts to guide business owners through the process. You can contact an eBay Seller OnRamp consultant at 1-866-325-3229. He or she will help you understand the best way to get your business online.

It is difficult to find this section of eBay. Go to the Site Map, under Selling Resources select See all Selling Resources, under Building Your Business select Small Business Center, then choose the Seller OnRamp link under Start a Business on eBay.

Seller News

Seller News is where you can receive the latest information about all aspects of eBay buying and selling. Discussion boards, general announcements, calendars, and hot lists are all provided in Seller News. The information is always timely, up-to-date, and thorough. Reading this information helps sellers make well-informed decisions.

◀ *SEE ALSO 16.3, "Chat Rooms and Discussion Boards"* ▶

Third-Party Services

Third-party services is the final section under Resources. Here you will find eBay's approved list of independent service or software providers for eBay sellers. Included are approved providers for several areas of eBay, including …

- ▶ Auction Management tools.
- ▶ SquareTrade for dispute resolution.
- ▶ Approved consulting and professional services from Elance.
- ▶ Links to the U.S. Consumer Product Safety Commission for recalled products.
- ▶ Warranty services for the products you sell.
- ▶ Escrow services for higher-end products.
- ▶ Authentication and grading services.
- ▶ Freight shipping services.

WORDS TO GO . . . *WORDS TO GO . . . WORDS TO GO*

The **friction points** of a listing are the key elements that can either clinch or lose a sale—for example, a poor-quality photo instead of a professional-looking photo.

Third-party services are software vendors or service providers that are independent from eBay.

15.4

16

STAYING CONNECTED TO THE EBAY COMMUNITY

16.1 COMMUNICATION

E-mail

Phone

Skype

Successful businesses need effective, efficient communication with their customers. In the corporate world, salespeople make a "pitch" to their customers using a sales presentation. Contact is maintained using the customary methods of phone calls, personal meetings, newsletters, and e-mail.

One of the key components of exceptional eBay customer service is prompt, professional communication. eBay sellers use the listing's description and photos to persuade potential buyers to bid on their items. They then communicate personally with their trading partner using e-mail, the phone, or Skype.

E-mail

During the eBay sales process, buyers sometimes have questions for the seller that they need to have answered before placing a bid. Post sale, buyers or sellers may have messages or questions for their trading partner before the item is shipped. If there is a problem with the item upon receipt, the buyer will need to contact the seller to solve the problem. In nearly all of these instances, eBay members communicate through e-mail.

Every eBay listing has an "Ask seller a question" link. Buyers use this link to send an e-mail to the seller. The e-mail is not sent directly from the buyer to the seller, but rather through eBay's own e-mail forwarding system. This intermediary system requires that all e-mail communication pass through eBay rather than directly from member to member. This is important because of spam and privacy concerns.

It is important when sending an e-mail to another member to check the "Hide my email address" checkbox. This is to stop unscrupulous spamming companies from gathering the e-mail addresses of eBay members. Additionally, this is important because many individuals now run spam filters on their computers. If a member sent an e-mail directly to another member running a spam filter, it would not be delivered, making communication among potential trading partners almost impossible. Note that Chapter 1 provides very good reasons not to run a spam filter on your eBay business e-mail account.

◄ *SEE ALSO 1.2, "Preregistration Preparation"* ▶

Find Any Member

You can find any eBay member using the Advanced Search link toward the top of any page. Next, select the Find a Member link in the search box on the left of the page. Enter the member's User ID to view the member's feedback profile, items for sale, and eBay store. Note that you will have to enter a verification code to perform this search.

E-mail Any Member

You can contact any member by e-mail by first clicking on the member's User ID anywhere on eBay. You will then see the member's feedback profile. At the top right of the page, click Contact Member and an e-mail form will appear for you to complete and then send. Again, you will have to type the verification code to do this.

eBay will then forward your e-mail to the member. Again, using eBay's pass-through e-mail delivery system will guarantee safe delivery, and provide privacy for both members and a record of the communication. However, if you want the member to have your actual e-mail address, leave the "Hide my e-mail address" box unchecked at the bottom of the e-mail form.

Phone

In some cases, it may be necessary to actually call your trading partner. eBay will provide more detailed contact information, such as a phone number, only between recent trading partners. Note that when you request this information, your trading partner will be e-mailed the same contact information about you.

To access this service, click the Advanced Search link toward the top of any page. On the left side of the screen is the link Find Contact Information. Click the link and enter the member's User ID plus the item number of the most recent transaction you had with that partner.

Skype

Skype is an eBay-owned company that provides free Internet voice communication. Each member must first have installed the Skype software and have a headset to connect to their computer. A Skype member can then make free Internet calls to other Skype members anywhere in the world.

Sellers can add a Skype button to their listings. Buyers can contact you by clicking on the button. Many sellers mention in their listings that "In the last 15 minutes of the auction we will be standing by on Skype for any last-minute questions."

Skype is very popular overseas, so if you have a high number of international buyers, consider using Skype. Learn more or download Skype from www.skype.com.

16.2 GETTING HELP

Help Link

Site Map

Answer Center

Learning Center

Live Help

Buying and selling on eBay can sometimes be very confusing. There will be times when a member needs more information or clarification. Because of this, eBay has created several levels of "Help" available on its website. PowerSellers and eBay storeowners are also given access to phone support. You should understand where and how to get help for the particular problems you encounter.

Help Link

Located at the top right of any page is the Primary Navigation Bar that contains eBay's Help link. This is where most eBay members begin their search for help.

Clicking this link provides access to eBay's Help database. Typing relevant keywords into the search box creates a search of the available help topics. Sometimes the keyword you use will not retrieve the proper information. Use different keywords or more generic keywords rather than specific words, and this will broaden your search.

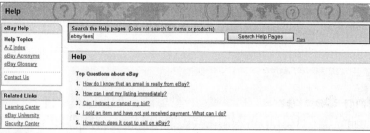

Help link.

On the left side of the screen are quick links to the most popular Help topics. Click the A-Z index and the first letter of the primary keyword for your question or problem.

Site Map

Also located on eBay's homepage under the Primary Navigation Bar is the Site Map link. This is probably the most important and most useful link for eBay sellers. The Site Map organizes all of the essential buying and selling informational links in one view. It is arranged using major categories, each with multiple subcategories. The user clicks through the subchapter links until they arrive at their desired subject.

The major category and subcategory links provided in the Site Map are ...

- ▶ **Buy:** Registration, Categories, More Ways to Find Items, Buying Resources
- ▶ **Sell:** Selling Activities, Selling Resources, Selling Tools, Web Stores (eBay Stores/ProStores)
- ▶ **My eBay:** My Account, My Selling Account, Dispute Console
- ▶ **Community:** Feedback, Connect, News, Marketplace Safety, More Community Programs
- ▶ **Help:** Resources, Help Topics

Answer Center

From the Primary Navigation Bar at the top of any page, click Community and then Answer Center. This will provide you with a member-to-member help link for a number of general eBay and PayPal topics.

Note that the Answer Center is considered a member forum, and the answers you receive are not from eBay representatives. Therefore, the accuracy of the information is not guaranteed. With that in mind, there is much to be gained by learning from more experienced eBay members who have practical experience in eBay buying and selling compared to an eBay customer representative who has most likely learned about eBay in a classroom.

Learning Center

The eBay University Learning Center is available from the Help link. It has training links and materials related to buying, selling, and increasing your sales. Provided are free tutorials as well as CDs and DVDs available for purchase.

You can also find eBay University classes available in your area. Click the links for the Basics of Selling or Beyond the Basics of Selling classes and enter your zip code. Any class in your area will be posted here. The instructors for these classes are not eBay employees but are approved Education Specialists trained by eBay and must use eBay-approved training presentations and materials.

Live Help

Sometimes you will need to interact with a live eBay representative. Located under the Primary Navigation Toolbar on the homepage is the link for Live Help.

When you click this link, a chat window opens and you can type your question in the chat box provided. The eBay representative will communicate with you using the chat method until your problem is resolved.

These eBay representatives are trained in specific areas and levels of eBay. In some cases, the question asked requires higher-level specialty knowledge and the representative may refer you to another help source. Note that sometimes during heavy-volume seasons such as Christmas, the wait times can be long. The rest of the year, the wait times are reasonable—especially during a workday.

eBay's E-mail Support

E-mail support is available as an alternative to Live Help. Log in to your eBay account, click Help, then Contact Us, and then the e-mail help link. Note, however, that eBay is usually slow to respond to e-mail questions. If you need an answer quickly, use the Live Help button mentioned above or eBay's Phone Support if you qualify (see below).

eBay's Phone Support

eBay offers phone support for sellers who have an eBay Store or are PowerSellers who meet the annual minimum sales or volume requirements. Phone support is available Monday through Friday from 6:00 A.M. to 6:00 P.M. PST. If you qualify, log in to your eBay account, click Help, and then Contact Us for your particular support phone number. If you do not qualify, use the Live Help chat window mentioned above to reach a live eBay representative.

◀ *SEE ALSO 9.8, "PowerSellers"* ▶

16.3 CHAT ROOMS AND DISCUSSION BOARDS

Chat Rooms

Discussion Boards

Members of the eBay community are encouraged to learn from and communicate with each other. Of particular help is communication with buyers and sellers of the items that you sell. This is a place to make new friends, meet business contacts, and learn from more experienced members.

Chat Rooms

eBay provides chat rooms where members can communicate in a casual setting. There are category-specific chat rooms for discussion of multiple collectibles, hobbies, and other popular categories. To enter a chat room, select the "Community" link on the Primary Navigation Bar and then click the "Connect" link.

You will see all the message titles and User IDs of those who posted the messages. The more popular postings tend to disappear quickly, as eBay will only hold 200 postings at a time. The older postings are removed as new ones are added.

General chat rooms are also available for discussing nearly any topic. The topics should be mostly for fun. No business should be conducted in the general chat room.

Discussion Boards

Discussion boards differ from chat rooms. The rooms are mostly for short discussions and the boards present discussion threads that can remain for longer times. A member starts a discussion thread by posting a question or comment. Other members are then able to continue the thread with their answers and comments.

Discussion boards are a great place to learn from more seasoned eBay sellers. You can post a specific question such as, "Where can I find cheap packing materials online?" Over several hours or days, more experienced sellers will see the post and give you their recommendations.

Currently, there are over 95 discussion boards on eBay. They are organized in the following groups:

▶ **Category-specific boards:** Post messages or browse to find answers and information about your favorite categories.

▶ **Community help boards:** eBay members answer questions and offer suggestions for specific eBay topics such as PayPal, shipping, or photography.

▶ **General discussion boards:** Are used to share opinions, suggestions, and comments about eBay or just have a friendly discussion with other members on any topic.

▶ **General announcement board:** Is where you can find the latest official eBay news. Each article is time stamped much like an online news service.

▶ **System announcement board:** All system problems, scheduled site maintenance, or system upgrades are posted on this board.

▶ **eBay tools board:** Discussion focuses on subjects involving eBay's selling tools such as Turbo Lister and Selling Manager.

▶ **Workshops board:** Online workshops are offered by other members, vendors, or eBay staff on a wide variety of topics. Workshops sometimes present lecture material and live interactive question-and-answer threads. See the board's workshop calendar for a current list of all upcoming workshops.

▶ **eBay Giving Works (Charity) Board:** eBay Giving Works discussions are designed to address buying and selling procedures required when designating a portion of a sale as a donation to tax-exempt, charitable organizations.

◀ *SEE ALSO 16.4, "eBay Connect"* ▶

16.4 EBAY CONNECT

eBay Blogs

eBay My World

eBay Wiki

eBay Neighborhoods

eBay Main Street

eBay Giving Works

There are many ways for eBay members to stay in contact with the eBay community. Many of eBay's Connect tools and services also help a seller promote their listings outside of eBay. The links for the services discussed in this subchapter can be found on the Community page located at the top of any page in the Primary Navigation Bar.

eBay Blogs

You can have your own **blog** on eBay! It can be a general blog for your friends and family or it can be business-related so new customers will find your eBay store or Internet site. Photos and videos can also be added to your blog.

Many sellers use eBay blogs as a way to drive traffic to their listings either from eBay or from the Internet. First, these sellers will create a newsletter blog. Next, major Internet search engines such as Google, MSN, and Yahoo!, use **spiders** and **crawlers** that will eventually find the blog. It is then catalogued and searchable when using these search engines. For more information on creating eBay blogs, use the following link: http://blogs.ebay.com/ebaynii@ebay.com.

eBay My World

The best way to profile your blog content is with eBay My World. As an eBay member, you already have your own My World page. Use this page to create informational content about your business and the products you sell, and provide the link to your eBay blog. The link to your My World can be shared with everyone and even printed on your business card.

eBay Wiki

Wiki is short for the Hawaiian word wiki wiki and means fast or quick. eBay Wiki is a web tool members can use to quickly write articles on a variety of topics (similar to Wikipedia but specifically for eBay). The articles can be written by any eBay member and amended by any other member. Because of this, information from eBay Wiki should not always be viewed as factual without verification.

The benefit is to have permanent, fact-based, impartial, and informative articles where eBay members can learn from more experienced members. The articles should be written to provide factual information about certain topics from an objective point of view. They should not be for the benefit of the author and no links to the member's listings are allowed.

eBay Neighborhoods

Neighborhoods are where eBay members share information about their buying and selling experiences and meet other members with similar interests. Many members post photos and links to their blogs.

Neighborhood members will have their neighborhood link automatically added to their My World page. You can invite friends to join your neighborhood, post reviews about products, or start a new neighborhood.

eBay Main Street

eBay is a serious lobbyist in Washington, D.C., and represents the interests of its eBay members. eBay Main Street is where you can stay up-to-date on the latest news and information concerning eBay's government relations or legislative issues that relate to eBay and Internet sales.

Topics generally covered in eBay Main Street are taxes, regulations, and other key legislative issues concerning Internet sales. You can search the issues posted for your particular state and at the federal level. Sign up for the eBay Main Street newsletter at www.ebaymainstreet.com.

eBay Giving Works

Giving Works is the program eBay has developed for charitable organizations. With this program, sellers can donate all or a portion of their eBay sales to a variety of charities.

Giving Works is administered by MissionFish, which is a charitable organization. MissionFish provides services and support for ...

- ▶ Managing the Giving Works nonprofit directory.
- ▶ Verifying nonprofit eligibility.
- ▶ Collecting and disbursing sellers' donations.

▶ Providing sellers with tax-deductible receipts.

▶ Tracking donations online.

Sellers may only list with eBay Giving Works if they …

▶ Are registered with MissionFish.

▶ Agree to donate at least 10 percent of the final sale price or $5 (whichever is greater) to a certified organization in the nonprofit directory.

eBay Giving Works listings are eligible for the eBay Giving Works Fee Credit Policy if or when the item sells. Under this policy, if your item sells, eBay will credit your Insertion and Final Value Fees back to you equal to the value of your donation.

MissionFish will provide the seller with a receipt for the tax-deductible donation if the item sells. Learn more about eBay Giving Works from the Site Map and then under More Community Programs.

WORDS TO GO . . .WORDS TO GO . . .WORDS TO GO

Blog is a shortened version of "web log," which is essentially an online bulletin board where individuals can post and respond to messages, questions, and comments.

Spiders and **crawlers** are automated software programs that major web search engine companies (Google, MSN, Yahoo!, and so on) use to scour the Internet in search of relevant and appropriate content for their search directory database.

A
WORDS TO GO GLOSSARY

Accounting Assistant An eBay-developed tool to easily and efficiently load all eBay and PayPal transaction information into QuickBooks and QuickBooks Pro. This feature is used for business accounting and tax purposes.

algorithm A series of carefully developed mathematical analyses and conclusions.

APO/FPO addresses The abbreviation for Army, Air Force, and Fleet Post Offices for overseas U.S. military personnel and their families.

B2B Refers to "business-to-business" sales as opposed to business-to-consumer.

blog A shortened version of "web log," which is essentially an online bulletin board where individuals can post and respond to messages, questions, and comments.

buyer requirements Preferences set by the seller to limit or block who they will allow to bid on their items.

calculated shipping rate The listing option where eBay automatically calculates the shipping rate using the seller's choice of either USPS or UPS. The shipping rate is based on the size/weight of the package, the shipping service, and the seller and buyer's zip codes. See also *flat shipping rate*.

checkout The post-auction process, when the buyer pays the seller for the item.

comma delimited A type of data file that uses commas to separate the data fields from each other. This format is used to transfer data files from one application or system to another.

commodity items Products that a seller has multiple quantities of in their inventory stock.

confirmed address A PayPal member's address that has been reviewed and deemed safe during the registration process. PayPal uses a credit bureau to compare the account holder's shipping address to their credit card billing address. The transaction details page will indicate to a seller whether the buyer's address is confirmed or unconfirmed.

critical mass When a business has grown to the point where its momentum has become self-sustaining and will fuel its further growth.

delivery confirmation Used by the USPS to indicate only when the carrier has delivered the package to the destination address. It is not the same as tracking used by UPS, FedEx, and DHL, where the package can be tracked throughout transit.

desktop based   An application that is installed and runs on the user's computer. The computer does not need to be connected to the Internet in order for the software to function. See also *web based*.

Detailed Seller Rating (DSR)   The portion of a seller's feedback profile where buyers can leave a more specific and complete review (such as item description or shipping) of the seller's performance and their customers' satisfaction.

drop shippers   Wholesalers that will ship individual items directly to the end customers for online sellers. The seller doesn't stock, pack, or ship the product.

eBay Store   Similar to having your own website on eBay; your own separate page(s) on eBay where buyers will see only your items for sale. The advantages are lower listing fees and longer durations compared to a standard eBay listing.

economy of scale   Refers to the per-unit cost savings of a product when introducing new manufacturing improvements or bulk procurement discounts. When used by eBay sellers, it usually means a quantity discount when purchasing inventory stock.

effort-benefit ratio   Measures how much effort is required to achieve a desired result. It is used to help determine whether a product is worth selling or a task is worth continuing.

feedback   The "self-policing" method eBay uses whereby both trading partners in a transaction can post a satisfaction score and make comments about the transaction for other members to view. New members start with a score of zero. A positive score is marked as +1 for a single transaction.

feedback rating   The cumulative score for a particular member derived from the total feedback scores they have received.

financial pro formas   Financial documents used during business plan development to project potential cash flow and income statements.

Fixed Price   A type of eBay listing where no bidding is allowed. The item is not offered at auction but for a particular stated price.

flat files   Computer files that have had all of their application format protocols removed. This allows the files to be easily shared and understood by other computer applications.

flat shipping rate   A listing option that allows you to charge the same shipping rate for all U.S. or all international shipping destinations. See also *calculated shipping rate*.

friction points   Key elements of a listing that can either clinch or lose a sale—for example, a poor-quality photo versus a professional-looking photo.

gallery pictures   Thumbnail-size pictures that are displayed next to the listing title from a keyword search.

general sell   Refers to selling all types of unrelated items much like a general store. The plan is not to build a business from related niche items, but variety and value.

Good 'Til Canceled (GTC)   An optional amount of time an item can be listed in an eBay Store. Under this option, the item will remain in the store until sold or cancelled by the seller.

HTML Builder   eBay's tool that storeowners use to insert hypertext markup language (HTML) code into their store design in order to create special design features.

ID verified   Means that a third-party credit bureau has verified your identity.

ideal niche   A market where there is very high demand but little competition for a particular product or group of products within a niche.

keystone   Pricing used by retailers to determine the price of an item. It is usually determined by doubling their cost.

keyword spamming   Occurs when the seller uses popular keywords in their title (that are not relevant to the item they are selling) to receive more search hits. All keywords in a title must be relevant to the item for sale.

lead time   The total time required from the product order to final delivery. When ordering from overseas manufacturers, it can take weeks or even months.

liquidation   Older-model, surplus, or closeout items that major wholesalers or retailers need to clear out of their store or warehouse. Many use professional, online liquidators to offload the items.

lot   Items sold by suppliers in bulk and in a certain quantity. A buyer may purchase a "lot" of 25, 50, or even 1,000 of a particular item.

metrics   Performance measurements used to analyze the effectiveness of different sales marketing techniques.

middlemen   Deceitful product suppliers who claim to be wholesalers. In fact, they are retailers who purchase products wholesale, add a markup, and sell them as wholesale to unaware online retailers.

Most Watched Items List   Allows sellers to view what items buyers most often add to their Watch Lists. This is a strong indicator of product interest and demand.

mouse over   When a computer user places the mouse cursor over an item icon or picture. With eBay's Gallery Plus, this results in automatic picture enlargement.

MSRP   Manufacturer's suggested retail price.

negative feedback   An unsatisfactory score left for another member. The negative score is marked –1 for a single transaction. Only buyers may leave negative feedback.

niche market   A much smaller segment of a larger market category.

niche sell   When all items sold by a particular retailer are related, complementary, and from the same niche.

P&L reports   Monthly or quarterly profit-and-loss reports for a business.

PowerSellers   eBay sellers that have attained a certain status level (Bronze, Silver, Gold, Platinum, Titanium) based on average sales or volume maintained over a three-month (or annual) period.

Product Finder   A search tool that appears only in certain eBay categories. Buyers use this tool to further narrow their search to the particular characteristics they desire.

product sourcing   The methodology sellers use to find their products and product suppliers.

profit margin   A metric business owners use to determine the relationship of profit to sales. Profit margin is a percentage determined by dividing Profit by Sales (P/S).

return policy   The section of a listing that provides a clear understanding about the seller's guarantees, refunds, and associated time limits.

sales channel   The method businesses use to sell items to their customers. Examples would be retail store, online store, or direct (in-person) sales.

search engine optimization (SEO)   The development of web page and keywords to receive a priority ranking placement in the results page of an Internet search engine.

Sell Your Item Form (SYIF)   The step-by-step online form that sellers use to create an eBay listing.

sell-through rate   The percentage of items actually sold when compared to the number of items listed over a given period of time. For example, if 50 of a particular item were listed in one month and 20 of the items actually sold, the sell-through rate would be 40 percent.

Selling Manager and Selling Manager Pro   Tools sellers use to easily create templates and new listings from existing listings. Selling Manager Pro has multiple features including inventory management and communication and feedback automation.

shill bidding   Occurs when a seller bids on his own item, or has a friend bid on his item for the purpose of running up the price. This practice is strictly forbidden and if caught by eBay's software, the seller's account will be suspended.

shipping calculator   A pop-up software tool eBay has developed to help sellers determine the shipping rate for their item. When the seller chooses "Calculated" rate for their listing, buyers can enter their zip code and click Calculate to see their shipping cost.

shipping policy   Part of the listing section that provides a clear explanation of the seller's method of shipment.

signature confirmation   Requires that a person at the destination address sign for the package.

SKU   Acronym for "stock keeping unit." It is more commonly referred to as a product, item, or inventory number.

Skype   An instant messaging and communication software application eBay members can use to chat over the Internet for free. Each member would need the Skype application software and a headset in order to speak to other members. Sellers who offer this feature can insert their Skype name into their listings so buyers can find and communicate with them.

spiders and crawlers   Automated software programs that major web search engine companies (Google, MSN, Yahoo, etc.) use to scour the Internet in search of relevant and appropriate content for their search directory database.

store referral credit   A 75 percent credit on an item's Final Value Fee when sellers send buyers to eBay from their own website. eBay tracks this activity and provides the credit to the seller's Final Value fee if the buyer purchases their items.

supply chain   The method by which products move: manufacturer, wholesaler, retailer, consumer.

tare weight Refers to the weight of the box and packing materials and excludes the weight of the items it will contain.

third-party software vendors Independent software development companies that are not owned or managed by eBay but develop software to be used by eBay buyers or sellers.

title The string of keywords sellers use in order to get the maximum number of search hits on eBay, and entice browsers to click through to their listing.

Turbo Lister An eBay-developed database tool to help eBay sellers easily and efficiently create listings. Turbo Lister resides on the seller's computer hard drive and replaces the need for the Sell Your Item Form (SYIF).

unique buyers Are only counted once for a particular period of time, no matter how many times or items they have purchased from a particular seller.

unique visitors Are only counted once no matter how many times they return to an eBay store within the month.

unpaid item (UPI) strike Occurs when a seller reports a buyer who hasn't paid for an item won from the seller. The buyer is given a clear warning and enough time to pay. If she does not comply, she receives an unpaid item (UPI) strike. After three UPI strikes, she is banned from eBay.

upselling Encouraging a customer to either upgrade the product, or purchase an accessory for the item they are buying. The term is sometimes used interchangeably with "add-on" sales.

USB (universal serial bus) cable Used to connect computers to peripheral equipment. The current standard interface USB protocol is 2.0. Older computers may not be compatible with this cable and may need an adaptor.

verified account When a PayPal member has confirmed his or bank account (confirmed the test transactions from PayPal to their bank) during the registration process, or was approved for a PayPal Plus credit card or PayPal Buyer Credit.

Verified Rights Owner (VeRO) eBay's policy to protect intellectual property such as copyrights and trademarks.

watermark A faint, translucent image, name, logo, or title that is cast over a photo to make online photo theft difficult.

web based A software application that does not reside on the user's computer but on a web server. The computer must be connected to the Internet in order for the software to function. See also *desktop based*.

webinar   A web-connected conference, meeting, or seminar where each attendee can view the presentation and communicate with the other participants from his or her own computer.

wholesalers   Buy products from manufacturers and sell only to retailers who have a business license. Consumers cannot buy from wholesalers.

B
RESOURCES

Following are the websites and link maps to eBay seller resources that are mentioned in the book. They are grouped alphabetically by category and then by the most often used links within that category. Note that a link map such as "eBay>help>type: fees" means to go to eBay's homepage, select the Help link, and then type "fees" in the search box.

Business License

Incorporation service providers:

▶ www.legalzoom.com/studentrate

▶ www.bizfilings.com/studentrate

eBay

eBay registration:

▶ www.ebay.com

eBay help:

▶ eBay>help

▶ eBay>site map

▶ eBay>live help

▶ For PowerSellers and eBay Storeowners *only*, phone support: eBay>help>contact us

eBay Express:

▶ www.ebayexpress.com

eBay disputes:

▶ eBay>site map>dispute console

▶ www.squaretrade.com

eBay, Other Helpful Links

Keyword finding tools:

▶ pulse.ebay.com

▶ keyword.ebay.com

▶ adwords.google.com/select/KeywordToolExternal

▶ Conduct Internet search for: "yahoo keyword finder"

▶ www.wordtracker.com

▶ Conduct Internet search for: "keyword finder"

eBay Toolbar:

▶ www.ebay.com/toolbar

eBay Seller Central:

▶ eBay>site map>seller central

What's Hot report on eBay:

▶ eBay>site map>seller central>what's hot

eBay blogs:

▶ blogs.ebay.com/ebaynii@ebay.com

eBay discussion boards, wiki, My World:

▶ eBay>site map>connect

eBay MainStreet:

▶ eBay>site map>more community programs>mainstreet

Selling Specialty Services:

▶ pages.ebay.com/sellercentral/specialtyservices

Find local eBay education courses:

▶ www.poweru.net/ebay/student/searchindex.asp

PayPal

PayPal registration:

▶ www.paypal.com

▶ Live PayPal representative phone support for Premier and Business levels *only* 1-888-221-1161. Other members call 402-935-2050.

Photography

Photography research and reviews:

- ▶ www.cnet.com
- ▶ www.dpreview.com
- ▶ www.calumetphoto.com
- ▶ www.photoflex.com

Cloud Dome, Infinity Boards, Cubes:

- ▶ www.trainingu4auctions.com
- ▶ www.trainingu4auctions.net (eBay store)

Photo Studio in a Box:

- ▶ www.americanrecorder.com

Photo file storage:

- ▶ eBay>help>type: "Picture Manager Overview"

Computer monitor calibration:

- ▶ www.epaperpress.com/monitorcal
- ▶ Google: "Computer Monitor Calibration"

Product Sourcing

eBay product sourcing, trending, and analysis:

- ▶ www.whatdoisell.com/studentrate

Find reputable wholesalers, liquidators:

- ▶ www.worldwidebrands.com/studentrate (OneSource)
- ▶ www.whatdoisell.com/studentrate

Find reputable drop shippers:

- ▶ www.worldwidebrands.com/studentrate (OneSource)

Purchase wholesale on eBay:

- ▶ www.ebay.com/reseller (for PowerSellers only)

Government surplus on eBay:

- ▶ pages.ebay.com/governmentsurplus/index.html

Find importers:

- ▶ www.globalsources.com
- ▶ www.worldwidebrands.com/studentrate (OneSource)

Importing research:

- ▶ www.globalsources.com
- ▶ www.importexporthelp.com
- ▶ globaledge.msu.edu
- ▶ www.busytrade.com
- ▶ www.rusbiz.com

Fulfillment centers:

- ▶ www.amazon.com/gp/seller/fba/fba_pricing.html
- ▶ www.moultonfulfillment.com
- ▶ www.mfpsinc.com
- ▶ Conduct an Internet search for: "shipping fulfillment centers"

Shipping

Free USPS/eBay co-branded Priority Mail boxes:

- ▶ ebaysupplies.usps.com

Corrugated boxes:

- ▶ www.uline.com

Packing supplies:

- ▶ www.uline.com
- ▶ www.papermart.com
- ▶ www.fast-pack.com
- ▶ www.ebay.com

Carriers:

- ▶ www.dhl.com 1-800-805-9306

- ▶ www.fedex.com 1-800-GoFedEx (1-800-463-3339)

- ▶ www.ups.com 1-800-PICK-UPS (1-800-742-5877)

- ▶ www.usps.com 1-800-ASK-USPS (1-800-275-8777)

Large item and freight carriers:

- ▶ www.freightquote.com

- ▶ www.uship.com

- ▶ dhl.com>ship>solutions

- ▶ UPS Freight Service 1-800-333-7400

- ▶ www.fedex.com 1-800-GoFedEx (1-800-463-3339)

APO/FPO (Military) shipping information:

- ▶ www.oconus.com/ZipCodes.asp

Private shipping insurance:

- ▶ www.u-pic.com

- ▶ www.dsiinsurance.com

UltraShip postal scales:

- ▶ www.trainingu4auctions.com

- ▶ www.trainingu4auctions.net (eBay store)

Shipping label software:

- ▶ www.pb.com (Pitney Bowes)

- ▶ www.endicia.com

- ▶ www.interapptive.com (ShipWorks)

Shipping label printers:

- ▶ www.pb.com (Pitney Bowes)

- ▶ www.brother.com

- ▶ www.zebra.com

- ▶ www.dymo.com

Exporting:

- ▶ www.export.gov
- ▶ www.wcoomd.org
- ▶ www.export.gov/exportbasics
- ▶ www.sba.gov/aboutsba/sbaprograms/internationaltrade

Shippers export declaration (SED) Form 7525-V:

- ▶ www.census.gov/foreign-trade/regulations/forms

Software Tools

Product analysis for eBay research:

- ▶ www.hammertap.com/studentrate
- ▶ www.terapeak.com/signup/studenttrial
- ▶ eBay>help>type: ebay marketplace research

Niche and product analysis for internet research:

- ▶ www.worldwidebrands.com/studentrate (Instant Product Analysis, Demand and Competition Research. All part of WWB's OneSource package.)

eBay auction management tools:

- ▶ eBay>site map>Turbo Lister
- ▶ eBay>site map>Blackthorne
- ▶ eBay>site map>Accounting Assistant
- ▶ eBay>site map>Sales Reports
- ▶ eBay>site map>Selling Manager

Third-party auction management tools:

- ▶ Auction Hawk: www.auctionhawk.com (web)
- ▶ Auction Sage: www.auctionsagesoftware.com (desktop)
- ▶ Auction Wizard 2000: www.auctionwizard2000.com (desktop)
- ▶ ChannelAdvisor: www.channeladvisor.com (web)
- ▶ DEK Auction Manager: www.dekauctionmanager.com (desktop)
- ▶ Infopia: www.infopia.com (web)

- ▶ Marketworks (owned by ChannelAdvisor): www.channeladvisor.com/mw (web)

- ▶ Spoonfeeder: www.spoonfeeder.com (web)

- ▶ Vendio: www.vendio.com (web)

- ▶ Zoovy: www.zoovy.com (web)

Other Helpful Sites and Products

Computer-related help and tips

- ▶ www.komando.com

eBay Seller Evaluation Checklist:

- ▶ www.trainingu4auctions.com

Escrow service:

- ▶ www.escrow.com

Foreign language translation software:

- ▶ www.freetranslation.com

- ▶ Google>Language (select the Language link)

Inexpensive logo design software:

- ▶ Logo Creator (electronics and office-supply stores)

- ▶ Logo Design (electronics and office-supply stores)

Interactive Video for eBay Listings:

- ▶ www.deal4it.com/studentrate

ProStores websites:

- ▶ www.prostores.com

Scams on eBay:

- ▶ www.millersmiles.co.uk/search/eBay

- ▶ Report Spoof E-mails: spoof@ebay.com

Skype (Internet voice communication):

- ▶ www.skype.com

Trade shows:

▶ www.tsnn.com

U.S. Consumer Product Safety Commission (recalled products):

▶ www.cpsc.gov/cpscpub/prerel/prerel.html

Author's website and eBay store for his students and readers (provides eBay buyer and seller tips, strategies, newsletter, postal scales, and photography equipment):

▶ www.trainingu4auctions.com
▶ www.trainingu4auctions.net (eBay store)

INDEX

G

V–W–X–Y–Z

Because time is the scarcest commodity of all

At *Your Fingertips* lets readers pinpoint the exact information they need without wasting time on unrelated material. Each book covers the gamut of information in concise but complete bites that are easy to find and easy to understand. Based on the notion that time is the scarcest commodity of all, *At Your Fingertips* offers readers the shortest path to the answers they need.

GRAMMAR & STYLE
AT YOUR FINGERTIPS

Nouns
Verbs
Adjectives
Adverbs
Pronouns
Interjections
Verb Tenses
Subject and Verb Agreement
Dangling Modifiers
Metaphors
Split Infinitives
Prepositions
Clauses
Sentence Structure
Compound Sentences
Punctuation
Numbers and Symbols
Capitalization
Abbreviation
Spelling
Exposition
Proofreading
Citations
Footnotes and Endnotes

Lara M. Robbins

978-1-59257-657-9

eBay® BUSINESS
AT YOUR FINGERTIPS

eBay® Registration
PayPal®
Account Types
Site Navigation
Fees
Creating Listings
Photos
Domestic Shipping
Returns and Claims
Product Sourcing
Selling Internationally
Global Communication
Advanced Selling
Unpaid Items
Non-Paying Bidders
PowerSellers
My eBay®
eBay® Stores
Growing Your Business
Competitive Analysis
Business License
Marketing
Auction Management Tools
Fraud Prevention

Kevin W. Boyd

978-1-59257-794-1

SPANISH
AT YOUR FINGERTIPS

Nouns
Verbs
Adjectives
Adverbs
Pronouns
Conjunctions
Verb Tenses
Subject and Verb Agreement
Gender
Subjunctive
Articles
Prepositions
Questions
Sentence Structure
Compound Sentences
Punctuation
Numbers and Measures
Capitalization
Forms of Address
Verb Tables
Idioms
Common Phrases
Pronunciation
Spelling

Clark M. Zlotchew, Ph.D.

978-1-59257-638-8

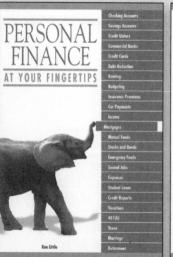

PERSONAL FINANCE
AT YOUR FINGERTIPS

Checking Accounts
Savings Accounts
Credit Unions
Commercial Banks
Credit Cards
Debt Reduction
Renting
Budgeting
Insurance Premiums
Car Payments
Income
Mortgages
Mutual Funds
Stocks and Bonds
Emergency Funds
Second Jobs
Expenses
Student Loans
Credit Reports
Vacations
401(k)
Taxes
Marriage
Retirement

Ken Little

978-1-59257-644-9

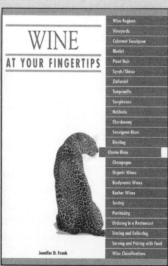

WINE
AT YOUR FINGERTIPS

Wine Regions
Vineyards
Cabernet Sauvignon
Merlot
Pinot Noir
Syrah/Shiraz
Zinfandel
Tempranillo
Sangiovese
Nebbiolo
Chardonnay
Sauvignon Blanc
Riesling
Chenin Blanc
Champagne
Organic Wines
Biodynamic Wines
Kosher Wines
Tasting
Purchasing
Ordering in a Restaurant
Storing and Collecting
Serving and Pairing with Food
Wine Classifications

Jennifer D. Frank

978-1-59257-789-7

ACCOUNTING
AT YOUR FINGERTIPS

Assets
Liabilities
Income
Sales Costs
Expenses
Debits and Credits
Depreciating Assets
Prepaid Expenses
Cash Operating Procedures
Cash and Credit Transactions
Accounts Receivable
Purchases
Inventory Costing
Discounts and Allowances
Accounts Payable
Cash Disbursements
Salary and Wages
Payroll Taxes
State and Federal Regulations
Cash Receipts Journal
Cash Disbursements Journal
Posting to the General Ledger
Producing Balance Sheets
Producing P&L Statements

George R. Murray, CPA, and Kathleen Murray, CPA

978-1-59257-649-4

ALPHA
Penguin.com